Phantasm Exhumed © 2014 by Dustin McNeill
ISBN: 978-0692203156
ISBN-10: 069220315X
Published by Harker Press

PHANTASM
EXHUMED

DUSTIN McNEILL

Edited by Olga Deutschberger

**With Additional Angus Scrimm and Reggie Bannister
Interviews by Todd Mecklem**

A NOTE ABOUT THE COVER

The cover art of this book was designed by the wickedly talented Stuart Manning from
original set photographs by Kristen Deem, whose striking photography appears throughout this book.
The author wishes to thank Kristen for so iconically preserving Angus Scrimm through her images
and Stuart for so wonderfully capturing the spirit of *Phantasm Exhumed*.

For my fellow phans...

TABLE OF CONTENTS

INTRODUCTION

Hallelujah, Dustin, you did it. You pulled it off! I don't know how many times these past decades since *Phantasm* appeared I've been approached at conventions and other venues by individuals who tell me they want to do a book about *Phantasm* and that's the last I ever hear of it. I can't remember how you and I first crossed paths. I do remember you were uncommonly diffident and respectful. And from the outset, your persistence, determination and devotion never faltered. Your sleuthing ability in turning up so many of the long vanished *Phantasm* folk is astounding, but not so surprising is their willingness to reminisce about those experiences they obviously remember joyfully.

I can't tell you what a thrill it is to hold in my hands this volume that encapsulates the phenomenon that is *Phantasm* within the covers of mankind's most glorious creation (possibly excepting movies), a book. I am elated to see the unique creative force that is Don Coscarelli honored and celebrated in this way. Along with the likes of George Lucas, Steven Spielberg and J.J. Abrams, Don exemplifies the prodigiously unfettered, almost child-blessed imagination that characterized earlier generations' Lewis Carroll, A.A. Milne and L. Frank Baum. It is my dream that I live to see this man so fully recognized and celebrated by the film industry and the world.

Kneel, o noble McNeill. For your unstinting efforts in creating such a celebration, and insofar as it is in my authority to do so, and excepting of course Michael Baldwin, I hereby dub thee the Boy of all BOYS. And to those readers yet to come down through the years, welcome, and...

XO

Angus Scrimm

Phantasm's creator.
(Photo courtesy Kristen Deem)

Chapter 0: Primordium

IN THE BEGINNING

According to co-director Craig Mitchell, it was with "blind confidence" that eighteen-year-old Don Coscarelli embarked on his first feature film. Speaking to the Associated Press, Mitchell traced their partnership back to a freshman science class at Woodrow Wilson High School in Long Beach. Ambitious and like-minded, they first teamed on an assignment involving saltwater aquariums. Upon completion, they submitted their report not on paper but as an 8mm short film, much to the delight of their instructor. Academic shorts in other classes soon followed as did a Wilson High orientation film, several television commercials and a brief job for Disney.

Following high school, the pair graduated from short subjects to their first feature-length production, *Jim the World's Greatest*. Coscarelli's mother, Shirley, graciously transformed their handwritten notes into a formatted script proposal for his father Dac to review for financial consideration. An investment counselor by trade, he agreed to grant his son an initial $20,000 budget. Years later, Dac Coscarelli would tell the Associated Press that his friends thought him crazy for taking such a risk. Then MCA/Universal President Sid Sheinberg was reported to have replied, "You are."

Coscarelli and Mitchell's story was surprisingly strong for a debut feature. A coming-of-age drama, it follows teen Jim Nolan as he attempts to hold together a family torn asunder by his unemployed father's alcoholism. Unbeknownst to anyone but the father, Jim's little brother is actually his half brother – their absentee mother's son, not the father's. Following a botched job interview, the abusive patriarch batters the younger boy to death in a drunken rage. Devastated, Jim sets out to kill his father and eventually finds him, though he spares the guilt-stricken man's life rather than become a murderer like him. After such a somber climax, the film ends on a faintly optimistic note, one that suggests healing will ultimately be possible for the young man.

That two teenagers were attempting a feature-length family drama would have been ambitious enough. That they

A much younger Don Coscarelli.
(Photo courtesy Darrell Kitchell)

were delving into the cinematically uncharted territory of child abuse was all the more remarkable. The film's early scenes, particularly those set at Jim's high school, flow so naturally that one can't help but suspect they were plucked from the directors' own time at Wilson High. Jim sleepwalks through science class, clashes with his guidance counselor, plays on the football team and watches girls – all common parts of the high school experience. The difference is that he wanders distantly through these traditions; merely going through the motions of parties, pep rallies and relationships. Jim's thoughts are preoccupied by a deteriorating home life.

NEW BREED PRODUCTIONS

The Coscarelli family formed New Breed Productions for the purpose of making *Jim the World's Greatest*. They soon began hiring a professional, albeit nonunion, crew. Problems quickly arose as the first-time directors clashed with their more experienced crew, all of whom were fired shortly into filming. The dismissal of the original cinematographer and lack of available funds to replace him prompted Don Coscarelli and Craig Mitchell to personally fill the vacant role. In addition to writing, directing and shooting, they would also edit the film together, though it is Coscarelli who receives producing credit.

To replace the missing crew, New Breed enlisted an eclectic mix of friends and fellow students, few with any relevant filmmaking experience. What this dedicated bunch lacked in knowledge they made up for in a willingness to learn and, more importantly, to work for deferred pay. Paul Pepperman, Coscarelli's former UCLA roommate, was brought on as first assistant director and unit production manager. Another UCLA student, Robert Del Valle, served as sound recorder. Aspiring stuntman George Singer Jr. boarded the film as set decorator. As with their directors, Pepperman, Del Valle and Singer had never crewed on a film before. They would all reunite on *Phantasm* four years later.

"I remember it well," Del Valle says. "The year was 1972 and I was attending UCLA's film school. A friend of mine heard about Don's movie and that they needed crew. There wasn't any pay, but when you're in film school you'll do just about anything for the experience. Also, when you're not getting paid for something, you can often get a better job than you would ordinarily with pay. Maybe you were an electrician and they make you a gaffer. Maybe you were a camera operator and they make you director of photography, although Don was his own DP. It's not uncommon in the film world and especially on student projects. It's mutually beneficial and a great way to build a résumé."

Apart from its rookie directors, the film's two most prominent players were Dac and Shirley Coscarelli, whose budget increases and boundless support helped propel the shoot forward. For their wide-ranging contributions, the Coscarellis received executive producer credit and brief cameo appearances. Dac can be seen as the gum-chewing assistant football coach during the big game and Shirley as a receptionist where the father has a job interview.

"Shirley Coscarelli was the den mother of our pack," Singer says. "She and her husband were always inviting us into their home and cooking great meals for everyone. They were frequently on set and willing to pitch in wherever needed. Some of us, including myself, were actually living out of their home during Don's early films. Thinking back on it now, it was strange having all these adults around who weren't telling us what we could and couldn't do."

Casting for the film took place in Long Beach and Los Angeles for non-Guild performers. Future *Trapper John, M.D.* heartthrob Gregory Harrison was found at Estelle Harmon's acting workshop and cast in his film debut as the title lead. Child-actor Robbie Wolcott was cast as the younger brother, Marla Pennington as a love interest, and stage veteran Ralph Richmond as Jim's football coach.

One newcomer destined to become a Coscarelli regular was actor and musician Reggie Bannister. The former Greenwood County Singers member had recently returned to acting with several plays and student films, but nothing in the way of features. He was discovered by the younger Coscarelli showcasing both talents on a Long Beach City College stage and immediately invited to join the cast. His brief appearance toward film's end would leave an indelible impression on the director, who would bring Bannister back for seven of his next eight films.

"I was basically comic relief," Bannister says. "I had about a five minute scene as this crazed hang glider pilot named O.D. Silengsly. The film had been pretty heavy up to that point, and my job was to take the kids on a little flying adventure. It was one of my favorite characters that I ever did with Don, because it was so outrageous. I really had fun with it. If you ever get a chance to see that, it's an interesting film."

TALL MAN FROM KANSAS

"Around 1972 <u>Variety</u> printed a one-inch casting ad that named the Century Plaza Hotel as the meeting place," actor Lawrence Rory Guy says. "I thought, 'This must be legitimate.' But I was, to say the least, bemused when the interviewers proved to be two teenage boys. I gave them my photo resume, and they called me down to Long Beach to audition on videotape for them. The teenagers were Don Coscarelli and his then-partner Craig Mitchell."

The chilling scowls that Lawrence Guy gave his intimidated directors are said to have
inspired Don Coscarelli to write the Tall Man into *Phantasm*.
(Photo courtesy Kristen Deem)

After the videotape audition, Coscarelli and Mitchell offered Guy (who would later come to great prominence as Angus Scrimm) the role of the alcoholic father. He admittedly had reservations about the project, particularly after a stormy reading with Gregory Harrison. "I'm not getting anything from your eyes," Harrison told Scrimm. "Oh, sorry," Scrimm responded. "Yours are lovely!" Even worse, filming would require constant trips from Los Angeles down to Long Beach for a meager (and deferred) pay. Still, he accepted the role and became at once the film's most experienced performer.

Though not always before camera, Scrimm's life had seemingly always been involved with the silver screen. Upon his 1943 arrival in Hollywood, the Kansas City native found employment first as a Paramount Theater usher and later as an RKO Pictures studio soda jerk. These jobs preceded his education at the University of Southern California where he studied drama under William C. deMille (playwright, film director and brother of Cecil B. deMille). Here he appeared in numerous campus sponsored stage productions as Rory Guy. Elsewhere, he coined the alias Angus Scrimm to avoid being caught in violation of de Mille's ban against off-campus appearances. Upon graduation, Scrimm shifted focus toward another passion at which he excelled – writing. He would join the writing staff of Capitol Records in 1961. Here he wrote liner notes for the likes of Itzhak Perlman, Frank Sinatra, Judy Garland, Nat King Cole and The Beatles, among others. He would later win the Grammy for Best Album Notes in 1975 for his work on *The Classic Erich Wolfgang Korngold.*

Just prior to his being cast in *Jim the World's Greatest,* Scrimm made nonvillainous appearances in two low-budget horror films. First was the Roger Corman-produced *Sweet Kill,* a steamy Hitchcockian thriller that marked the directorial debut of Oscar winning filmmaker Curtis Hanson. The second was *Scream Bloody Murder,* a public domain shocker remembered today mainly for Scrimm's all too brief scene as the doctor on a doomed house call. Curiously, both films feature psychopathic killers deeply affected by the Oedipal complex.

"After that, I floundered," Scrimm says. "I had no agent. I wasn't in the Guild. I answered misleading casting ads that turned out to be softcore porn or required a $400 fee to apply; offices that you'd give a swift glance and walk right out again."

AN EDUCATION

Full-time production of *Jim* began in September 1972 and then was suspended a short while for the aforementioned restructuring. After the initial breakdown, New Breed worked primarily on weekends. Unable to afford constructed sets, the film was shot entirely on location. Interiors for the Nolan family apartment were staged at a rented residence in a crime-ridden section of Long Beach. Scenes of Jim working at Jack In The Box restaurant were done during off-hours. Four different Orange County high schools stood in for the one seen in the film, including the filmmakers' own Wilson High. A scene in which the father goes for a job interview was shot in the real-life investment office of Dac Coscarelli, with Shirley at the reception desk.

Jim proved to be an intense training ground for both the directors and crew. This often meant learning from mistakes, of which there were many. Scenes were executed with technical flaws which then required re-shooting. Substantial dialogue had to be looped. Actors were detained on set all day without ever going before camera. The chilling scowls that Angus Scrimm gave his intimidated directors on such fruitless days are said to have inspired Don Coscarelli to write the Tall Man into *Phantasm.* Scrimm's on set rapport with Gregory Harrison improved greatly after their initial reading together. They would reunite years later when Harrison called Scrimm in for a guest role on an episode of *Trapper John, M.D.* that Harrison both starred in and directed.

"After a take," Scrimm says, "Craig Mitchell would come to me and say, 'That was very good, but we're going to do another take and this time could you give it just a little more?' Craig would drift off and Don would mosey over with his congenial smile and say, 'Really nice work! Now on this next take, maybe give it just a little less.' We'd shoot again, I'd let the

George Singer, Don Coscarelli and Paul Pepperman at the camera.
(Photo courtesy Darrell Kitchell)

character do whatever he felt like, and both gentlemen would find a moment afterward to tell me, "That worked just fine!"

"I adored working with Don on *Jim the World's Greatest*," Robert Del Valle says. "I say that not only because it was my first film, but because it was like '*Hey kids, let's go make a movie.*' Because it was such a low-key affair, Don was able to keep a fun mood going onset. It's tough to recreate that kind of experience today when I'm on a show like *Six Feet Under* and I've got seventy-five crewmembers hanging around. That's a much different vibe than when you've got ten or twelve crewmembers at most. With smaller crews, you're able to have more fun because it's so much more personal to work on. That's how I look back on *Jim* and *Phantasm*."

New Breed wrapped principal photography in March 1973, but not before exhausting the film's paltry budget. A reluctant Dac Coscarelli agreed to supplement them an additional $80,000 in production funds to complete the film.

The younger Coscarelli would later advise prospective directors not to live under their investor's roof, telling The Philadelphia Inquirer that his father "was always bitching about this $100,000 home movie he was going to end up with."

Coscarelli and Mitchell spent the next five months editing the prior seven months of footage until they arrived at a rough but coherent version of the film in late summer 1973. Unsure of how to proceed, the elder Coscarelli put in a call to screen the film for Los Angeles Times entertainment editor Charles Champlin. As a judge for KCET's Young Filmmakers Competition, Champlin had expressed interest in Coscarelli and Mitchell's work years before when they took home third prize in the contest. The circumstances of his screening were disastrous with film breaks and unsynchronized sound. Yet despite these conditions, Champlin wrote that *Jim the World's Greatest* "came through with its power and assurance intact." The film now had a strong advocate.

A young Don Coscarelli at home.
(Photo courtesy Darrell Kitchell)

UNIVERSAL APPEAL

Shortly after screening the film, Charles Champlin suggested to Sid Sheinberg that he look into New Breed's debut feature. A print was shipped to the studio. Sheinberg saw great potential in their work and had MCA/Universal secure distribution rights almost immediately, more than repaying Dac Coscarelli's investment. While the studio had been trending younger with twenty-something filmmakers George Lucas, Steven Spielberg and David Ward, they would be setting a record with nineteen-year-olds Don Coscarelli and Craig Mitchell. It was with great fanfare that MCA/Universal's publicity department announced the film and its young directors in newspapers throughout the country. The Schenectady Gazette called it "Universal's most interesting imminent acquisition."

Though distribution had been secured, there was still much work to be done on *Jim the World's Greatest,* especially

now that it was an official MCA/Universal picture. Coscarelli and Mitchell were moved into a backlot office to oversee improvements to the film, which included new scenes and a revised conclusion. To this end, MCA/Universal underwrote several days of additional photography at a cost of $50,000, half what New Breed had spent for an entire year of production. The studio also paraded numerous composers before the directing duo from which future *Phantasm* collaborator Fred Myrow emerged. In an attempt to cross-market the film, it was paired with a single from folk rock band America titled 'Story of a Teenager.' Although the title words appear nowhere in the song lyrics, it does play over the opening and closing credits.

In the hands of MCA/Universal, the project underwent several title changes including *Teenager, Teenage Man, Cheers, Story of a Teenager* and the final *Jim the World's Greatest* which was "not the world's greatest title" according to Champlin's review.

DISAPPEARING ACT

After spending the better part of a year in limbo, the completed film was finally released in 1975 as *Story of a Teenager,* but only in select markets where it subsequently failed to make a box office impression. Given their wildly profitable summer run of *Jaws,* Universal could well afford to risk releasing New Breed's family drama even if it underperformed. The film was re-released the following year as *Jim the World's Greatest,* but once again only in a limited number of theaters where it garnered weak profits. Film critic George Anderson lamented it was "the most poignant disappearing act of the year" in his syndicated column.

Profits aside, the film generated positive reviews from critics. The Deseret News applauded *Jim*'s three unknown leads, predicting that Gregory Harrison, Robbie Wolcott and Rory Guy "are expected to be heard from later." At length, Charles Champlin gave the film high praise in his Los Angeles Times assessment, commenting that *Jim* had "pathos and tempo, warmth and a lot of sly, wry humor." He continued by

Top: A lighthearted Paul Pepperman.
Bottom: The "Den Mother" of New Breed Productions, Shirley Coscarelli.
(Photos courtesy Darrell Kitchell)

"They made a fascinating little film that was way ahead of its time..."

- Angus Scrimm on *Jim the World's Greatest*

saying that the film is worthwhile regardless of the directors' ages, that "their work demands no allowances or forgiveness because of their youth. Many an older work has been far less true to itself."

If only MCA/Universal had shared Champlin's faith. In retrospect, the entire transaction has the distinct outward appearance of being a record-setting gimmick for distributing the work of two teenage filmmakers. Trailers, posters and newspaper ads all boasted how "two teenage boys with no background or professional experience" had made "a remarkable film," a fact that so often overshadowed the plot itself. Had MCA/Universal truly thought *Jim the World's Greatest* "remarkable," perhaps they might have invested more weight behind its release, given it due advertising and not shelved it for nearly a year upon completion. Had the time between procurement and release not been so great, the film could have benefited from the front-end wave of publicity surrounding its young creators.

"They made a fascinating little film that was way ahead of its time in depicting child abuse and the predicament of a teenage boy who has to take charge of his family when his dad - my role - gets lost in alcoholism," Scrimm says. "Gregory Harrison in his first film role is sensational in the lead, Reggie Bannister has a wackily charming scene as a glider pilot, and an appealing kid actor named Robbie Wolcott was heartbreaking as the abused son."

"I think the first time I saw it was after it had been released to theaters," Ralph Richmond says. "I was quite impressed with it and very disappointed when after about six weeks they pulled it. I guess people objected to the child-murder. Of course, that's certainly something to object to but

I thought we handled it well in the film because it was done with jump cuts so you never really saw it. You only had the impression that it had happened. I think we would've done better if that scene hadn't been included. Certainly that was a realistic place for the story to go, but it became too much. It wasn't even that the little boy died, in my opinion, it was just that we bothered to actually show it happening. It's still a good film, though. A powerful film."

"Even with all of its high school antics, Jim was a very mature film," Robert Del Valle says. "Don Coscarelli and Craig Mitchell took their subject matter very seriously. It was certainly a much better film than you would've expected two teenagers to have written, directed, shot and edited and it remains a huge accomplishment for them both. I haven't seen it in years. I wish it could get a home video release because I'd love to see it again."

In the years that followed, *Jim The World's Greatest* was seldom seen, though it did enjoy the occasional HBO broadcast. It was also screened for the cast and crew of Coscarelli's next two films. Universal has since forgotten the entire ordeal, never having released *Jim* to home video throughout their decades-long ownership. Distribution rights have since reverted back to New Breed.

GOING SOLO

Writing in the Los Angeles Times, Charles Champlin congratulated Don Coscarelli and Craig Mitchell for having the courage to write about the world around them rather than working with more "standard commercial forms." Young

Shirley Coscarelli, flanked by her son.
(Photo courtesy Darrell Kitchell)

writers and directors, he continued, too often distrust their own experience, which is the ultimate lesson of *Jim the World's Greatest*. While the film itself is pulled from neither director's personal history, it does exist in a world they know, which at the very least can be taken to mean Long Beach. This important piece of advice, like so many hard learned lessons about independent filmmaking, was not lost on Coscarelli as he began his second feature.

As MCA/Universal held *Jim* in limbo, the filmmakers behind it announced an amicable end to their partnership. Speaking to an Associated Press reporter, Coscarelli revealed that he was working on a story about a rock musician. His parents, happy to have gainfully made it out of *Jim* no worse for wear, made public their retirement from the movie business. These plans, like the rock musician story, were soon thwarted as their son shifted focus toward another project entirely.

Before his first film had even seen release, Coscarelli was hard at work on a second, *Kenny & Company*. His script presented a slice-of-life tale chronicling the days leading up to Halloween in the lives of three suburbanite twelve-year-olds: the likable Kenny, his mischievous best friend Doug, and their pesky-yet-lovable pal Sherman. Together they attend school, build costumes, go trick-or-treating, prank the neighbors and attempt to understand girls, death, school and sex. The film concludes with Kenny defeating bully Johnny Hoffman with a little help from his pals. If *Jim*'s failure was due to its overtly dark tone, Coscarelli was not going to make the same mistake again. Instead, he presents a lighthearted family-comedy about life growing up in Long Beach, though the town is never identified in the film. The proceedings feel loosely autobiographical as though a window into Coscarelli's childhood.

"I wasn't surprised at all when Don called me back to do *Kenny & Company*," Ralph Richmond recalls. "Even though *Jim* didn't do well, I never once thought it was the end of the road for him. I could tell that directing was simply in Don's blood, something he wanted as a major part of his life. With his father running an investment company, it looked to me like he wasn't going to have any trouble getting the backing he needed."

"It's not really a kid's film as far as I'm concerned," production assistant Dennis Kitchell says. "It's geared toward people who are just out of the last stages of childhood, heading into young adulthood. I think that's why Don was able to create it. He was so close to these experiences that they weren't lost on him yet. I really can't think of anything else like it because most of the time, kid movies have a very different tone than ours did. It reminds me most of the *Peanuts* cartoons because it's a kid's eye view of the world. The adults are on the periphery. You don't see that in a lot of movies. "

COSCARELLI & CO.

Returning to fund and executive produce were Coscarelli's parents who again appeared on camera. This time, Dac cameod as the victim of a Halloween prank and Shirley played a sizable

Darrell Kitchell and Don Coscarelli preparing a shot.
(Photo courtesy Darrell Kitchell)

role as Kenny's mother. For the production crew, New Breed sought to repeat the formula used on *Jim the World's Greatest* and invited back several players. Chief among the returning crew was Paul Pepperman, who was now elevated to associate producer and unit production manager. George Singer also returned, this time as key grip and stuntman. One notable addition to the crew was film professor Darrell Kitchell, whom Don Coscarelli hired to serve as director of photography.

"I think Don was lucky to have found Darrell Kitchell," second assistant cameraman Steve McKenzie says. "Darrell actually brought some experience to the film because he had been teaching at Long Beach City College and done some other stuff in the business. Basically, he knew what the heck he was doing. Everyone else? We were all pretty green."

"Don went into production with a very distinct vision for the film," Darrell Kitchell says. "He wanted to shoot it from a kid's point-of-view by never bringing the camera more than three feet off the ground. Certainly that seemed interesting on paper but we discarded it early on because it didn't work. We also shot through a D4 fog-filter lens to give it a fantasy feel, but that didn't work either and looked awful in dailies. Although we got rid of it pretty quickly there are still a few fogged out shots in the film, maybe in the classroom scenes. We were all for experimenting until we found what worked best."

"I was told about the film by Mimi Townley, who taught a film class at Wilson High that Don and Craig Mitchell had taken," transportation captain Stephen Elders says. "I knew about *Jim the World's Greatest* because she would mention it in class from time to time. Just before school let out for summer, Ms. Townley asked my best friend, Steve McKenzie, and me if we wanted to crew on a feature film during break, knowing that we were avid film fans. Of course we did and were sent to the Coscarelli home in Bixby Hills where we were put to work right away!"

Casting for the film took place in Long Beach and Los Angeles, which netted newcomers Jeff Roth as Sherman, David Newton as the pesky schoolmate Pudwell and Terrie Kalbus as love interest Marcy. Non-actor Dan McCann won the title role after being discovered at a school carnival and invited to audition by Pepperman. Adult cast returnees included Ralph Richmond as FBI agent Big Doug and Reggie Bannister as schoolteacher Mr. Donovan. The adult cast also featured Ken Jones as football coach Mr. Soupy, Mary Ellen Shaw as a neighbor, and Long Beach City College professor James de Priest as Kenny's father.

"The younger cast members were terrific for their age," Dennis Kitchell says. "Dan McCann was your typical neighborhood kid and Jeff Roth was exactly how you see him in the film. Jeff never broke character when the camera stopped rolling because he was that character! All three boys were very patient with the demands put on them. A film set is quite an environment for kids that young to cope."

"As an actor, you're always happy to have a bigger part," Richmond says. "As Big Doug, I was the principal adult player in *Kenny*, the first billed of the adults. That meant that I had a lot more to do. *Kenny* was about fourteen days of shooting for me whereas *Jim* was only two or three. I thought the three main kids were very talented young people who were intent on the work at hand and not so much on fooling around, as a lot of children tend to be. It was a great experience, all around, and I like the film we made. I think my favorite line was 'And that's how handcuffs work.'"

"I was singing in the Long Beach Civic Light Opera at the time," Jones says. "I was Johnny Leadville in *The Unsinkable Molly Brown*. Shirley Coscarelli, I think, introduced me to Don who had me read for a film he was doing. They liked what I did and soon after cast me in *Kenny & Company*. So I wasn't just someone they pulled off the street to be in the film. I had been involved with acting for a long, long time. I'm still

surprised at how young Don was when I first met him. To be making films at his age was amazing. Hell of a nice guy, too."

HOLLYWOOD'S ORIGINAL BALDWIN

Years before Alec, Stephen or Daniel, there was another Baldwin in town – Michael Baldwin. While he wasn't cast as the lead in *Kenny & Company*, he did give the film's breakout performance as Little Doug. Born to multiple Emmy-Award winner and animator, Gerard Baldwin of Hanna-Barbera and Jay Ward Productions fame, the future *Phantasm* star was by far the most experienced child actor cast in the film. Prior to this, his first feature role, Baldwin had made guest appearances on shows such as *Starsky & Hutch*, *Sesame Street* and *The Electric Company*. He was twelve years old when he met Don Coscarelli.

"The first film I ever did was called *The Sense of Hearing*, which was an animated educational film that my father made," Baldwin says. "I was quite small, probably five years old, and we shot it in Bradford Park on a rainy day. My character was walking around, listening to all of the auditory input until eventually the camera pushes in on his ear and it goes into the animation."

Following appearances in several school plays, Baldwin expressed a serious desire to pursue acting professionally. A family friend arranged a reading with a local child talent agency and he was quickly signed to a contract. Television appearances and commercial work came shortly thereafter. *Kenny & Company* marked one of Baldwin's first cattle call auditions where he was up against dozens of other hopefuls. He was offered a role in the film the very same day he read lines for Coscarelli. "I guess I must've done something right," Baldwin says.

"You could always tell which one of the kids was the more natural actor," Stephen Elders says. "It was very clearly Michael Baldwin and I'm not surprised that Don went on to use him in *Phantasm*. He was very comfortable in front of the

Top: Hollywood's original and still most interesting Baldwin - Michael.
Bottom: Darrell Kitchell, Don Coscarelli, Dan McCann and Michael Baldwin watching a scene.
(Photos courtesy Darrell Kitchell)

camera and seemed to have an actor's instinct even at a young age. Sometimes Dan McCann could be a little wooden during a scene and it would require a few takes before Don could coax him into being natural, but for a newcomer to acting, Dan did a fine job. It just came easier to Michael."

"At some point after I was cast, there was a screening of *Jim The World's Greatest*," Baldwin says. "At that time, I think it was being called *Story of a Teenager*. I felt it was an incredibly dramatic film. I remember being particularly impressed by a younger Angus Scrimm, not having any idea that I would wind up working with him later on. Greg Harrison was good in it too. I actually met Greg years later when he was on Broadway in *Steel Pier* with my best friend Daniel McDonald. We wound up going to a party at Greg's house and I remember pointing out to him our mutual Coscarelli connection. He was a cool guy."

CAMP KENNY

Kenny & Company's production would be far more orderly than Don Coscarelli's first film had been, even despite having children now thrown into the mix. Amazingly, production went smoothly and managed to stay within the summer schedule. The film was made for less than *Jim the World's Greatest* at a cost of only $65,000 for all of filming and $130,000 for post-production. These outcomes can likely be attributed to Coscarelli having written a more solid script this time around, one that didn't require massive reshoots or cuts.

"We shot *Kenny & Company* mostly on weekends for an entire summer," Darrell Kitchell says. "We would shoot Friday night, Saturday, Sunday and sometimes Monday morning before we had to check the equipment back in at Alan Gordon Enterprises in Hollywood. With them, you were supposed to pick your gear up at 5:00 PM on Friday, which put us driving back to Long Beach right in the middle of rush hour traffic. Ordinarily, you could make the trip in forty minutes but in traffic it could take you hours. So they wound up letting us pick our stuff up at 2:00 PM on Friday, which allowed us to

shoot that night for free. Since they weren't open on Sunday we only paid for Saturday and shot throughout the entire weekend. This saved us tons of money."

Another budget saver was a decision to shoot extensively at the Coscarelli home in Bixby Hills, which alleviated New Breed of both rental and permit costs. So much filming was done here that partitions went up to separate living space from shooting space. As her home became production central, Shirley Coscarelli took on the roles of art director and caterer in addition to acting and executive producing. Once a place of residence, the Coscarelli home was now a movie set and summer camp.

"Don's parents made a big impression on me," Steve McKenzie says. "I'll be blunt here; these people had money. They lived in a rich part of Long Beach but they could not have been nicer to us. They were so deeply involved with the film and welcomed us into their home for an entire summer without hesitation or complaint. I'll never forget how truly warm they were to everyone. I'm not sure I remember a single day where either Shirley or Don's father wasn't on set."

"Steve McKenzie and I were the youngest crewmembers on the film," Stephen Elders says. "We were still in high school and because of that, we had a pretty good rapport with the kids. One of my regular tasks was to chauffeur Dan, Michael and Jeff around from their homes to set in the mornings. Don's parents always let me drive the Coscarelli family Oldsmobile on these runs, which was a new experience for me since I'd only had my license for a year. They were very trusting people! Later on, we had to find a used school bus to handle all of the kids for the crowd scenes. I think they wound up calling me transportation captain in the credits, but my job wasn't limited to just that."

For the sharp-eyed viewer, *Kenny & Company* is brimming with cameo appearances. George Singer has a bit part as the Corvette driver who runs over Kenny's dummy. Darrell Kitchell plays a policeman during the end chase. Best boy Corey Leedom appears as a car crash victim and his dog, Hardy, doubles as Kenny's dog, Bob. Paul Pepperman makes two cameo appearances, one as the haunted house monster and

Top Left: Dan McCann as the title character during school scenes.
Top Right: Jeff Roth with Don Coscarelli.
Bottom: Darrell Kitchell, in costume as a police officer, holds a light meter to Jeff Roth.
(Photos courtesy Darrell Kitchell)

Paul Pepperman watches a test run of the skateboarding-through-fire stunt.
(Photo courtesy Darrell Kitchell)

another alongside Coscarelli himself as construction workers when Doug skateboards through fire. Even rock band America has a blink and you'll miss it cameo on a poster in Kenny's garage.

"We all did a little bit of everything," McKenzie says. "That meant occasionally getting pulled into a scene for whatever reason. Steve Elders and I got pulled into a crowd scene near the end. Back then, he had long dark hair and I had this big mustache so, needless to say, we did not blend in with the kids! I can't imagine why no one thought how out of place it was to have two grown men watching children fight one another and not break it up!"

"Practically every crewmember is in the movie somewhere except for me," Dennis Kitchell says. "But my car made a dramatic appearance. When the uncredited Paul Pepperman is chasing the kids down the street on Halloween, he runs smack into my orange Volkswagen. Paul hit it so hard that he dented the fender and cracked the windshield, which

they fortunately paid for. It was a small sacrifice for the movie. If it looks like Paul hits the moving Volkswagen hard, it's because he did. That's how you take one for the team."

"Interesting to hear that Don later shot too many scenes on *Phantasm*," Darrell Kitchell says. "Interesting because I thought we had the opposite problem on *Kenny & Company*. Right after we'd screened the married print of the film, we got into it over that. I told him, '*Don, this needs more scenes. The story moves too quickly. You need more foreshadowing.*' He felt differently about it. Obviously, I lost that argument. But when the film underperformed upon release, I always thought it was partly because of the editing. I know that's a bad thing to say because I like the film a lot, but it could've benefited from additional shooting and slower pacing. More of a good thing."

With production's end, Coscarelli began editing the film at his parent's home, with regular assistance from Pepperman. Despite the film's greatly reduced music budget, Fred Myrow agreed to return as composer with help from

Reggie Bannister and future *Phantasm* player Bill Cone, the latter of whom formed two parts of the three member Good Band. Bannister and Cone were billed as The Otis Players for their musical contributions, taking their name from Kenny's prank dummy in the film. Lee Mishkin, an associate of animation director Gerard Baldwin, handled the film's opening title sequence. Upon completion, Coscarelli personally shopped the film around to prospective studios. The response was lukewarm. Twentieth Century Fox would eventually purchase domestic distribution rights.

NOT A SKATEBOARDING MOVIE

One facet of *Kenny & Company* that would go on to plague its eventual release was the inclusion of a resurging pastime then sweeping Southern California. Both Kenny and Doug skateboard their way through several perilous scenes that leave

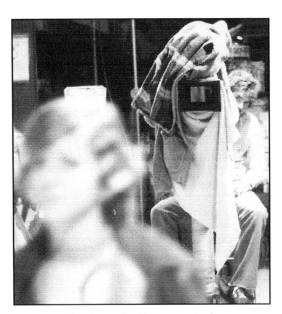

Don Coscarelli with camera trained on
Michael Baldwin at the toy store location.
(Photo courtesy Darrell Kitchell)

you wondering if Michael Baldwin shouldn't have abandoned acting for a career on wheels. In reality, the production enlisted professional skateboarder Steven Monahan to double Baldwin on such scenes. The one exception was the skateboarding-through-fire bit, for which George Singer fearlessly stepped in. To Baldwin's credit, he really did ride his skateboard while doing a handstand.

"Skateboarding was my main mode of transportation for years and years," Baldwin says. "There was a solid five year period where I didn't go anywhere without a skateboard. I had started riding in elementary school around fourth or fifth grade when skateboards were becoming popular again. So imagine how cool I thought it was to actually be skateboarding in a movie that I was also acting in. In reality, I wasn't that great at it, which is why they brought in a superstar skateboarder to double me on all of the stunts."

The release of *Kenny & Company* coincided with the creation of an infamous downhill event, the Hill Street Speed Run in Signal Hill. In the film, the heroes traverse this very same incline, Kenny in a homemade go-kart and Doug on skateboard (Monahan doubling). The combination of Monahan's involvement and Signal Hill was enough to earn the film publicity in skateboarding magazines that in turn presented their readership with a skewed image of the film; it was not at heart a skateboard movie. Sensing the sport's rising popularity, 20th Century Fox strongly emphasized the sport's prominence in their advertising, which only added to public misconception about the film. Both theatrical posters highlighted skateboarding and the sport was incorporated into the film's official logo in newspapers.

"Don Coscarelli was concerned about the way the studio marketed that film," Ralph Richmond says. "They made it look like a skateboard picture and it wasn't that at all. In fact, we had very little skateboarding in it. Consequently, when skateboard enthusiasts came to see the film and it didn't have enough skateboarding scenes to satisfy them, they bad-mouthed it. *Kenny & Company* wasn't getting good press and we all felt the studio was to blame because of how they were marketing it."

An original newspaper advertisement for *Kenny & Company*.
(Hey look, *The Omen* is playing!)

SHELVED

In a discouraging repeat scenario, *Kenny & Company* underperformed in what little distribution 20th Century Fox gave it, prompting them to shelve it entirely. This time there would be no Charles Champlin to advocate on the film's behalf and no re-release the following year. If the only bad press is no press, then by all means, *Kenny & Company* had bad press. In the wake of *Jim*'s botched release, Don Coscarelli's sophomore effort failed to generate the same kind of national coverage afforded him previously. In fact, it was barely reviewed by anyone.

What little press the film did garner was positive. Variety said of the film: "Modest in the best sense of the word, *Kenny & Company* unfolds simply and enjoyably as a series of believable incidents in the lives of its young characters." Writing in the All Movie Guide years later, Hal Erickson noted, "The end result makes one wish we'd seen a lot more of both Dan McCann and Don Coscarelli after the limited release of *Kenny & Company*."

"I thought the film turned out really well," Ken Jones says. "Everyone I ever spoke to thought it was a pretty good picture too. Can't say it made much money, though. For one thing, they weren't fast enough in releasing it. They needed to beat *The Bad News Bears* to the punch because they were aimed at the same crowd. That was a baseball picture and we were, what? A touch football picture? They couldn't or didn't get it out in time to beat *Bears*. Still, it was a fun show."

"I was pretty aware of the rivalry between our film and *The Bad News Bears*," Michael Baldwin says. "It annoyed me that we made our movie before they made theirs, but that they had this wide release and we had a bullshit release. It also annoyed me that they got all of this press for being a film where kids actually acted like kids when we had already done it. We were a pre-*Bad News Bears* fuck-shit-piss kid movie, where the kids said words they weren't supposed to before *The Bad News Bears* made it cool. Although they certainly didn't do it without class or style."

"I knew once it disappeared that something had gone wrong," Dennis Kitchell says. "That it wasn't successful here didn't surprise me much. It was an odd film and I don't think they marketed it the right way. I sometimes wonder if I like this film just because I remember working on it or if it's really as good as I think it is. I think it's the latter. Other people seem to hold this film with real affection, like it was part of their own childhood and you know what? Maybe it was. It seems to cover a pretty broad range of experience, which makes it timeless. I also see a lot of my own childhood in it, but people who weren't even alive when we made it can relate to it as well. It's quite universal that way. It resonates with people."

"Here's the lousy part about the whole experience," Steve McKenzie says. "After the film was done, Don asked me if I wanted to get involved with his next project but I politely declined. I said '*Eh, I need to get a steady job. Thanks for the invitation, but I can't.*' And of course that film turned out to be *Phantasm*, which would have been a blast to work on. I wish I'd taken him up on that offer."

TURNING JAPANESE

One bizarre footnote to the legacy of *Kenny & Company* was where it eventually found success, which was in Japan through film distributor Toho-Towa. Even before release, Japan's enthusiasm toward a film about American kids that Americans didn't even care about was astonishing. To celebrate Kenny's release, Toho sent Don Coscarelli, Dan McCann, Michael Baldwin and Jeff Roth on a whirlwind promotional tour through the country where they received a rockstar welcome. Translated, the title read *Boys, Boys, Boys.*

"The trip to Japan was such a good time," Baldwin says. "We were big stars all of a sudden. But there was something puzzling about the Japanese and the way that they viewed the movie. They laughed at all the wrong places. There was something they were getting from that movie that no other culture was getting. I remember watching it with a large Japanese audience and seeing where they reacted to the film, and being baffled. These people were liking the movie but not for the same reasons I would like it."

Combined with the future success of *Phantasm*, Baldwin would remain a celebrity figure in Japan for years to come, prompting a stream of fan mail and the occasional house visit. "That wasn't as much of an issue back then as it could've been," Baldwin says. "But people have found my address before and shown up at my door. They're usually women, so it's not so bad. When cute young Japanese girls show up on your doorstep, you invite them in. You say, '*Come on in, let's have breakfast.*' It's harmless."

POST-KENNY

By late 1977, Coscarelli had two very credible films to his name. Then only twenty-two years old, he briefly considered helming a pirate film next. He had long thought that Angus Scrimm would make a splendid buccaneer with the piercing scowl that is now so indelibly linked to the Tall Man. The idea was scrapped as New Breed would have struggled to fund such an expensive endeavor in a then-dead genre.

"While we were making the film," Darrell Kitchell says, "Don never mentioned wanting to do horror next. As a matter of fact, he spoke as if he wanted to do another kid's picture that would use girls more than *Kenny & Company* did. He was really impressed by Terrie Kalbus and Starla Dotson. Both were just local junior high girls and non-actresses that worked great in those roles. That's probably why he brought Terrie back for *Phantasm*. For a non-actress, she was terrific."

In the years since its release, *Kenny & Company* has enjoyed a modest cult following through airings on television and interest from the *Phantasm* fan base. In 2005, it saw home video release through Anchor Bay Entertainment with a DVD special edition personally supervised by Coscarelli. Along with *Jim the World's Greatest* it stands as a worthy predecessor to *Phantasm* with no less than fifteen cast and crew carrying over to New Breed's third production.

"Honestly, I'm shocked," Steve McKenzie says. "I'm shocked that thirty-five years later there are people still interested in this little low-budget film made by a bunch of kids in Long Beach about a bunch of kids in Long Beach. The summer we spent making that movie was one of the best I've ever had and I'll always look back fondly on my time with those guys. That anyone else liked the film, that's just great."

The Coscarelli's on set - Dac, Shirley and Don.
(Photo courtesy Darrell Kitchell)

"... I'll always look back fondly on my time with those guys. That anyone else liked the film, that's just great."

- Steve McKenzie on *Kenny & Company*

Chapter 1: Morningside

By 1977, Don Coscarelli had independently written and directed two feature films. That both underperformed at the domestic box office, while disheartening, did not prevent him from mounting a third. His father, an investment counselor, had seen healthy returns on both ventures, even if the distributors had not, and was keen to fund another. The younger Coscarelli would need to generate more than just favorable reviews if he were to continue making movies. Now was the time for a hit.

SOMETHING WICKED

Phantasm legend has it that Don Coscarelli was test screening *Kenny & Company* when the idea of making a horror film first occurred to him. As the picture ticked past the seventy-two minute mark, Paul Pepperman's haunted house monster appeared and filled the screen with its grisly visage. This sudden scare caused the audience to jump, flail and scream – much to the surprise and delight of Coscarelli who hadn't counted on such a visceral reaction. Never before having wielded such an awesome power over his audience, he longed to make them jump like this again!

The horror genre was not unfamiliar territory to Coscarelli. He had grown up an avid fan of movies that made people jump. In *Kenny*, the director paid subtle tribute to James Whale's *Frankenstein* by listing Pepperman's monster without a performer (à la Boris Karloff's monster in the 1931 film). Coscarelli's plan was ambitious – to scare his audience silly with an abundance of shocks, one every five minutes if possible. He also hoped that a horror movie, hailing from a traditionally lucrative genre, would give him the box office success so desperately needed.

"I remember all of us having lunch one day while recording the music for *Kenny*," Bill Cone recalls. "It was Don, Paul, Reggie and myself. Don said something to the effect of wanting to make a horror movie but not having a story for it yet. I said, '*Don, if you're going to make a horror movie, please make Ray Bradbury's Something Wicked This Way Comes.*' I thought it

was a terrific story and I just knew it would make a wonderful movie. We all then started throwing around ideas after that. Most of what we brought up that day wound up being what *Phantasm* was all about. I told him that I would do the music if he wanted, but that I also wanted to be in it. Don said, '*Well, sure. You'll all be in it.*'"

Coscarelli soon read the Bradbury novel and was immediately smitten with Cone's suggestion. He began plans to direct a film adaptation of it. Early on, he decided that Michael Baldwin and Dan McCann would do nicely as the young leads, Jim Nightshade and Will Halloway. An inquiry into film rights, however, revealed that Michael Douglas had already purchased them. Down but not out, Coscarelli forged ahead, reasoning that if he couldn't make *Something Wicked*, he could evoke it using roughly the same idea.

Poster for the eventual 1983 film adaptation by Walt Disney Productions.

While promoting *Kenny & Company*, Coscarelli announced his new direction in September 1976 by telling The Deseret News about his next project, a horror film called *The Immortals*. This title, which mirrored a central theme in Bradbury's novel, was soon dropped.

THE ORIGINAL SCREENPLAY

To write his horror film, Don Coscarelli left Long Beach for a secluded cabin in Big Bear. The tranquil mountain-lake community offered him a sanctum ideal for channeling a macabre muse previously untapped. When he finally returned several weeks later from his cabin retreat, Coscarelli held in hand the story and characters that would endear his film to millions contained within a script titled *Morningside*.

The narrative follows orphaned brothers Mike and Jody Pearson and their friend, ice cream man Reggie, as the trio uncover and attempt to stop an evil plot underway at the

Has the most creative cabin fevers *ever*.
(Photo courtesy Kristen Deem)

local Morningside Mortuary. An alien mortician known only as "The Tall Man" has been unusually proactive in procuring customers whom he has converted into hideous dwarf-slaves. Otherworldly horrors await them inside Morningside including a deadly aerial sphere and a dimensional doorway. By and large, this was *Phantasm* by another name. The basic story and key ideas were all there along with an hour of additional subplots involving secondary characters. As such, *Morningside* envisioned a much broader story than *Phantasm* did, particularly where characterization was concerned.

At the core of Coscarelli's script, beyond all the extraneous material he would later trim, was *Morningside's* emotional foundation – the story of Mike Pearson. A troubled youth, Mike feels forsaken by his older brother for leaving him in the wake of their parents' deaths. Even worse is that Jody assumes that Mike's imagination is merely a ploy for attention and fails to heed the young boy's warnings about Morningside. Mike's solitary vantage is a perfect perspective from which to experience the story. Coscarelli infuses the role with great pathos and taps into the universal angst of growing up (a recurring theme in both his previous films).

Notably absent from this original draft is the Tall Man's alter ego, the sultry Lady in Lavender. Not until nineteen-year old actress Kathy Lester read for another role was Coscarelli inspired to create the part. Lester wore a lavender dress to her audition. "Originally, I was only supposed to read for some girl that Jody meets at a bar," Lester says. "She takes him to the cemetery to make out and ends up getting killed by one of the dwarves. Don said after the screen test that he thought I had a devious, sensual quality about me and decided to turn me into a villainess. I thought it was a lot better than getting killed off!"

Early script drafts also contained an alternate version of the silver sphere, one that more closely resembled the nightmare vision that first inspired Coscarelli to include it. "Originally, it was a big ball that had a hypodermic needle attached to it," Robert Del Valle says. "It would fly around until it found a victim and then inject them with a poison and they'd keel over and die. *Phantasm* was being shot at the same time that *Star Wars* was about to come out and I remember seeing in that film's trailer the scene where Darth Vader held Princess Leia hostage and was about to question her. In floats a big ball with a hypodermic needle that's going to inject her with some kind of truth serum and I went, '*Oh my God! That's what we're doing!*' So I called Don and he said, '*Well, we've gotta do something else.*' Then it became the ball we know as it is today."

The most significant difference between *Morningside* and *Phantasm* was in how they concluded. *Phantasm* ends with Mike waking from a bad dream only to have the Tall Man reemerge in a shock appearance, skewing the line between nightmare and reality. *Morningside*, on the other hand, ended more poignantly with Mike waking to reality and remaining there to face the hardship of grief, his brother and parents lost to him by ordinary forces. In this more somber conclusion, alien morticians and silver spheres were not real. Death, however, *was*.

The shift from *Morningside* to *Phantasm* encompassed a great deal more than simple rewrites or scene deletions. The film's evolution inched forward throughout production, climaxing in the reflective days that followed the first test screening in January 1978. The film's back-end metamorphosis was still more than a year away at this point. For now, it was going to be called *Morningside* and short of some tweaking, such as the originally scripted 'dog in heat' becoming a 'gopher in heat,' it would be filmed as Coscarelli had envisioned.

PHAMILIAR FACES

During casting, Don Coscarelli sought to bring back no fewer than seven New Breed veterans for *Morningside*. Several appeared in tailor-made parts. The roles of Mike, Reggie and the Tall Man were written specifically for Michael Baldwin, Reggie Bannister and Angus Scrimm. Other returning cast members included Ken Jones as the mausoleum caretaker, Terrie Kalbus as a fortuneteller's granddaughter, Ralph Richmond as a bank guard and Mary Ellen Shaw as the brothers' Aunt Belle. Good

> # "I think Don saw these characters as sort of like us if we were involved in this situation..."
> ## - Reggie Bannister on characterization

Band bassist Bill Cone was cast as the film's first victim, Tommy.

The majority of *Morningside*'s cast agreed to act for deferred compensation and few were required to audition for their parts. Most performers were without a contract at the start of filming, much less an agent to negotiate one. The cast agreed to appear in the production before ever reading the script. Some even finished their work without ever receiving the elusive document. Coscarelli's enthusiasm alone - not the strength of the material - convinced prospective cast and crew to join the production.

"I think Don saw these characters as sort of like us if we were involved in this situation," Bannister says. "You know, Reggie is everyman's man. If you're going to go through the gates of hell, this is the guy you want next to you because he'll give it up for you. Something I like about the character is that I've become known as the ultimate sidekick."

"Once we finished *Kenny & Company* I stayed in contact with Don and Paul Pepperman on a regular basis," Baldwin says. "As far as I was concerned, we were like buds. What I didn't know at the time was that they were negotiating *Phantasm* behind my back with my agent and my parents. They couldn't tell me about it because they'd been sworn to secrecy. Had I found out, I probably would've been really excited and wanted to do it for free like everyone else, which I didn't. My agent saw to it that I was paid weekly for my work. I do remember getting a script in the beginning but I don't think it was more than sixty pages or so. I never had what we were shooting in advance. I'd just get the necessary pages on the day we were going to shoot them and go from there."

One newcomer to the production was actress Bettina Viney, whom Coscarelli had cast at Scrimm's suggestion: "All the way back to *Jim The World's Greatest*, I'd been telling Don that there was a terrific actress who worked at the Callboard Theatre. The audiences there adored her. Bettina was an Englishwoman who had been over here for years, tall, rail-thin, with dark red hair. She could play a villainess who could chill your bones, or the sweetest, most understanding, heartwarming nun. When Don did *Phantasm*, he said, '*All right, we'll give your English actress the part of the fortune teller.*' It was perfect for her."

THE MAN WHO WOULD BE JODY

Don Coscarelli first offered the part of Mike's footloose older brother to Gregory Harrison, for whom he had written the role. When Harrison declined the part, an extensive casting search was held from which up-and-coming musician Bill Thornbury emerged. He was immediately brought in to read lines with Michael Baldwin. "It was a little awkward when I first met Bill," Baldwin says. "We did some fairly dramatic scenes in the Coscarelli's backyard by the pool. I think we were just sort of feeling each other out and seeing how it would go, how the chemistry was going to work. It worked out great and we became fast friends. Bill is an awesome guy."

"Acting was never really what I wanted to do with my life," Thornbury says. "I was open to it because I had signed with a theatrical agency. My agent signed me because she thought I could make her some money doing television commercials. That eventually led to a few film gigs, which led me to Phantasm." Prior to joining the cast of *Morningside*, Thornbury had gained significant exposure and entry into the Screen Actors Guild with Richard Donner's *Sarah T. - Portrait of a Teenage Alcoholic*. His fellow cast included Mark Hamill, Larry Hagman and Linda Blair, who joined Thornbury on guitar for a duet performance of Carole King's '*It's Too Late.*'

Just after *Sarah T.*, Thornbury recalls being sent by his agent to MGM where a young director named George Lucas was making a new sci-fi movie. He was admittedly not thrilled by the idea. "I kind of snickered to myself because I thought that had already been done with *Star Trek*," Thornbury says. "The only other person in the waiting room was Mark Hamill, whom I knew. He was excited and I wasn't and I think I took that kind of ridiculous, absurd attitude into the meeting with George Lucas. I met with him by myself but I didn't read. He said, '*I'm just looking right now and I know you're involved in another project,*' and I remember not being particularly charming or even trying to be. It was not one of my more intelligent days."

Lucas eventually cast Hamill in *Star Wars* and Thornbury soon received another call from his agent about a young director named Don Coscarelli. "My wife, Sharon, and I saw *Star Wars* the night that it opened," Thornbury continues. "We had perfect seats at Grauman's Chinese Theater and the place was packed. I knew then that I had made a terrible, terrible mistake in not putting my best foot forward. I'm not saying I could've gotten the job, but I could've given it my best. It was a perfect example of how you don't know everything when you think you might and that you should always share in other people's enthusiasm on whatever they're doing. It might come back and bite you if you don't. That's what I took with me into *Phantasm*."

TALL, DARK AND SCARY

According to his own record, Angus Scrimm officially signed on to play the Tall Man on January 3, 1977. He recalls first hearing about the role from Coscarelli's parents at a Writer's Guild screening. "They tapped me on the shoulder. We embraced and they said, '*Did you know that Don has written a new script and there's a part in it for you? You're going to play an alien.*' I thought, '*How intriguing, a film about a European immigrant*

The mild-mannered Lawrence Guy.
(Photo courtesy Kristen Deem)

coming to America, that's going to be a real challenge! Great!' Then I read the script. A *different* kind of alien!"

Though he knew at once he was game for another Coscarelli project, be it about aliens or immigrants, his involvement would come second to the duties involved in caring for his terminally ill mother.

"Making the film entailed great sacrifices with my blessed sister Lucille subbing for me at home," Scrimm says. "But all recent literature on caring for an Alzheimer's patient stresses the need for the caretaker to get away from time to time. My sporadic absences to play the Tall Man provided just this outlet and, together with my in-home work writing liner notes about Beethoven, Mozart, Shostakovich, et al., for Angel Records, helped me stay in balance."

In a journal dated 1/28/1977, Angus Scrimm wrote:

I joined the Coscarellis at 4:30 for makeup tests at Shirley's hands. I'd mentioned at our last meeting, as a possibility, that my combed-over hair conceals a bald forehead, which might create a very effective elongated face. Shirley's first act -- with a mixture of tentativeness and decisiveness -- was to comb back the superstructure of hair that conceals my gleaming pate. She then used a pale base to make me look deathly, shadowed in the temples and cheek hollows, and I was already transformed into something sinister. We then tried four more makeups, the shadowing in of the eye sockets and other tricks, with Shirley occasionally consulting huge elaborate, lavishly illustrated makeup guidance books she'd brought along. The first remained the best. Don Jr. took photographs. We'll know Wednesday which makeup photographed best.

On February 9, Scrimm met once more with Shirley Coscarelli at the world-famous Western Costume Company for wardrobe ideas - ideas being all the production could afford there. The two decided that the Tall Man's uniform should consist of a tight-fitting black suit, red tiepin and elevated boots. The black suit was supplied by Dac Coscarelli and altered to fit the towering performer at Benny the Tailor's in Long Beach. The persona of the Tall Man took a little more time to develop. Scrimm would eventually find the character's menacing voice after rehearsing his dialogue into a tape recorder. The mannerisms, walk and facial movements would be perfected before a mirror.

There exist three origin stories for the Tall Man's signature stare, all of which date back to the filming of *Jim the World's Greatest*. Coscarelli repeatedly incurred it by summoning Scrimm to location without ever getting to shoot his scenes. The performer was also said to have scowled in the direction of a misbehaving child on set, who straightened up immediately. As Scrimm recalls, a light-hearted moment may have brought about its first issuance.

"On one of those days when I knew it was going to be a long time before they got to me, I drove down to the beach area of Long Beach, which still existed back then. There I found one of those kiosks where, for a quarter, you could take your own photos and they would come in a strip of four. I was making faces and being funny and one of the faces I made was the Tall Man, which stayed with me when I got the photos back."

NEW BLOOD FOR NEW BREED

Don Coscarelli welcomed back five New Breed stalwarts to work as crew on *Morningside*. These included Paul Pepperman as Co-producer, George Singer Jr. as Key Grip/Stuntman and Robert Del Valle as Unit Production Manager. Eager to see a return on their largest film investment yet, the senior Coscarellis reassumed their customary roles as Executive Producers. Shirley Coscarelli so immersed herself in filming that she resorted to using aliases in the film's credits (S. Tyer, Shirley Mae and Shirl Quinlan are all her). Her contributions included wardrobe, makeup, set decorating, production design, catering and the occasional special effect.

In addition to these five veterans, the crew was comprised of new recruits. Notices were left on local college bulletin boards, attracting Grip John Zumpano and Assistant Editor Bruce Chudacoff, who subsequently brought on board Boom Operator Colin Spencer and Editorial Assistant Jim Becker. Trade ads and word of mouth lured in the remainder.

"It was a deferred show," Chudacoff says. "That meant if the movie got distributed and if they made their initial costs back, people would get paid. I've worked on a number of deferred shows over the years while trying to get established in the business and this was the only one that ever paid me. I eventually got a check for $1,688 which was the largest check I'd ever seen in my life. Well, the largest check that had my name on it anyway."

"I was a student at USC," Zumpano says. "One day, I saw an index card on a bulletin board looking for crew members on a 35mm film shooting on weekends. It sounded perfect. I set up an interview and went out to this house in Van Nuys. It was Pepperman who let me in, I think. The place reeked of pot smoke and there was Panavision equipment scattered everywhere. I immediately thought, 'You know, I think this is going to work out just fine...' (laughs). I think I knew It was a horror movie going in. They were making prosthetic hands in the sink when I arrived and the house was overall a disaster."

"I was working at CBS with a guy named Phil Neel," Visual Consultant and Gaffer Roberto Quezada says. "We were assistant editors there, in the union and everything. Phil had worked on Don and Paul's previous movie, *Kenny & Company*. They called Phil to work on *Phantasm*, something Phil really wanted to do. The trouble was there was no pay offered up front. It was all deferred. So Phil thought long and hard about it and finally decided to pass and stay on at CBS in his union job. Phil then told me about this movie that his friends were interviewing crew for down in Long Beach. Assistant editing at CBS meant I was basically a gopher for the real editors and this was not my idea of filmmaking. So I went down to Long Beach for the interviews and got the job along with absolutely everybody else they interviewed!"

"I was hired onto the film through Roberto Quezada," grip Daryn Okada says. "He was doing a foreign film series at East L.A. College and I was projecting them in the auditorium there. He told me about Don's new film and that they were always needing crew. On set, I was basically a grip. There wasn't much else I could do at that time since this was the first real film I ever got to do anything on. It was a great learning experience. I was just getting out of high school at the time and trying to decide whether I was going to pursue photography or cinematography. I think *Phantasm* helped me decide that, although I had no idea how far I would get into filmmaking."

While Coscarelli's parents were eager to fund another feature, they were less than thrilled to donate their home to filming for fear of reliving Camp *Kenny*. Consequently, the production acquired a two-story home near the Van Nuys airport for shooting and housing, which became a perk to crewing on the film. Coscarelli, Pepperman, Singer, Quezada and Script Supervisor Dena Roth stayed upstairs while less frequent crewmembers stayed downstairs, all of which doubled

Behind the camera.
(Photo courtesy Kristen Deem)

as the Pearson home interior. Here at *Morningside* headquarters the special effects were created, equipment was stored, and several crewmembers (mostly Quezada and Roth) pieced together dailies using a vintage Movieola editing machine. This was communal filmmaking at its best!

This grouping of cast and crew, both seasoned and inexperienced, would become affectionately known as "the phamily," a league that would grow with each new sequel. These loyal veterans were and remain today a familial unit, evidenced by the return of no less than a dozen alumni for the 1988 sequel.

PRODUCTION PREP

With a script, cast and crew all in place, Don Coscarelli moved quickly toward production. Continuing in the New Breed tradition, *Morningside* would shoot mostly on weekends and largely on location, but at a slower pace than either of its predecessors. The absence of a shooting schedule made it difficult to predict when filming would be complete, though it is doubtful anyone expected it to last quite so long. This laid back approach is often cited as having been vital to the film's quality. Compared to independent horror films of the period, this was extremely atypical. *The Amityville Horror* completed filming in seven weeks, *The Texas Chain Saw Massacre* in just four weeks and *Halloween* in a mere three.

"It was a herculean effort but we didn't know it at the time," Roberto Quezada says. "It was more like something done for Peter Pan. We were just a bunch of lost kids in Don's back yard making a movie in between gobbling down every issue of American Cinematographer, every interview with Stanley Kubrick, Laszlo Kovacs, Vilmos Zsigmond, every *Star Trek* episode, and all the beer we could get our hands on. Every movie after that had SAG, teamsters, unions, grip trucks, DGA, schedules, budgets, studio executives – everything the first *Phantasm* didn't have and everything that made every movie after *Phantasm* a grown-up movie. And that sucks."

New Breed's most ambitious production would soon find itself under pace, over budget and extremely disorganized. Part of this was due to the script not being nearly as lean as *Kenny & Company* and its story not as focused as *Jim the World's Greatest*. If ever there existed rules on how to make a movie, *Morningside*'s team wasn't abiding by them. The production was trial by fire, ingenuity born of necessity. They don't make movies like this anymore. They never really did to begin with.

Morningside's preproduction involved securing several product placements which included Hodaka's "Road Toad" motorbike and most notably Dos Equis beer. Hodaka supplied a brand new bike for Mike to ride and a poster advertisement for his bedroom wall. The Cuauhtémoc Moctezuma Brewery supplied ample cases of the amber Mexican lager which can be seen throughout the film in numerous scenes. The free Dos Equis became a major perk to crewmembers, making up for the deferred pay!

THE TALL MAN COMETH

On the evening of Monday, February 21, 1977, Angus Scrimm stepped before camera as "the Tall Man" for the very first time. Having received a completed script only two weeks prior, he eased into the role that first night with only one scene and absolutely no dialogue. His sole task was to crash through a window and look very scary. For this effect, several sheets of breakaway sugar glass were purchased, an expensive stunt material that remains quite sharp upon shattering. While such scenes are generally safe, cast members were aware that more daring feats would be asked of them. *Morningside*'s meager budget could not afford to double performers with professional stuntmen. The one exception was Michael Baldwin who was often doubled by Key Grip George Singer Jr.

In a journal dated 2/21/77, Angus Scrimm wrote:

The first time, the crew gasped and shrieked, though they knew what was going to happen. We took a second take to be safe but I think the first was a little better. Bill Thornbury, who plays Jody, serenaded me while Shirley put on my makeup with some of his own songs and some old standards. He has a caressing voice, like a silken night breeze. His mother was a music teacher. Little Michael, who plays the younger boy, is a hard-bitten pro of fourteen. But he wasn't so much of a hard-bitten pro that he didn't laugh like hell during every rehearsal and during every take when I burst through the window making my scowl at him.

"I was intrigued and game at the opportunity to shine in an area a bit foreign to me," Scrimm says, "but also a little antsy that a stunt gone wrong might impair my ability to serve my little patient's dire need of me at home. Paul Pepperman worked out every stunt and performed it himself till he was convinced I could do it safely, and the crew -- particularly a fellow named Doug Cragoe and another named Colin Spencer -- went out of their way to prepare the physical aspects of the set for maximum security. In the end, it was all great fun."

"People are always asking me if I thought Angus was scary to work with," Baldwin says. "The answer is absolutely not. I didn't find him scary because he's such a nice guy. A lot of people feel that way about him. On the screen, he comes across one way because he's acting as the Tall Man, but in person he's just a really nice guy. Keep in mind that I had met him long before *Phantasm*, back when we were doing *Kenny & Company*,

"It was a herculean effort but we didn't know it at the time."
- Roberto Quezada on the original *Phantasm*

Angus Scrimm in costume and out of character as the Tall Man.
(Photo courtesy Kristen Deem)

so he wasn't a complete stranger to me when we started."

Van Nuys filming continued the following night with Jody's abduction by the Tall Man which was omitted from the theatrical cut but eventually used in *Phantasm: Oblivion*. The scene was conceived as part of the original ending. Jody Pearson is alone in his room, shortly after vanquishing the Tall Man with Mike. He is shocked to see a reflection of the mortician – very much alive – dagger in hand. Scrimm recounts that eight takes were needed to align his reflection with the camera, a precision shot that was later recreated for the film's revised ending with young Mike.

"Meeting Reggie and Angus came later for me," Bill Thornbury says. "Both I liked immediately and both I relied on a lot for their experience having worked with Coscarelli before. I just felt more confident around them and we got along great. I think the whole company was receptive to people that shared their same ideals, dreams and thoughts. It's like bringing home a girlfriend to meet your parents. Sometimes there's an immediate sort of rapport and I think maybe I had that effect on those guys because they just accepted me. It was mutual."

CREATING PHANTASMS

Several days later on Thursday, February 24, the company forged ahead with an early special effect. The evening's task was to simulate a door bursting from its hinges and soaring across the room to reveal the Tall Man. The crew considered a complex rope and pulley system before Roberto Quezada suggested a simpler approach. His method saw an unhinged door fashioned like a shield, with leather straps for gripping. On cue, Paul Pepperman – garbed in skateboard pads and a motorcycle helmet – bolted across the room carrying the trick door before him. With proper lighting and the door held at just the right angle, Pepperman was cleverly shielded from camera.

"We had that perfect blend of knowledge and stupidity among all of us put together to accomplish things that were completely new," Quezada says. "Or if re-inventions of the wheel then re-inventions that had not been done that way

before. The rush that each success engendered not only kept us high and going at it for many months of principal production, it still exists up on the screen thirty-five years later. Whatever the hell it was, we nailed it and then we bottled it."

This night was Angus Scrimm's third scene without dialogue. The actor wished to vary his performance beyond making what he called "Halloween faces." After discussing this with Coscarelli, they both decided that the Tall Man should grin wickedly midscene. To be safe, the door scene was filmed both grinning and straight-faced in case test audiences took the grin as a cue to laugh (they didn't). Scrimm also theorized that while the Tall Man respected Mike as an adversary with whom he enjoys toying, the mortician ultimately planned to kill him.

"Early on, I formed the opinion that the Tall Man represented Death in young Mike's mind," Scrimm says. "I had as a kind of reference to playing the role that the Tall Man was actually the Grim Reaper."

A HANGING IN AGOURA

On a weekend in mid-March, the production traveled to Agoura Hills. There they prepared for the film's most infamous cut sequence: the Tall Man's death by hanging. The scene entailed the brothers lynching the Tall Man from a gnarled old tree, leaving him for dead. In revenge, the undead mortician plunges the world into permanent darkness by preventing the sun from rising. A bewildered Mike returns to the tree and warns his adversary, "You're killing the world." The Tall Man proposes a bargain. If the boy cuts him down, he'll release the sun and leave town. Mike complies. Once free, the Tall Man reneges on the deal and resumes his deadly chase. As originally written, "killing the world" referenced the mortician's hold on the sun, not the town by town plot of the sequels.

The hanging scene was a late addition to the script, envisioned by Coscarelli in January 1977. To Angus Scrimm's delight, his character finally had dialogue – and plenty of it. Work on the first half of the sequence began the evening of Friday, March 18. For the spirited crew, winter filming in Agoura

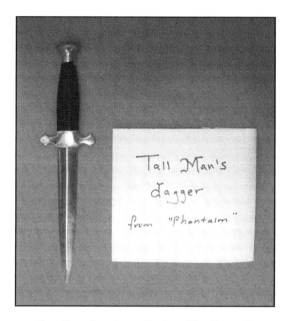

Above: From the private collection of Don Coscarelli.
Below: The hanging tree as it appears today.
(Dagger photo courtesy Kristen Deem)
(Tree photo by the Author)

would be an exercise in endurance and dedication. Shot during two of the most frigid nights in March, the company employed blankets, thermal underwear and canned Dennison's Hot Chili (dutifully prepared by Robert Del Valle) to ward off the freezing cold. Coscarelli and Paul Pepperman alternated as cameramen, both braving the unsteady scaffolding to film high up in the tree. When the exhausted crew finally wrapped at 5 AM, they adjourned to find layers of ice on their car windshields.

In a journal dated 3/18/1977, Scrimm wrote:

> My first act on the bill was to be hanged experimentally. A knotted rope in the traditional style was put around my neck. Concealed behind somehow was a thin but strong wire, which looped through a pulley attached to the tree branch. The wire's end was fastened to the bumper of a truck, which was driven cautiously forward and backward to raise or lower me. My mark was about eight feet off the ground, not the two to five feet I'd been told. I must've presented a startling sight indeed to the freeway drivers as they passed. In the earlier part of the night, we attracted an audience of onlookers down below.

Top and *Bottom:* The interior of Fosselman's Ice Cream Company remains remarkably unchanged by time.

"'That scene was lit completely different at first,'" Roberto Quezada says. "Don didn't like what I had done and finally told me to just put a big light directly behind the tree so that rays of light emanated from it and lit up the atmosphere around it. This seemed really unnatural to me and was counter to the pact that Don and I had that all lighting in *Phantasm* was to have a logically explainable source. I was dead set against doing this, told him so, and then went and did what he wanted. The shot was stunning. So much for source lighting."

In spite of the grueling hours, unfavorable conditions and deferred pay, morale remained surprisingly high on *Morningside*. Only a few crewmembers were fired or walked off. "You have to keep things light on set because you can't always focus people who aren't being paid," John Zumpano says. "You have to allow for a certain amount of frivolity and off-the-cuff activity because you're just happy the crew showed up and you want them to show up again next week. So no matter how cold or late it was, we always had a good time making *Phantasm*."

"People came and went on the crew," Daryn Okada says. "Our core group was very small. As a crewmember, you either clicked with everyone and stayed on or you decided it wasn't quite what you thought filmmaking was supposed to be and you left. Those people never returned. By the time the movie was over, I thought we had become a really tight-knit group of people that worked well together. *Phantasm* taught me how important total dedication is to a project. You've got to give it all you've got."

"I seem to remember that we filmed at all hours, day or night," Michael Baldwin says. "They would just send a car whenever they needed me. I did plenty of night shoots like the hanging tree, regardless of whether we were inside or on location. It was quite common on that show, although highly illegal now with child labor laws. You couldn't get away with that shooting schedule today, but I never minded. It was too much fun for me to mind."

Agoura filming continued the following evening with a conclusion in which Mike cuts down the Tall Man. One of the night's more daring shots entailed Pepperman capturing the action from a lofty branch high above the actors. Scrimm recalls that Baldwin, perched on a high tree limb, twice dropped the dagger on him from above. The knife was "not a rubber prop but real and dangerously sharp," and the teen's frigid hands were unable to grasp it. He also recounted a handful of problems that plagued this second night including camera malfunctions and a noose rope that continually unraveled. By 3 AM, their perseverance paid off; the location was a wrap.

DOS EQUIS & ICE CREAM

Another cutting room casualty unfolded some forty miles east down the 10 Freeway in Alhambra. In this scene, the Pearson brothers, drunk on Dos Equis, make their way to Reggie's Ice Cream shop where a playful food fight ensues. The interior for Reggie's shop was the world famous Fosselman's Ice Cream Company. The management agreed to let *Morningside* film during off-hours for a $50 location fee. The family-owned parlor is still open for business today and remains remarkably unchanged by time. Many of the original signs, tables, chairs and light fixtures are the same as of this writing.

"This whole thing ends up in a big food fight, throwing ice cream and seltzer water," Reggie Bannister recounts. "We had a lot of fun doing it. The punch line to the scene was a close-up of an ice cream sundae. You pull back on this ice cream sundae, and you realize that it's huge, and it's been built on Mike, who's lying on the parfait table passed out from the Dos Equis. So everybody's sort of got the munchies, sitting around eating the ice cream. [...] Reggie was an ice cream man, but he was also a musician, and in this ice cream parlor we built a little stage, and this was where Reggie played his music. So people had their ice cream late at night and he also sold Dos Equis beer. It was kind of fun, because they filmed me singing three of my original songs, and they were going to edit that in at various places. Didn't make the cut."

"I just remember this huge mound of ice cream on Michael's torso," Bill Thornbury says. "Everybody would take a spoon and eat ice cream off of him when we weren't shooting.

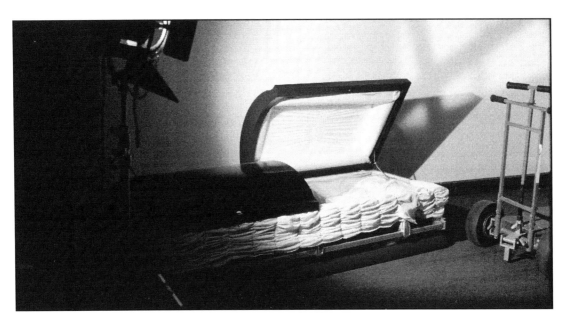

The Tall Man's victims don't rest in peace for very long.
(Photo courtesy Kristen Deem)

That was a really fun evening. I saw that scene on one of the DVD releases some time ago and wasn't particularly impressed with my depiction of somebody who was under the influence. I'm just being honest here."

"What a waste," Michael Baldwin says. "That was a heck of a lot of work for no payoff. I haven't seen that footage, ever. I'd love to see it."

DIAL M FOR MORTUARY

After two freezing nights in Agoura, the crew gladly welcomed a move indoors at Long Beach's Sunnyside Mortuary on Sunday night, March 20. That Sunnyside sounded very much like Morningside was no mere coincidence. The first scene slated found the Tall Man dashing after Mike through the casket showroom following the caretaker's death, which was yet to be filmed. The chase would require flawless synchronization since the actors would be running toward Don Coscarelli on camera, who would in turn be running backwards through the narrow

showroom. The potential for injury or damage to person, camera or casket was immense. Angus Scrimm notes that Coscarelli ran through ten rehearsals altogether until he felt confident enough to roll film. Four takes were then recorded.

In a journal dated 3/20/1977, Angus Scrimm wrote:

I had congratulated myself midday on feeling no real ill effects from Friday and Saturday night's hanging tree exertions, but on the second running rehearsal, the upper part of my thighs, where the harness straps had supported my weight during the hanging, began to hurt. I said nothing hoping that each rehearsal would be the last. But by the tenth rehearsal, both legs were killing me. On the second take, I feared I could run no more and told Don my troubles. I limped in agony to the trailer and stooped on the backbench. Ten minutes later, Don came in looking abashed. 'Rory, I hate to have to tell you this, but we're afraid the handheld camera might have jiggled and we want to cover ourselves by filming the chase again with a stationary camera.' I couldn't even move my legs. 'How long can you give me to recover?'

In an effort to balance Scrimm's needs with those of production, Coscarelli called for an hour's lunch break to allow his ailing performer time to recuperate, after which the chase was re-filmed twice more. The night's second scene saw the first on set appearance of Ken Jones as Morningside's Caretaker. In it, the hulking henchman enters the casket room in search of Mike, who is hiding nearby in a Batesville Autumn Oak model. Just before discovering the boy, the Caretaker is summoned by the Tall Man who has appeared in an opposite doorway. Not fond of being shut inside an actual casket, Michael Baldwin armed himself with a flashlight for the claustrophobic shots.

"Just being in that place scared the hell out of me," Jones says. "At one point, Angus and I were in a room inside the mortuary where they had real bodies waiting to be embalmed the next day. This place was no joke. The thing I remember most about working with Angus is that he liked to stay in character as the Tall Man even when we weren't shooting. If you were to walk up on him and you weren't expecting him, he could scare the hell out of you. Personally, I think he enjoyed doing that."

"Ken Jones and my only scene together involved merely a bit of wordless business while standing in the doorway to a casket room in which Mike was hiding in a coffin," Scrimm says. "We'd both been summoned to the Long Beach location in the wee hours of the night. My recollection is that Ken regularly appeared in productions of the Long Beach Civic Light Opera, but in the unsavory makeup Shirley Coscarelli created for him he looked like anything but the Baron Von Trapp, and as the Tall Man I must have looked equally appalling to him."

The following weekend saw three additional night shoots, again at Sunnyside, concluding the afternoon of Sunday, March 27. At the memorial chapel, the production shot scenes of Jody and Reggie chatting over a postmortem Tommy, all flanked by a roomful of mourners consisting of many of the crew. Dailies from the prior week revealed that the casket showroom material was blurred and unusable. A retake would be needed. Coscarelli planned to wrap chapel photography as early as possible, then move back into the casket room for a brief pickup shot with Scrimm and Jones – neither of whom were scheduled for that evening…

Just before 2 AM, Paul Pepperman began the dreaded task of dialing the actors to request their presence on location. While the co-producer managed to rouse a slumbering Tall Man, repeated calls to Jones's home were met with a busy signal. It was later revealed that his phone had mysteriously slipped off the hook. Scrimm's journal reveals that in order to bring Jones to set, Coscarelli and Pepperman had to first travel to Bixby Hills to wake Dac Coscarelli so that he could accompany them to his investment counseling office. There they hoped to find a copy of Jones's *Kenny & Company* contract, which would contain his home address. The pair then traveled to his home in Whittier, woke him and had the performer onset by 6 AM. During this madcap manhunt, the crew remained on standby at Sunnyside. A brisk two takes with Scrimm and Jones were filmed before the night was called a wrap.

"My God, that was such a late night call," Jones says. "They hadn't told me beforehand that they were going to need me so I had no clue about the reshoot. Both Don and Paul came for me and personally knocked on my door to get me out to that mortuary. I wound up leaving with them and the moment we arrived, I hurried into costume and makeup and we started shooting."

TEENAGE TERROR

Three months into production, advancement on *Morningside* had slowed due to the weekends only routine. In an effort to play catch up, Don Coscarelli filmed continuously from Friday, April 1 to Saturday, April 9, in conjunction with Michael Baldwin's school dismissing for Easter Break. Given his performer's newfound availability, Don Coscarelli sought to capture as many scenes with the adolescent lead as possible. As filming contoured to his schedule, Baldwin began to realize his weighty position amongst the cast as a lead performer.

"Actors have power, definitely," Baldwin says. "If they have a big enough part and once there are enough days shot and in the can, filmmakers can't go back and recast those people. When something would happen that I didn't like and it would keep happening over and over again, I would just say 'Well, I'm done. Goodbye!' and I would walk off. Then the crew is standing there with their hands in their pockets like 'Well, what do we do now?' Though you have to understand that I was a child and when you realize that you have the power to stop a show, the filmmakers make it a point to see that you're being served and getting what you need so that you don't wind up stopping the show. Kids on movie sets can be dangerous and I'm pretty sure I abused my power on *Phantasm*!"

One such show stopping incident involved the scene where Mike blasts his bedroom doorknob off with a shotgun cartridge and a hammer. The stunt's precarious setup involved pyrotechnics, much to Baldwin's dismay. A small explosive was taped to the end of the hammer, which was then attached to a wire that ran down the actor's jacket sleeve, pant leg and across the floor to Paul Pepperman who would manually detonate it as the hammer made contact with the door. The first take went exactly as planned and despite his continued unease, Baldwin

agreed to a second. Pepperman began to rerig the special effect. "I was still nervous about it," Baldwin says. "And Pepperman is trying to reassure me with, '*It's fine, don't worry, there won't be a problem*' but as they're re-rigging the hammer, the thing all of the sudden goes off in my face. It just explodes and it really pissed me off. I dropped the hammer and said, '*I'm not doing that again,*' and left out of there. So the one shot they got of me doing it was the one they had to use."

Despite such incidents, Baldwin is reported to have gotten along famously with *Morningside*'s predominantly adult cast and crew. He was especially well regarded by his director, who praised him as one of the most appealing child actors he'd ever worked with. When pressed about what he liked least about filming, Baldwin laughs, "I remember hating having to scream and act scared. I thought it was too girly. Whenever I had to do it, I always tried to scream in a lower register. So imagine prepubescent Michael Baldwin trying to scream like a man, not a girl. I'll let you judge how successful I was with that."

The "Last Perfect Day" street in Sherman Oaks where Mike chases after Jody.
(*Author photo*)

WAREHOUSE MAUSOLEUM

The filmmakers had logically reasoned early on that no self-respecting funeral establishment was going to let their cameras anywhere near it given the film's high quotient of gunplay and bloodletting; at least not for any reasonable fee. Instead, the crew would need to build their own mausoleum. As filming proceeded on location, a construction team labored in Chatsworth to convert an ordinary warehouse into the film's then titular structure. Wilson High alumnus Mark Annerl drafted plans for the façade, which by design appeared much more grandiose onscreen than it actually was in reality. The mausoleum was a mere single corridor with an octagonal rotunda at one end, a doorway to the spacegate room at the opposite end, and an intersecting hallway bisecting the middle. By switching out the set decoration, this one hallway could become many, sometimes even within the same scene.

Working from a rented space on Variel Street, Construction Supervisor Marc Schwartz led the mausoleum project, which involved a steep learning curve since neither he nor his team had ever built a film set before. They were well versed in actual construction and built the structure accordingly. What resulted was an uncommonly sturdy mausoleum set capable of withstanding any number of weight-loads and abuses without toppling over. The walls regularly supported cameras, lights and even crewmembers.

"One thing about the film that amazed me was that mausoleum," Ralph Richmond says. "There was a small room in the back of the warehouse for one of my bank guard scenes, so I went out to Chatsworth in order to film it and saw this huge set they'd built. The whole thing was done up in plywood covered in plastic contact paper. It was the kind of stuff you'd use on your shelves in a cupboard. In person, it didn't look like anything special but in the movie it looks like real marble! They say that burlap films like velvet and, apparently, contact paper films like real marble. I guess that's the magic of film!"

"We spent a lot of time in the contact paper mausoleum," John Zumpano says. "That stuff took forever to

shoot and we never had enough lights for what we were doing in there. You couldn't ever leave them standing either. We'd go to light one scene but then another actor would become available and we'd have to tear down our setup to go film their material. Then you ran into the problem of trying to match lighting between shots when you came back. Roberto was a master at that. He could relight a scene in the mausoleum exactly the same way even if the two shots had been done months apart, which they sometimes were."

By Monday, April 4, enough of the mausoleum had been completed to allow filming on set. One of the earliest scenes captured was Jody's encounter with the Tall Man just prior to Tommy's service ("The funeral is about to begin, sir!"). Once on set Bill Thornbury, who was of no small stature, seemed to diminish the Tall Man's colossal height when standing next to him. To compensate, Angus Scrimm did the scene from atop an apple crate. Now two months into filming, Scrimm had begun to doubt his performance as the Tall Man, a role he took very seriously. He had studied the script closely and consulted biographies of Boris Karloff and Bela Lugosi for inspiration. Coscarelli, having already witnessed dailies of the hanging sequence and other Tall Man scenes, doubted nothing and harbored great confidence in Scrimm's abilities, continually assuring him of such.

> "They say that burlap films like velvet and, apparently, contact paper films like real marble. I guess that's the magic of film!"
>
> - Ralph Richmond on the mausoleum

In a journal dated 4/4/1977, Angus Scrimm wrote:

I feel my every scene is done at the same slam-bang intensity and there's no variety whatsoever. Moreover, I'm vexed because I've not seen a foot of my work to get a hold on the character. I didn't begin to do a good characterization of Russell Nolan in Jim until I finally saw some of the footage. I'm acting blind here.

As it turned out, Scrimm wasn't the only one who held such doubts. Many cast and crew felt similarly, particularly those without a copy of the script such as Reggie Bannister. To them *Morningside* appeared to be veering off into strange directions which, in fact, it was. Acting in the film often meant learning lines on the same day as filming. There was seldom any content or characterization beyond that day's work. As filming continued, more than a few cast members shared silent skepticism about the film they were making.

"I got onboard the whole idea eventually," Thornbury says. "It was certainly out there but the longer I was involved with the project, the more I started to care. I started seeing what was going on and that we were onto something that really would be good. Initially, I didn't even know if we would ever get released. That's the truth. I honestly didn't know if it would ever be distributed or anyone would get to see it. As we got on with it, I believed more and more that we had a good shot at somebody picking it up. Don had the vision for it, you know? He knew what he was doing even if I didn't."

Prior to mausoleum photography, the Chatsworth warehouse was used to fake roadside night exteriors such as Reggie's overturned ice cream truck and the subsequent dwarf attack on Mike, Sally and Suzy. The latter scene's production saw George Singer Jr. pulling double duty, both as the dwarf that attacks Mike and then as Mike himself as he's thrown through the rear windshield. "That was the only scene where I was two characters," Singer says. "I essentially threw myself out the window of the car."

"I really liked our warehouse setup," Daryn Okada says. "To think that we were making a movie in a warehouse and not a soundstage was cool. That happens every day now, but it didn't back then. In fact, movies seek to do that now. But back then; it was like we were making our own giant playground in a warehouse. Also, a very young Industrial Light and Magic had recently carried out the effects for *Star Wars* in a Van Nuys warehouse. That always seemed like a fun parallelism in terms of breaking away from the norm and doing whatever you had to do wherever you had to do it to get your film made."

THE SILVER SPHERE

With mausoleum construction complete, Don Coscarelli was free to begin work on the pièce de résistance of his magnum opus: the attack of the silver sphere. Although New Breed preferred to handle most effects in-house, the more complicated sphere effects required outsourcing. To this end, they turned to Mechanical Engineer Willard Green, owner of Hollywood Turntable Rentals and Sales. In his hands, the balls were refined both in design and in function. It was Green's suggestion that the sphere drill into its victim's head. This prompted someone else to suggest the blood spurting. Green would bill *Morningside* a scant $1,163 for his services. Sadly, he would pass away before ever getting to see his masterful handiwork on the big screen.

Rather than build one fully functional prop, which New Breed had requested, Green recommended a multi-sphere approach in order to keep the effects as simple as possible. To simulate flight, the balls were filmed being thrown down a mausoleum corridor where they would shatter spectacularly. When reversed, this footage appeared to show them floating upward and soaring offscreen. A similar reverse shot was used when the ball first strikes the caretaker: it was actually yanked away from the actor's head using monofilament wire. Coscarelli had planned on shooting this effect in close-up so that the audience could see the blades stabbing into actor Ken Jones. This was changed to a medium shot, however, when Jones's forehead prosthetic proved noticeably unrealistic.

The actual drilling required a much more elaborate setup whereby Green fitted a half-sphere with a rotating drill bit. In order to preserve the illusion, this stationary setup

The screen's first "digital vampire," according to critic Charles Champlin.
(Photo courtesy Kristen Deem)

could only be filmed from one angle so as not to reveal the blood tubing and electrical wiring that protruded from the ball's hidden backside. Such close-ups yielded new challenges, however, since the ball very clearly reflected both camera and crew. To this end, a false mausoleum wall was created to conceal the crew with only a lens-sized hole cut in the wall for filming. For the long shot of the caretaker being drilled, a handheld sphere was manufactured that spurted blood. A concealed tube ran from Jones's sleeve down inside his coveralls, and then across the room to a drum of fake blood.

Another challenge involved how to light the spheres. The false wall solution that concealed the camera and crew would not work with stage lights since shielding a light source would effectively render it useless. "Don absolutely would not accept a pin source of light reflected on his precious balls," Roberto Quezada says. "It finally occurred to me that what defines a reflective surface is not the light hitting it, but the light hitting everything else. So we stopped lighting the ball

and started lighting everything else around it. This created the problem of how to hide the camera from reflecting in it."

"When we started working with the ball, that's when it got complicated," Jones says. "That darn ball was the most troublesome part of the whole show. Once they finally figured out how to make it work, and I say finally because it took them a good long while, I'd say we spent maybe two nights to do the drilling that you saw in the film. I don't think we did too many takes of that one either. I think they shot it from several angles and cut together the best of each take to make the scene. It was such a messy thing that you wouldn't want to have filmed it any more than you had to."

"One of the worst things about shooting *Phantasm* was trying to get the blood out of the equipment," John Zumpano says. "Our gear was always sticky with that red Karo syrup. After you kill someone and they bleed all over the place, you have to start mopping it up right away. You never quite get it completely off the floor and after that your shoes start to stick

How tall is the Tall Man? About 6-foot-4 in *Phantasm*.
(Photo courtesy Kristen Deem)

when you walk. Then later someone asks, '*How did your shoot go this weekend?*' and you answer, '*Oh, it was good. I spent most of it mopping up red and yellow blood off the floor.*' It wasn't always about making movies. Sometimes it was just about keeping the place together."

"Don taught me something very important with regard to the silver sphere," Bruce Chudacoff says. "One of his techniques was to not have the device that's either drawing the audience in or repulsing them away onscreen for too long. Just give them a glimpse of it and cut away because you don't want to be gratuitous with it. If you count the sphere's screen time in terms of minutes, it's not in the picture for very long at all. Don wisely chose to cut away and let the sound enhance the scene rather than linger on the ball. That's why it works so well."

"The silver sphere scenes were painstakingly difficult," Daryn Okada says. "I say that because we didn't have any immediate verification that we had gotten it right. It was all up to Don to figure that out and he did so with incredible simplicity, I might add. It was great to see him take a practical approach to those scenes instead of resorting to extensive optical effects, not that we could afford them. I think the incamera stuff really resonates with audiences because those effects have an unmanipulated feel to them. The spheres are an unworldly threat and yet visually they're very organic looking."

"After one of the nights on which we shot the sphere scene," Jones says, "I was too tired to stick around and remove all of my makeup, so I just drove home with it on. I was wearing this really ugly pale makeup that Don's mother had cooked up for me and on top of that, I still had some of the blood from the ball on me. I was a mess. Part way home, I got pulled over by a cop who got one look at me and said, '*Alright, buddy. Where's the party?*' and I told him, '*There's no party, officer. I'm making a movie in Long Beach and I didn't have time to take my makeup off.*' He didn't buy it and went back to his car to make some calls on the radio. I'm not exactly sure why, but he eventually let me go. I can't imagine what he was thinking at that moment. I knew what I was thinking, though! I was embarrassed as hell to be seen looking like that in public!"

"If you count the sphere's screen time in terms of minutes, it's not in the picture for very long at all."

- Bruce Chudacoff on the silver sphere

FREEZING THE TALL MAN

On Tuesday, April 5, mausoleum filming continued with an action scene later cut from the film. The Pearson Brothers, while under attack from the Tall Man, destroy a charging sphere with a shotgun blast. The mortician then grabs Jody and lifts him effortlessly against a marble wall. Thinking quickly, Mike grabs a nearby fire extinguisher to douse his enemy with a paralyzing icy spray. The scene introduces a classic Tall Man quip originally spoken to Jody but later recycled in *Phantasm II*, "You think you go to heaven. You come to us!" Don Coscarelli would write the scene into *Phantasm: Oblivion* where it would again suffer deletion.

Had this scene been included, it would have confirmed for audiences an important detail – that the Tall Man could not withstand cold. It would have been the culmination of an earlier, yet unfilmed scene that showed frigid mist billowing from Reggie's ice cream truck, momentarily paralyzing the mortician. By having observed this eerie paralysis, Mike astutely knows to grab the fire extinguisher with which to blast his nemesis. The nonresolution of this plot thread due to the scene's deletion would result in years of speculation with many wrongly assuming that the Tall Man enjoyed the cold billowing from the truck freezer. The correct interpretation had always been pain, not ecstasy. The debate would continue on until a flashback in *Phantasm III*. Cold was no friend to the Tall Man.

In order to simulate the Tall Man singlehandedly lifting Jody by the throat, Bill Thornbury was filmed sitting on a camera operator seat and hydraulically lifted. Though the scene utilized dry ice, most of what hit Angus Scrimm came from an actual fire extinguisher.

In a journal dated 4/5/1977, Angus Scrimm wrote:

I don two sets of thermal underwear and huge plastic baggage to ward off the cold. Paul Pepperman operates the extinguisher and we filmed it several times. In the script, the cold of the extinguisher causes me to melt into a jelly. I feel only a faint coolness, though a piece or two of dry ice hits my neck and causes a burning sensation. Today we're celebrating Mike's birthday. We have a cake at 5. He's disappointed because they didn't let him man the extinguisher, but he's allowed to ride the motorcycle in the fields behind the warehouse. Mike is fourteen.

The following day, Scrimm and Thornbury continued work in the mausoleum. The scene entailed Jody's nightmare vision in which a malevolent Tall Man strides menacingly towards him in slow motion (a striking scene that padded much of *Phantasm*'s theatrical trailer). At 7 PM, Coscarelli announced a retake from the previous day as the Tall Man staggers away from Mike's chilly assault. Once again, Pepperman manned the extinguisher. "On the last take," Scrimm says, "Paul sprayed higher than usual and gave my neck an icy blast which made my whole head steam most picturesquely. I unleashed my finest scream and the crew was so entranced that they applauded after Don said '*Cut*'."

The scene's original finale was captured the following day. After hoisting his brother onto a chandelier for safety, Jody disappears around a corner to look for help. No sooner does he vanish than a pack of dwarves, one of them brandishing a sphere, rounds the corner. The situation worsens when the chandelier begins dropping several inches at a time from Mike's added weight, slowly lowering him toward his doom. Mike

Promotional yellow finger given out at the film's premiere.
(Author photo)

gets away safely, however, when the chandelier comes crashing down, crushing the dwarves below.

THE DARK RECESSES OF MORNINGSIDE

The evening hours of Saturday, April 23 found the crew laboring in a corner of the warehouse now converted into the gloomy basement of Morningside Mausoleum. Mike was to sever the Tall Man's fingers, trapped in a doorjamb, from which would flow thick yellow blood. As seen in Sound Recordist Michael Gross's home movies, the scene's setup was quite bizarre. Atop a platform four rubber fingers squirm in yellow alginate. Beneath the staircase landing, Shirley Coscarelli puppeteers the Tall Man's severed digits (cast from Paul Pepperman's hand) using a mirror to monitor the scene. Above, Michael Baldwin garners laughs by pretending to lick blood from his knife.

In a journal dated 4/23/1977, Angus Scrimm wrote:

Coscarelli and Pepperman commenced shooting at 4 PM so they could get to me earlier tonight. My call was for 8 PM. At 7, I went out to the car to leave for Chatsworth and decided to go back inside the house to take some Vitamin C capsules. As I entered the door, the phone rang and it was Bob Del Valle postponing my call till 9. The crew had constructed a barely secure platform on stilts leading to a massive looking door. Beyond the door was a stairway leading to a corridor lined with cardboard packing boxes and strewn with cobwebs. An interesting set. […] This is the culmination of the chase through the casket room we filmed several weeks ago when my legs gave way. We rehearsed often and shot it several times before Don was satisfied. […] Don told me that he'd set up the next shot and use his own fingers - I could go home. It was not yet midnight. I was delighted. I went into the trailer, dressed, removed my makeup and Don came in. 'You know, I planned to have Mike in the shot when he sees your fingers moving and I'd like to supervise him through the camera, so would you mind staying and doing the shot? It would take about fifteen minutes.' I stood with my fingers caught in that bloody door in a little cut out place made for them for two hours while lights were fixed, Mike went off ward and had to be found, a little piece of the door was painstakingly pasted back with gaffers tape, etc. etc. It was after 2 before I got away.

"That night involved a lot of waiting around," Baldwin laments. "I remembering being in the makeup trailer waiting on them to get it ready for hours on end. At around 3 in the morning, I finally just walked onset and yelled, "*Oh my God! Aren't we ready to go yet?*" and I can remember Don's Mom, just her voice, going, "*Oh, shut up!*" It was one of the few times that she ever raised her voice to me. She was one of the few people that could actually wield that power over me because she was a mom! She was able to successfully get me to shut up and slink away into the dark, tail between my legs. Those guys, Coscarelli and Pepperman, they couldn't control me at all. But Shirley, being a mom, could totally do it."

Later that night, the crew prepped for a second basement scene of Jody sneaking into Morningside in an attempt to verify Mike's claims. While Jody scans the darkened room with a flashlight, a concealed dwarf abruptly leaps onto his back in a frenzied assault. Jody dispatches the creature with a headshot, mere inches from his own, before making a hasty exit through a broken window. The dwarf's airborne recoil was achieved using a shock cord, which was harnessed to a child actor and pulled forcefully back by the crew.

"Bill nearly set fire to himself [shooting the dwarf]," Roberto Quezada recalls. "This was years before the tragedy on another movie, *The Crow*, where an actor was accidentally killed by having a blank shot in the direction of his head. Not too different from what we asked Bill to do in the throes of battling a hooded dummy on his back."

On May 25, 1977, *Star Wars* burst onto theater screens across the country introducing audiences to an alien race of hooded dwarves known as Jawas. Their resemblance to the Tall Man's robed minions was uncanny.

"You couldn't help but notice the similarity between the hooded characters in *Star Wars* and ours," Thornbury says. "Did we somehow catch wind of it and borrow the idea of the dwarves? No, I don't think so. I think Don was just on the pulse of what was happening at the time and came up with a great character, as did George Lucas. It certainly makes for a visual coincidence but the similarity ends there. Personality wise, the two creatures aren't anything alike."

LOST SCENES

A significant cut made in the transition from *Morningside* to *Phantasm* was a subplot involving the Pearson family bank. The removal of this subplot reduced Jody's role and expunged those of the branch manager, Mr. Norby, and a bank guard, Ralph (named for performer Ralph Richmond). These bank scenes established Jody's public image as an anti-authoritarian, footloose youth. They also depicted his rocky relationship with a bank teller, Suzy. With the omission of the bank, so

went corresponding scenes involving Jody's personal life. Consequently, the Suzy character is first introduced at the antique shop, then abruptly dispatched by a pack of dwarves ravaging her VW Bug, backstory be damned.

Bank scenes were partly filmed on a small set inside the Chatsworth warehouse and partly on location in Julian, California. "The first scene in the script that I received was set in the bank," Bill Thornbury says. "They obviously changed that opening but originally Jody had inherited a bank in the movie from his parents. His girlfriend was a teller and I walked in and acted like I was going to rob the place with a water pistol and we all cracked up. Then she comes into my office and sits on my lap. It was just playful. I think I was holding a cigar or something."

"The way Don pitched *Phantasm* to me was to simply describe what my role was," Richmond says. "And there was nothing strange about my role. I was supposed to be a guard at the bank the older brother is operating. We planned for five days of filming and I completed my role in just four. It was only after I was finished that Don began to change up the story and wound up cutting out all of the scenes in which we see Jody running the bank. That meant that my four days were suddenly on the cutting room floor. I remember one bank scene they had me do I wasn't really keen on. As the older brother came into the bank in this scene, I was supposed to turn and goose him as he went by. I guess because they thought it'd be funny. It didn't seem to me like it really had a place in the film, but they wanted it so I did it. Don could come up with some pretty bizarre things with that imagination of his, not all of which made it into the film, I'm glad to say!"

FUNERAL FOR A FRIEND

On Sunday, May 7, New Breed congregated at Chatsworth Park North to capture scenes of the Morningside Cemetery. Armed with a truckload of prop tombstones on loan from the 20th Century Fox prop department, the crew would spend the next several weeks entrenched here, often under unfavorable conditions. Their first measure of business was to stage Tommy's graveside service. The scene played out amid atmospheric showers, which accounts for why background mourners can be seen clutching umbrellas as the principal cast soaks in the foreground. Because rain barely registers on celluloid, the inclement weather was not an issue. The incessant wind, however, proved far more troublesome, repeatedly toppling the makeshift cemetery.

As the most populated scene in the film, Tommy's funeral allowed for numerous cameos. Both Dac and Shirley Coscarelli can be seen among the mourners, as can actor David Arntzen (Toby), Reggie Bannister's mother, investor Bob Bixby and Good Band drummer David Seachrist, who was also present during the earlier memorial chapel filming. Although Horace Bannister (Reggie's father) appears to recite the Lord's Prayer near scene's end, the voice is actually that of Angus Scrimm who dubbed the role during post-production. The fake casket so freely wielded by the Tall Man was crafted from lightweight balsa wood and, according to the performer, just as easy to break as it was to lift.

Mike's initial Tall Man encounter was a late addition to the script, added some two months *after* filming began. The alien undertaker telekinetically causes Mike's motorbike to stall as the boy attempts to flee the cemetery. The bike restarts only to crash soon after, tossing Mike over the handlebars. Don Coscarelli considered making this scene much more diabolical by having the bike take on a life of its own and even run over the prone teen. It was dialed back, however, and a close-up shot of the Tall Man smirking at his own mischief was filmed but not used.

Privately, Scrimm formulated his own take on Mike and the Tall Man's cemetery meeting, likening it to Pip's graveyard encounter with the convict in Great Expectations. His idea began with Mike stopping to admire a flock of birds. All fly away, save for one who remains happily singing on its branch. Suddenly, it stiffens and falls dead to the ground. Mike looks up from its feathered corpse and into "the deathlike face of the Tall Man." Musing over the idea thirty years later, the actor comments, "It might've worked nicely."

While Michael Baldwin did much of his riding for the cemetery scenes, George Singer Jr. performed the riskier wheelies and high-speed bursts. "The funny part about that scene is that I had never ridden a motorcycle before in my life," Singer says. "I just told them I knew how to ride it so that they'd let me do it. Somehow, Don figured out that I hadn't and wound up letting me do it anyway so long as I practiced beforehand. I remember being in the backyard of wherever we were shooting and doing wheelies and rehearsing on the bike right up until the scene. I was pretty crazy back then, always up for whatever Don wanted to throw at me."

"I remember the motorbike scenes well because we were all worried that Michael was going to plow into a gravestone and injure himself," John Zumpano says. "We also used to tease George when he'd go to play Mike but that's when the rest of us would do George's job and learn another part of the craft. Those scenes look great too. I was looking at the film recently, trying to remember how we did the shots where the camera is attached to the bike because we certainly didn't have the money for a proper mount, a camera car and a teamster driver. I have a feeling we just came up with a rig that would barely hold together, and hold together it did because it was pulled off wonderfully."

"Look at how gorgeous the day exteriors on *Phantasm* are," Roberto Quezada says. "That's because Don and Paul and I absolutely refused to shoot one frame of film until the clouds, the sun, and all the planets were all perfectly aligned. For each and every shot I took very detailed notes on lighting ratios between bright and dark sides of a subject, between foreground and background, and what light did on different colors and surfaces. Then I pored over the footage all day long, all week long. I would apply what I learned from this regimen each following weekend. If there was anything that Don or I did not like about the lighting on any scene - and I mean anything on any scene - we reshot the following weekend. We had total access to practically every location we used on the movie so this was not impossible to do."

Top: Mike senses he is not alone on his ride home through Morningside Cemetery.
Bottom: Horace Bannister poses with future hearse coordinator Guy Thorpe and son Reggie.
(Dwarf photo courtesy Kristen Deem)
(Bannisters photo courtesy Guy Thorpe)

TALL MAN ON MAIN STREET

Production moved to the quaint mountain town of Julian on Tuesday, May 10. This allowed Don Coscarelli to open up his film beyond the familiar Morningside Mortuary and Pearson household. Situated three hours south of the Van Nuys base camp, Julian was the first and shorter of two long-distance location shoots. The former gold mining town's Main Street had been chosen for the central artery of Mike and Jody's hometown (unidentified in the film but called China Grove in the novelization). Centered on the cozy Main Street was the Julian Café. With some set dressing, the exterior became Reggie's Ice Cream. Across the street and several storefronts down was the Pearson family's bank, a real-life bank now occupied by Rabobank. This stretch composes the entirety of downtown Julian.

In a journal dated 5/10/1977, Angus Scrimm wrote:

We were in a line of about six or eight vehicles with Don Jr. leading the way in the Cadillac with Mike and Bill as his passengers, the courier with equipment next, the ice cream truck driven by Roberto, my car with Shirley Coscarelli and Doug as passengers, the big van, the car with the dressing room trailer and Paul Pepperman bringing up the rear. In Escondido, the ice cream truck stalled at a red light and had to be pushed from the left turn lane to a gas station. The town section of Julian is a single main street with a hotel, two small restaurants and some nondescript stores.

On location, the crew filmed the surreal moment when Mike spots the Tall Man slowly approaching Reggie as he loads ice cream into his truck's freezer. Suddenly, the mortician pauses, engulfed in the billowing mist. He seems paralyzed, hands raised as if to ward off the icy fog. Mike watches, terrified and amazed. As the cloud dissipates, the Tall Man continues on his way. Intended to set up the aforementioned fire extinguisher scene, this Main Street encounter was not without merit even when the payoff Tall Man death was removed; it was chilling.

"The scene on Main Street is my favorite in the entire picture," Bill Thornbury says. "Angus and Reggie are great in it, but Michael's performance just sells it to you. His kind of aimless, meandering walk down the street at first and then the look of horror in his eyes as he sees the Tall Man just come across as so genuine. I think he really nailed that scene."

"I had to crawl inside of a rancid old ice cream truck in order to waft the cold mist," George Singer Jr. says. "It was all wood inside and smelled like rotten eggs. I was the only one small enough to fit inside so I had to do it. It was pretty bad but the show must go on! No whining, soldier! I just kept wondering what I was breathing in there. But I don't look back at it as a bummer. When you're on a show working those long hours, you're bummed out at the elements, but that's just life, you know? You're supposed to look back at it and go, '*Oh, it wasn't that bad. I can't say I've done it again since then, though.*'"

"We came back from Julian in the rain," John Zumpano says. "Sort of far from the border, there was an immigration checkpoint on Interstate Five. Roberto Quezada was driving the ice cream truck, totally exposed to the rain, and he didn't have a raincoat on or anything. We had put a garbage bag over him to try and keep him dry but I don't think it was working too well. At some point, we realized that we'd never checked to see if the truck had any registration in it. We'd just never bothered to ask Don if the ice cream truck was a real vehicle or a movie vehicle. I don't know if it ever did have the paperwork onboard but Roberto got through the checkpoint fine. Maybe he charmed his way through it, I don't know. He was always such a character, a very funny man."

BEDSIDE MANNER

The early morning hours of Saturday, May 14 found the production back at Chatsworth Park North to capture Mike's horrifying nightmare as he wakes in bed surrounded by Morningside Cemetery, the Tall Man looming over his headboard. After a beat, zombies burst from the ground and viciously grab hold of the struggling boy. This iconic scene,

Top: The Tall Man's side of Main Street circa 1986. Reggie's truck would have been parked on the left.
Bottom: Mike's side of Main Street circa 1986 including the original phone booth from the scene.

(Photos courtesy Kristen Deem)

which would rank a respectable twenty-fifth on Bravo's *100 All-Time Scariest Movie Moments*, introduces what would become a *Phantasm* series hallmark – temporal displacement. The smooth transition from Mike's bedroom to the cemetery is masterfully executed: the camera zooms in on the sleeping boy in his bedroom, then subtly cuts away to an identical close-up before zooming back abruptly to reveal the cemetery. The location switch is so deft that until the camera reveals tombstones, the audience is unaware that a change has occurred.

"When you pull something like that," John Zumpano says, "you've got to relight your shot exactly the same way so that it matches up with what came before it. You then have a challenge to figure out what's required of you to fool the audience into thinking nothing is different between setups. I'm sure those two shots were done weeks if not months apart, but you wouldn't have known it by the way it was filmed. That's because Roberto Quezada was so good at lighting for film."

"Don gave me total freedom to light *Phantasm*," Quezada says. "But he is a perfectionist, a complete director, and someone that could inspire me and others to walk through fire for him, so I never wanted to disappoint him. I also worked very hard to make sure the lighting would be completely to his liking. Don and I have always thought very similarly on what a film should look like so this was not difficult for me to do."

In a journal dated 5/14/1977, Angus Scrimm wrote:

> The holes were dug on either side of the bed when I arrived. Camera and light in place, bed in place, but the leopard spotted sheet and pillowcase had been forgotten, left behind in Long Beach. Kent was sent to get them because he was the fastest driver by far. Kate proceeded with my makeup and we waited on set while she did very elaborate corpse makeups on George Singer and Robert Del Valle. Kent was back before she'd finished. We finally started at 4 AM and did two takes, both of which Don had printed.

"If you're the Tall Man looking down, I was the zombie on the left side," Singer says. "It was trippy because there was ice on the ground as we shot this. The girls made mud patties with icy water and dirt and these were rubbed all over our clothes. The only way to stay warm was to get into the grave and let the floodlight in there warm you up. Looking back, it's a great cameo to have in the film."

THE ORIGINAL 'CUDA

For some, the true star of *Phantasm* was not a character but instead the 1971 Plymouth 'Cuda. The sleek ride was a jet-black 440 six-barrel model with flared fenders and Cragar S/S wheels. Don Coscarelli's decision to so prominently feature the vehicle stemmed from a lasting desire to own one after first beholding the remarkable muscle car in high school. Filming the vehicle for Phantasm was an easy way to finally get behind the wheel of one of the greatest vehicles of all time. The 'Cuda would instantly become an indelible part of *Phantasm*'s identity.

"You have to wonder if Don intended for the 'Cuda to become a celebrity within *Phantasm*," Bruce Chudacoff says. "Certainly it has become that because now you've got a *Phantasm* model 'Cuda and it's well known throughout the world as being part of the series formula. It almost became a character unto itself."

On-screen, the 'Cuda was the epitome of cool on four wheels. Offscreen, it was anything but this. Having been "enjoyed" for several years prior to filming, it was purchased on the cheap and badly in need of work. The car was given a last minute going-over by Bill Thornbury's brother, Skip, who enhanced the body with gold pin stripes. Beyond cosmetic touches, the car's electrical wiring was reportedly on its deathbed and the aftermarket sunroof leaked.

"It was a great ride," George Singer Jr. says. "Great... so long as you could get it started. It seemed like we had trouble with that every single time we went to film."

"I learned how to drive in that car," Michael Baldwin proudly exclaims. "It was great fun getting to take that thing out on the open road but the truth is that I never drove it by myself or for long distances. Never on the freeway or anything like that. But to a thirteen year old, it was the coolest thing ever."

"Hot as love!" - the 1971 Chrysler-Plymouth 'Cuda.
(Chrysler publicity photo)

"I was raised in a car family," Thornbury says. "I've always been a car guy and appreciated quality cars, and the 'Cudas are definitely worth appreciating. My father was a Chevrolet Oldsmobile dealer so I grew up accustomed to driving good cars. The 'Cuda was the one that I really fell in love with during the making of the film, though."

WESTLAKE BOUND & DOWN

On Monday, May 30, a skeleton crew ventured into the Westlake Village district to shoot evening hearse driving scenes. In the film, the Tall Man's ride back to Morningside abruptly ends when a captive Mike shoots out a back tire and window before jumping free of the coach. The careening hearse plows into a tree and explodes, mortician inside. Barely visible inside the rear cab with Mike is what appears to be a motionless dwarf.

Westlake Village roads were vacant enough by night that driving scenes would not attract unwanted attention, namely the police. One of the evening's riskier shots involved Angus Scrimm driving without his glasses. Scrimm, manning the coach, was required to look away from the road to gaze back sardonically at Michael Baldwin (and Don Coscarelli on camera), yet miraculously keep from off-roading the hearse.

An uncredited Roger George, who went on to handle pyrotechnic duties on *The Terminator, Night of the Creeps, The Lost Empire* and Coscarelli's own *The Beastmaster,* handled the magnificent hearse explosion. The scene's fiery climax attracted a sizable crowd from the nearby expressway.

"Don and Paul were very open to hearing other people's ideas," George Singer Jr. says. "Like the time that I went up to them and said, *'Why don't you light me on fire and let me crash the hearse into the tree?'* No kidding. I actually asked Don if I could build a protective suit and be lit on fire for the scene! I think it was his dad who decided that it wouldn't be too good of an idea and it was scrapped. Probably for the best."

Moments before exploding, the Tall Man guns the hearse through Morningside's majestic gates. These gates belonged to the Cobb Estate in Pasadena where they still stand today. Built in 1915, the Estate went through several owners including the Marx Brothers, before being bought by the city in 1971. Eight years earlier, local citizens had blocked an effort to convert the property into, of all things, a cemetery. The gates are situated some four hundred miles south of the Dunsmuir Estate, later used as the mortuary's exterior, making this a sure candidate for the longest driveway in film history.

"We were all so enamored with the location that no one realized a bright yellow sign warning drivers of a ninety degree curve in the road was right in the middle of the frame," Roberto Quezada recalls. "So Coscarelli, in his inimitable last minute way, mentioned the problem of the sign in the shot to me since I was the one who found the goddamn place. His way of bringing up stuff like this was to get Socratic on me with a question like, '*Um, what did you think we were going to do about that sign in the middle of the shot?*' So I hopped into the grip van, asked Pepperman to guide me backwards so I wouldn't hit anything except what I was aiming at, and proceeded to run the offending yellow sign over. It snapped off at the base, we threw it into the bushes and got the shot. Pepperman had a conscience, or a good sense of a lawsuit waiting to happen, and kind of leaned the sign back up against a tree by the side of the road the next morning after we all left for home."

A DWARF NAMED TOMMY

Later in the year, the production captured another dangerous driving scene in which the white hearse chases down the Pearson's 'Cuda. Clutching a pump rifle, Jody climbs through the muscle car's sunroof to blast away their assailant, whose hearse soon veers off road into yet another tree. To film Bill Thornbury firing the shotgun, Don Coscarelli and Roberto Quezada wedged their bodies and the camera into the car's limited trunk space. The crew thought it wise to tape a protective seat cushion to the director's face to prevent disfiguration from shell rebounds.

"So now we're ready to go," Quezada says. "We hop into the trunk of the car, take off way down the road and Don yells, '*Action!*' I'm sitting right next to him to steady the camera and make sure that we're passing under the lights correctly. Bill throwing off the glass of the sunroof nearly takes our heads off. I'm not kidding. Do you have any idea what the g-force of a pane of Plexiglas is at fifty miles an hour? Neither did we. Immediately, in fact, instantly, after the first shot out of the gun, Don and I each quietly realize to ourselves that we forgot our earplugs. The sound of a full load three feet from your head is, well, let me put it this way: Going deaf was the least of our immediate concerns. It fucking hurt. There were three more shots to go and we didn't even have a bullet between us to bite down on. But we nailed the scene, did a victory lap around the set, hopped out of the trunk, and promptly noticed that the cushion we had so permanently taped to Coscarelli's head was on fire. I'm talking engulfed. I mean flames two feet off the top of the cushion. Half the crew is burning their fingers trying to find the untabbed ends of the tape to get the cushion off Don's head. The other half is beating the shit out of Don to put out the flames. In retrospect, he wished it was a more padded cushion."

Following the hearse crash, Mike and Jody circle around to investigate. They find the Tommy-dwarf impaled by a tree branch, oozing yellow blood from its hideous maw. Horrified, they realize the creature is their friend. At a nearby phone booth, they call Reggie to bring his truck. As with his prior funeral makeup, Bill Cone's dwarf visage was designed and applied by Shirley Coscarelli.

"I had to do that scene in the hearse about four times, spitting out that yellow stuff," Cone says. "I'd fill my mouth up with it, spit it out and then they'd wash me off so we could go again. It was made out of flour and food coloring, so definitely not tasty. As soon as I arrived on set, Shirley put all of that makeup stuff on me and since I had to go to a party that night, I thought I'd just leave it all on for fun. As I drove back, I stopped off at a gas station and got the weirdest looks from everyone there. I guess I was a little early for Halloween."

"That phone booth was rented from the phone company and we had to return it after we were done filming in it," John Zumpano says. "I remember that we loaded it up in George Singer's yellow Datsun truck to take it back. Neither of us knew much about how to tie these things down. So on the way to return it, the phone booth spills out onto the freeway and we have to go retrieve it. Needless to say, it was a little

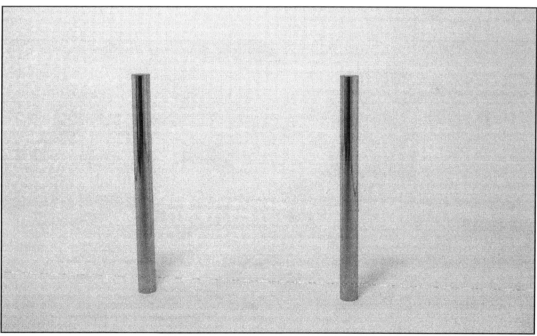

Top: The dwarf barrels were actually A.C.T. Polydrums, intended for transporting toxic chemicals!
Bottom: The original spacegate poles would return for each sequel.
(Photos courtesy Kristen Deem)

An illusion - the Red Planet skyline actually extends upward rather than outward.
(Author photo)

dinged up. The people who we returned it to, miraculously, didn't bother to inspect it and George and I just kind of looked at one another, nodded, and then skated out of there as fast as we could."

SPACEGATE TO INFINITY

From behind an ominous black door there resonates a peculiar hum. The room beyond glows brilliant white and houses an interdimensional doorway. In the story, Mike discovers that the Tall Man is shrinking and shipping Earth's recently deceased to another planet to use as slaves. Most alarming for the youth is that his parents' crypt is unusually vacant. *Phantasm*'s abrupt switch from horror to science fiction reinvigorates the film in its third act. This development bears a likeness to Ed Wood's *Plan 9 From Outer Space* which was originally named *Grave Robbers from Outer Space*, a title that could equally have belonged to *Morningside*.

Though the spacegates were Coscarelli's vision, their functionality as a tuning fork-inspired device owes to Susan and Reggie Bannister. "Don had the design for this room in his head, and it was more imagery than anything," Bannister says. "Don has terrific imagery, you know. You can see it in his scenes, the way he builds things. You can see it in his camera work. He took me into this room with these two chromium

steel bars coming out of the floor and he goes, '*Well, this is the spacegate, Reg. One thing we really can't figure out is how it works.*' I was with my wife at the time, Susan, and Don left us in the room and said, '*Think about this, how this thing would work...this door into another world.*' That's the way Don likes to work. So we were looking at the canisters in there, and the spacegate, and Susan goes, '*You know, it looks like the ends of a tuning fork*'. I said, '*It really does...Wow, that's really far out!*' We ran out to Don and said, '*Hey Don, we've got it. It's a tuning fork. And it sets up this vibration; it actually causes a rent in this reality.*' And Don said, '*That's it.*'"

Being solid steel, the spacegate pillars were massively heavy. Though lightweight duplicates have been fashioned over the years, this original pair would return in all three *Phantasm* sequels. The disappearing effect of Michael Baldwin passing through the gate was achieved by carefully lodging a mirror between the poles so as to reflect only white, same as behind it. By reaching past the mirror, Baldwin's hand would seem to disappear. Roberto Quezada's blinding light scheme was a nod to Stanley Kubrick's *2001: A Space Odyssey*, a personal favorite of Quezada, Coscarelli and Baldwin. Not coincidentally, *2001* Cinematographer John Alcott would later enlist on Coscarelli's tumultuous fourth feature, *The Beastmaster*.

"I really liked competing with Paul and Don to figure stuff out," Quezada says. "They taught me that all filmmaking is really just optical illusion. Mike sticking his hand through the

Reggie Bannister - faithful friend, ice cream man and spacegate imploder.
(Photo courtesy Kristen Deem)

spacegate and into the other dimension was Paul. I don't know what kind of hallucinogenic his brain naturally produced, but it really kicked ass."

The spacegate sequence ends with Reggie accidentally initiating an implosion, creating a powerful vacuum that ultimately consumes the entire building. As the portal opens, Reggie barely manages to escape its massive pull. The vacuum effect was created by attaching shock cords to Bannister's ankles and having crewmembers pull back violently as he crawls away. Just off-camera, more crewmembers hurled polyethylene barrels toward the poles to create the illusion of their being sucked off world. More than one of these 55 gallon drums struck Bannister as he crawled along the floor; just one of the workplace hazards one finds on a *Phantasm*.

The sequence depicting the Red Planet was filmed at the Santa Fe Dam in Irwindale. Although the landscape appears to extend off into the horizon, it actually is a steep, rock-strewn hillside that rises upward instead of outward. Roughly a dozen of the foreground dwarves were played by children. The robed youngsters were culled from Art Director David Gavin Brown's neighborhood and were all thrilled to pile into the back of the Tall Man's hearse for the ride to Irwindale. The remaining slaves, particularly those closer to the horizon, were robed cardboard boxes. As Mike Pearson tumbles through the violent red sky, the scene alternates between Baldwin in close-up and a head over heels George Singer Jr.

"If I remember correctly, we had a pulley attached to the roof with a line tied around me," Singer says. "This was in the warehouse. We had painted one of the walls bright red. Some people were on the other end of the line and they pulled me off the ground so that I could do flips, which Don cut in very quickly with Michael's material."

Bill Thornbury and Kat Lester reminisce about their scene thirty years later.
(Photo courtesy Scott Pensa)

When *Phantasm* arrived on home video, it was inadvertently missing part of the spacegate sequence; the moment where the room loses power while the heroes are trapped inside. The absent footage, which appeared completely dark, was situated at the end of a reel and mistakenly trimmed by a lab technician who was unaware that dialogue had been layered over the blank screen. The scene was restored on MGM's 1998 video release, which was advertised as the "original theatrical version" to consumers.

"It was funny dialogue," Bannister says. "I had no idea why they cut it out. It was great. The lights go out, and there's all this scuffling, the door opening, closing...and then, with the screen dark, there's this moment of silence. And then you hear my voice go, '*Jody? Mike? Oh, shit...*' I realize I'm alone in this stone dark room. Then it goes to the next scene."

THE ONLY THING TO DO IN THIS TOWN

One *Morningside* sequence both recut and recontextualized was Jody Pearson's initial visit to Dunes Cantina. Jody finds the seductive Lady in Lavender seated at the bar and quietly sidles up to her. One can only imagine that this is how Tommy's final evening began. The original motivation for Jody's drinking was to help forget that his discontented girlfriend, Suzy, was now on a date with another man. With the deletion of the bank scenes, Jody seems to drink merely to break up the monotony of small town life. Dunes Cantina was located on the Pacific Coast Highway in Sunset Beach. Owner Señor Corky Gill had only two requests of Don Coscarelli: that his crew pay for their drinks and that he receive a cameo. He can be seen in the film behind the counter sporting a cowboy hat.

After his bank guard performance was deleted, Ralph Richmond was recast as the Dunes Cantina bartender. His new scene with Bill Thornbury took place the morning after Jody's Lavender encounter. "The filming I did at the bar took one day," Richmond says. "The location was an actual bar in Sunset Beach, a ratty-looking two-story bar with a balcony on one side. I used to drive past it all the time. I went from having a decent-sized part as a bank guard to only having one line as the bartender. I say it to the older brother after he'd left with a gal in the previous scene. I go, '*You get a hold of something you couldn't handle?*' and that was my performance in the film. At least I wasn't out completely!"

"In the film, you just see me sitting at the bar," Kathy Lester recalls. "Then Bill walks up and we leave together. You see it all through the window from Mike's eyes. We actually shot a whole interior scene with dialogue at the Dunes that didn't make the film. Don wanted us to improvise and we were both just at a loss. We had been talking so much before the scene that we didn't know what to say. And then Bill was to look at the bartender and say, '*One Dos Equis, por favor*' and the bartender is supposed to slide it down to him and he would take a drink. We wound up doing too many takes and before long, Bill was pretty tipsy!"

Jody's night out continues at Chatsworth Park North, where the film's memorable opening scene between Tommy and Lavender would also unfold. Although a brief affair onscreen, the prologue's filming was a drawn-out process. Shooting was first delayed by Lester's reticence to so intimately straddle Bill Cone, whom she had only just met. Her anxiety was greatly compounded by the location's openness and numerous onlookers.

"Almost none of that scene did I actually shoot with Kathy," Cone says. "It was right there at her wedding day in real life and in the film, she was supposed to be sitting there naked on someone else's lap. Awkward, right? We had one shot where she was sitting on top of me, but that was it. Then they brought in the doubles." The scene's first substitution was Thornbury for Cone, whom Lester had known prior to that night of filming and was more comfortable acting opposite. A second double was brought in when Lester began to reconsider her decision to disrobe.

"I wasn't really excited about it," Lester says. "I thought it would be fine, not much different than wearing a bikini. I'll just be sure to find something not too revealing, I thought. So I was getting my makeup done in the trailer and there's a knock on the door, time to shoot the scene where I kill Bill Cone's character. I started to come out of the trailer and I see all of these guys drinking beer and they're like, '*Bring out the bimbo,*' and I just said, '*I'm not doing this scene.*' It was supposed to be a closed set and I wasn't going to do it. Don said, '*Okay, we'll shoot around this scene. Do you mind if we get a body double?*' and I said, '*Hell, no! I don't mind because I'm not doing it.*' I was nineteen. I didn't get any specifics on this."

With Tommy's murder scene incomplete, warehouse reshoots were in order. Laura Mann, credited in the film as Double Lavender and believed by some to be a pseudonym, was enlisted to perform the nude portion of the Lavender role. The substitution of Mann for Lester and Thornbury for Cone meant that four performers were now part of a scene that featured only two characters, not counting Angus Scrimm's Tall Man. For her warehouse close-ups, Lester sat atop an apple crate and was asked to simulate "great sex" for the camera.

"So I started ooing and ahhing, and Don started moving in closer and I would start cracking up. I said, '*I just can't do this.*' I don't know how many times I tried. He asked '*What can I do to make you comfortable?*' and I said, '*I need a prop!*' (laughs) I asked if Bill Thornbury could come over and could I sit on him? Bill said, '*Sure,*' so that's what I did. Needless to say, we got the shot. We got it in one take."

Back on location, the company was to encounter another setback, this time while filming Jody and Lavender's graveside sex. Now Thornbury was refusing to submit to nudity. An uncredited crewmember volunteered to substitute as Jody's naked backside. "My butt is in the movie," John Zumpano says with relish. "I play Bill Thornbury's butt in the love scene because, quite frankly, no one else wanted to do it. At first, I thought, '*Sure, why not?*' But then I started wondering, '*Am I going to be embarrassed by this later on?*' I got stage fright all of a sudden. Hiking down your pants for the camera wasn't the most glamorous work out there but it had to be done. The show must go on, you know."

"About seven or eight years later," Cone says, "I ran into Kathy at a shopping mall in Orange County. I walked up to her and said, '*Hello, you probably don't remember me, and don't take this the wrong way, but you actually murdered me once.*' Then she realized who I was and we had a good laugh about it."

BURYING THE TALL MAN

On Sunday, June 5, New Breed convened at Quail Creek in Chatsworth to begin work on the Tall Man's final demise. Despite having already been hanged, melted and blown up, the mortician would now suffer a nasty fall down a mineshaft that would be sealed by giant rocks. Situated west of Tampa Avenue, the location boasted a steep hillside ideal for bowling Styrofoam boulders downhill. Unlike his previous feats, there would be no illusory stunt this time for Angus Scrimm. He would actually have to fall into an open pit and act as if he didn't already know it was going to happen.

Two months prior, the Kansas-born thespian had portrayed a monk opposite Bill Cosby and Sidney Poitier in *A Piece of the Action*. For the role, Scrimm had offered to cut the Tall Man's long locks. Fortunately, director Poitier deemed it unnecessary. Now Scrimm found himself repeatedly crawling on hands and knees out of a dirty pit at an ungodly morning hour, mouth full of dirt and body bruised. According to a fellow cast member, there was usually one person often tasked with making such arduous requests of the performers on behalf of *Phantasm*'s creator.

"With Paul Pepperman, I always felt like he was trying to get us to do something that we probably didn't want to do," Michael Baldwin says. "He was a perfectly nice guy and would never ask us to do anything that he wouldn't first do himself but, of course, the difference was that he was a

grown man, I was thirteen and Angus was older than both of us combined. So there was always a bit of push and pull going on there. He was never heavy-handed with us but I was always very suspicious whenever Paul would come over, like '*What the hell does he want me to do now?* (laughs)"

In a journal dated 6/5/1977, Angus Scrimm wrote:

> *I ran perhaps eight paces and then right foot first, left foot following, plunged into the pit. My arms struck the right rim and I fell into the foam rubber with a mouthful of dirt. We did it again. This time as I approached the pit, I cut my steps a little closer and went down cleanly but it was obvious that I anticipated and calculated the drop. Take no good. The third time, I ran hell for leather, cracked both arms a painful crack as I hit the far rim and dropped backward into the pit. Don decided he liked that one. Then the camera was set up at pit left. I charged forward twice more, filmed from a side angle, emitted a wild yell and threw my arms above me as I fell. Don pronounced himself satisfied.*

Completion of the Tall Man's plummet wrapped Scrimm for the evening, though he remained to watch Bill Thornbury and crew roll several massive boulders into the pit. Despite their Styrofoam composition, the props were enormously heavy, even more so when barreling downhill. Their trajectory was calculated to stop just short of Coscarelli and camera. During filming, the first boulder overshot the pit and crashed into the director, causing contusions and more than $1,000 in damage to the rented Panavision equipment. Scrimm recalls that on the first take the crew mistakenly rolled only one boulder. This misfire was fortunate as multiple boulders misfiring "might have killed" Coscarelli on camera. After prepping the scene a second time, the boulders were rolled, this time with *Pepperman* on camera. On this second roll, they hit their mark splendidly without further injury to anyone.

"I've never witnessed anything so riveting, so spectacular, as that boulder's descent," Scrimm's journal reads. "Paul, Don, Shirley and I watched transfixed and if it had come at me, I don't think I would have moved."

FEAR IS THE KILLER

On June 10 and 11, the production filmed scenes involving the fortuneteller and her granddaughter. Both characters remain unnamed in the film but had been identified as Mrs. Starr and Sarah Starr in Shirley Coscarelli's novelization. Interiors were captured at the crew's Van Nuys residence. The fortuneteller's house exterior was a private residence in Woodland Hills, which New Breed secured for its standard $50 location fee. Angus Scrimm notes that Don Coscarelli and Paul Pepperman ran into trouble when they announced the shoot with only a day's notice to the performers. Michael Baldwin and Terrie Kalbus were available to film. Bettina Viney, however, was not. Several months had passed since she was given the fortuneteller role without an audition or a contract and she was unwilling to miss her nephew's birthday party that weekend for filming.

Unable to reschedule the shoot, Coscarelli and Pepperman recast the role with Mary Ellen Shaw, who had already filmed scenes as Mike and Jody's aunt. Shaw's heavy costuming was an attempt to conceal her dual casting as Aunt Belle.

"It was obviously the same actress," Scrimm says. "So the aunt was eliminated, and Mary Ellen as the fortuneteller became one of the unforgettable images in the film. I've wondered since if Bettina's nephew might not have preferred to have his aunt's artistry preserved in a classic film. Still, there's something endearing about a woman who unhesitatingly puts love of family above a shot at being in the movies."

Drawing from Frank Herbert's <u>Dune</u>, Coscarelli included a variation on the novel's Bene Gesserit "Pain Box." In <u>Dune</u>, a religious group uses the box to test human reactions to mind over fear/agony. In *Morningside*, the fortuneteller uses the box to teach Mike not to fear that which he doesn't know or understand, an important lesson at the film's conclusion.

The Fortuneteller's House as it appears today.
(*Author Photo*)

The Pearson family homestead.
(Photo courtesy Kristen Deem)

In both Herbert's novel and Coscarelli's film, the boxes are completely empty and the pain is merely psychosomatic.

A subsequent scene was filmed, and cut, in which Mike returns the next day to find the house dark. The fortuneteller appears, quite distraught, and tells him that Sarah hasn't returned from visiting her grandfather's crypt at Morningside. In the film, the girl is last seen approaching the cemetery and entering the spacegate room. Thus, it was originally Sarah's disappearance, not curiosity, that motivated young Mike to trespass into Morningside.

THE ORIGINAL ENDING

On Wednesday, June 29, New Breed traded its faux-cemetery in Chatsworth for a real cemetery in Long Beach. The day exteriors captured at Sunnyside's Memorial Park encompassed what Don Coscarelli had first envisioned as the film's conclusion. Mike was to wake in his bedroom surrounded by empty Dos Equis bottles, discounting the entire film as a drunken dream. Then at Morningside Cemetery, he would solemnly stand over Jody's grave. The camera would pull back, passing a funeral where the Tall Man would be revealed as a harmless mortal. The scene would finally crane to a wide shot of the entire cemetery before cutting. No last minute jump scare. No reemergence of the Tall Man. Truly, it would only be a dream.

"I don't remember much about that ending but I'm glad Don changed it," Michael Baldwin says. "Had we gone the only a dream route, I think we would have pissed off the audience. You feel cheated when a film does that because no one wants to go on this journey for ninety minutes only to find out that it's not real. I can't speak for Don, but I imagine that's part of why he changed it. And the great part is that he didn't really change it, he just built onto it in a more satisfying way for the audience because all in all I still think it still could have been a dream. It's really up to the audience to decide."

The shot of Mike gazing down at Jody's grave was later incorporated into the film's revised ending as a flashback during Reggie's fireside chat. The extended version of the scene with an ordinary-looking Tall Man was later written into the script for *Phantasm: Oblivion*, but trimmed to stop just short of Angus Scrimm's big reveal.

THE PACIFIC PALISADES

On Friday, July 1, the crew gathered outside a modest one story home in Pacific Palisades. The day's work included both day and night exterior shots of the Pearson household. One scene was Jody and Reggie's porch duet of '*Sittin' Here At Midnight*'. The song was written by Bill Thornbury and augmented by Reggie Bannister's impromptu guitar solo. This phan-favorite tune has never been released on any of the *Phantasm* commercial soundtracks, though Thornbury did studio record it in 1995. Bannister's oft-quoted line, "hot as love," was supplied to him by fellow Good Band bassist David Seachrist.

"I've always been a feel guy and that song has a feel to it that I like a lot," Thornbury says. "I didn't particularly love how it came off in the movie. I would've preferred that we recorded it and then lip-synched it for camera because the audio quality would've been better. But hey, everybody seems to like that scene. I wound up finishing the tune long after we shot it. I did an acoustic-vocal version of it which had no bass, no drums, nothing. I like both versions, though. The "*Uh!*" in the film bothers me a little bit, but I still like the tune. It works."

The location was also the backdrop to a deleted scene in which Mike arrives home still rattled from his cemetery encounter with the Tall Man. He and Jody proceed to drink Dos Equis well into the evening until they decide to pay an inebriated visit to Reggie's Ice Cream.

"It was really beer in the Dos Equis bottles," Michael Baldwin says. "Totally less touchy back then. It was a different time and they were just kids themselves, the crew. I mean how old was Don Coscarelli? Twenty-three? Not that old. When we went and shot in Julian later on for the exteriors of ice cream store in Alhambra, the whole crew would be partying in someone's hotel room when we were done at night. I would be right there partying with them. It was a lot of fun. I was always older than my age."

Filming temporarily stalled later that night due to an ineffectual prop. A wooden, fingerless hand that Angus Scrimm was to utilize for the remainder of the film (due to Mike's finger-chopping) proved too unrealistic. The inanimate device extended conspicuously farther than the actor's true hand. Scrimm suggested that the Tall Man was indestructible; therefore his fingers should be the same. The scene was revised on the spot so that the Tall Man would initially pretend to still be missing fingers only to open his hand a moment later, revealing the restored digits. Scrimm single handedly carried his co-star by the nape of the neck by having Baldwin step onto a camera dolly, which was then wheeled by off-camera crewmembers to the waiting coach.

DUNSMUIR HOUSE

On Friday, December 9, the company headed four hundred miles north for its biggest location shoot yet. Their destination was the stately Dunsmuir House in Oakland. The estate had been chosen to serve as the face of Morningside Mortuary. Built in 1899 by Alexander Dunsmuir, the son of a wealthy coal baron, the mansion was a wedding present for his bride, Josephine.

The historic Dunsmuir.
(*Photo courtesy Kristen Deem*)

"The funeral is about to begin, sir!"
(Photo courtesy Kristen Deem)

The thirty-seven room manse was never lived in by its owner, who died while on honeymoon. The widow Dunsmuir did take up residence following her husband's passing only to die herself two years later. The property was eventually purchased by the City of Oakland and included on the U.S. National Register of Historic Places in 1972. The mansion is presently open for tours, weddings and film production. Most notably, Dunsmuir appeared in the 1976 chiller *Burnt Offerings*, written and directed by *Dark Shadows* creator Dan Curtis. The film starred Karen Black, Oliver Reed, Bette Davis and Burgess Meredith, and is likely what attracted Don Coscarelli to make the long trek north to Dunsmuir. It would later appear in Roger Moore's final Bond film *A View to a Kill* and the Mike Myers comedy *So I Married an Axe Murderer*.

The high intensity shoot required both day and night exteriors captured within a single weekend. "God, the house was just fantastic," Reggie Bannister says. "All the shots you see of that house were done in a weekend. One weekend.

And that was the longest, hardest shoot that I remember. We had to get it all, because we couldn't go back. We couldn't afford to go back."

The trip roster included Don, Dac and Shirley Coscarelli, Michael Baldwin, Bill Thornbury, Bannister, Angus Scrimm, Kathy Lester, Paul Pepperman, Roberto Quezada, Robert Del Valle, George Singer Jr., Bruce Chudacoff and Colin Spencer, among others. Most drove, some flew, and a handful of crew members piled into the back of the Tall Man's hearse and joined a procession with the Cuda, motorbike, makeup trailer and Econoline van up to location.

"It was stressful," Scrimm says. "My family was four and a half years into the relentless, ongoing deterioration of our mother from an Alzheimer's-like affliction complicated by recurring respiratory infections. Don and Paul made an earnest effort to find a location in Southern California that would keep me close to home but at length settled on Dunsmuir House. On December 7, 1977, my mother's condition had so worsened

Available for weddings.
(Photo courtesy Kristen Deem)

that she was admitted to Hollywood Presbyterian Hospital at Vermont and Sunset for tests and treatment. On Saturday, Dec. 10, after a night at the hospital, I drove myself to LAX and caught an 11:15 AM flight to Oakland. The *Phantasm* scenes involving the funeral home had to be shot."

"Don Sr. met me on my arrival and drove me to Dunsmuir House," Scrimm continues. "After Shirley applied the Tall Man's makeup, I donned the black frock coat, Inverness cape, and Dickensian top hat, and in late afternoon a gleaming glass hearse with black and gold decorations arrived with two horses to pull it. I mounted the driver's seat and Don and Paul took endless color and black and white photos in a process that lasted, what with repeated trips back to the supply trailer for film magazines, cord, lenses, etc., for some ninety minutes until we lost the sun. After a dinner of pizza and root beer, I retired to the drafty interior of Dunsmuir House while exteriors with

Mike, Bill, Kathy and Reggie were filmed, and spent the hours chatting with the mansion's caretaker, David. Sometime after midnight I was called out to do the scene in which the Lady in Lavender, who has just thrust a knife into Reggie's chest, morphs into the Tall Man. A giant wind machine just at camera left was blowing with gale force straight at me, propmen were flinging dried leaves into its path, the Dunsmuir porch lights behind me were swinging crazily, and my instructions were to look sinister and enigmatic and keep my eyes wide open and unblinking in spite of the wind and pelting leaves as I drew the knife from Reggie's chest."

"I constantly thank Don for giving me one of the longest death scenes in the history of cinema," Bannister says. "It was terrific."

"I was inside the mansion at that point," Zumpano says. "My job was to be at the light switches that control the

The entrance to Morningside. Also the longest driveway in history.
(*Author photo*)

The Tall Man and the original *boooy* thirty years later.
(Photo courtesy Paul Miser)

porch lights so that once we started rolling Paul would go out and tip all of the light fixtures on the porch so they would sway. Then you start throwing leaves into the fan and during that time, I was inside the mansion flipping the porch light switches on and off like there was an electrical storm or something. It was a really low-tech combination of special effects trickery but when it all synchronized, it looked stunning onscreen."

"Here is why I was so impressed with Don and Paul," Chudacoff says. "They knew that they wanted to have leaves blowing in the last scene at Dunsmuir. They also knew that to guarantee those leaves being there that they would have to bring them. So it's my recollection that out of the back of a van came several bags full of leaves that were brought up from Southern California. They were very good at thinking ahead."

"It was barely fifty degrees," Lester says. "Everyone's in jackets and scarves and I'm in my little lavender dress with no stockings and Don tells me to lay down on the grass, wet with morning dew. They're supposed to be only throwing leaves into the fan and there is Michael throwing twigs and stones into the mix. So now I'm freezing and feeling sharp pains. I had to throw my hands up and yell for them to stop filming because of it."

"Now that's a true story," Baldwin says. "I do recall it. I liked messing with people, so did I put rocks into the leaf mixture for the wind scenes? Hell, yeah!"

"Then there's another scene we filmed in Los Angeles where Michael's trudging through the woods and all of the sudden he sees me with a knife," Lester says. "I'm supposed to be staring expressionless at him. We had to shoot that more than a couple times because Michael was making horrendous faces at me. It was ridiculous! Sticking his tongue out, crossing his eyes, mouthing things. He would do anything to piss me off. And it worked. I came to find out later that he had a crush on me the whole time and that was his way of expressing it. He sure was an incredibly cute pain in the ass."

"What you have to remember is that we all had lives outside of *Phantasm*," Chudacoff says. "Except for maybe Don and Paul, this was a part-time gig that we came and went for many months. Coming back from Oakland, several of us went right into finals week once we touched down. We had to take our books with us and study when we weren't filming at the mansion. We didn't wind up studying very much but had to at least take the books along."

"I got a Sunday 8 AM flight back to LAX," Scrimm says. "At the hospital, my mother was so glad to see me. We were told we could take her home in two or three days. She died suddenly that night while I was with her, just after midnight."

FINAL DAYS

As a long year drew to a close, so did production on *Morningside*. Only a handful of scenes remained to be shot. The campiest of this leftover lot was the attack of the Tall Man's finger-turned-insect on Mike and Jody. The bug prop was hand crafted from a model kit by Shirley Coscarelli and brought to life by monofilament wire (and convincing performances from the cast). Don Coscarelli would later tell <u>Fangoria</u> magazine that he was so unsure of the bug sequence that it was nearly cut from the film. A subsequent bit where Mike encounters a larger version of the bug was excised. While the scene draws Reggie's character into the brothers' misadventure, the actual day of production wrapped Reggie Bannister's work on the film altogether.

"If you had to explain what that movie was about," Bannister says, "and you could extract one line out of the picture, it would probably be when the bug circles around Reggie's head, and he falls down and he goes, '*What the hell is going on?*' (laughs) That would definitely be it. We felt that way many times making it. What the hell's going on here? I don't know. *You* made it. I don't know."

"It's much easier to do those kinds of scenes when you're a kid," Michael Baldwin says. "When you're still young, the world of pretend isn't as far away as it is for an adult. You have fewer qualms about acting like you're wrestling with a bug creature inside of a jean jacket or that your hand is trapped inside of a black box. Kids' imaginations are much more fluid than adults so it's no big deal to them. I don't know that I'd want to redo those scenes today because they seem much more silly to me now than they did then."

POST-PRODUCTION

Unique for its time, *Morningside*'s post-production ran parallel to its filming. This meant that scenes were being cut together during the week between weekend shoots. Much of the film had already been assembled by December when the cast and crew reached Dunsmuir. Scenes involving Jody and the family bank were struck. More trimmings hit the editing room floor after a January 1978 test screening. These additional cuts included chase scenes and Tall Man deaths.

"It didn't strike me as being odd that we were editing the film as we made it," Bruce Chudacoff says. "If you're only shooting on weekends, what else are you going to do during the week if not edit? It made sense. Let me give you *Phantasm* Editing 101. I would take the 35mm film reel that contained a copy of the film negative and the separate audio track reel, run them through the sync block, find the frame where the slate closes, mark with an 'X', find the slate sound on the 1/2" audio track, mark it, place the film reel and audio track reel on the Moviola, separate the 2 marks by 24 frames, watch it, rewind, add it to the collection of film to be viewed by Don and Paul."

In a journal dated 9/24/1977, Angus Scrimm wrote:

Phone chat with Don's mother: "My son just came home. They've timed the film as it's now cut and it runs two hours and ten minutes so they want to go back and cut out another half hour. My scene is already out."

Next came the music. Don Coscarelli again enlisted Fred Myrow for a uniquely original horror score. For this, Myrow teamed with collaborator Malcolm Seagrave. The score's eclectic instrumentation featured a Yamaha YC30 Synthesizer, Clavinet, Fender Electric Piano and, according to Scot Holton's liner notes, "virtually the entire percussion section of a symphony orchestra." The hypnotically cyclic eight note melody at the heart of their *Phantasm* theme would become an instantly recognizable trademark of the film and its sequels.

"Fred Myrow was a classically trained composer of great gifts and had a terrific instinct for the special needs of film composing, and Seagrave an admirable collaborator," Scrimm says. "Their music was an incalculable contribution to the film's power and effectiveness."

Music aside, there was still much work to be done. Dialogue had to be looped. The Chatsworth mausoleum had to be torn down and was removed by Christmas 1977. A teaser poster was commissioned for Jim Warren to design. Completed in just one week, the artist painted a medium close-up of the Tall Man, fingers bursting from his head. Bizarre and surreal, the poster was used to advertise the film to critics, test audiences and distributors. The original oil painting would be sold to an anonymous collector in 2003.

"I was friends with Paul Ratajczak," Warren says, "who owned the recording studio in Long Beach where *Phantasm*'s soundtrack was being recorded. Don Coscarelli saw my artwork there and asked me to do the painting. This was used for the first ad for the movie in the <u>Los Angeles Times</u> and for a fifteen foot poster for the festival premiere of *Phantasm*."

There still remained the issue of what to name the film. Not content to stick with *Morningside*, Coscarelli regularly solicited the input of cast and crew for a new moniker. Scrimm recalls that he briefly considered calling it *The Dark* until another horror film beat them to the punch. Shortly thereafter, Paul Pepperman suggested *Phantasm*, a word popularized by Edgar Allen Poe in works such as The Black Cat, The Masque of the Red Death and The Fall of the House of Usher. The word had an eerie ring and was rather imprecise. So broad were its definitions that the film's theatrical trailer would try to answer the question "What is *Phantasm*?" by volunteering several suggestions: a nightmare, an illusion, an evil and a fantasy. The trailer concludes with the famous tagline: "Whatever it is, if this one doesn't scare you… you're already dead!"

Excerpt from The Fall of the House of Usher:

> To an anomalous species of terror I found him a bounden slave. "I shall perish," said he, "I must perish in this deplorable folly. Thus, thus, and not otherwise, shall I be lost. I dread the events of the future, not in themselves, but in their results. […] In this unnerved—in this pitiable condition—I feel that the period will sooner or later arrive when I must abandon life and reason together, in some struggle with the grim phantasm, FEAR."

Above: We have him to thank.
Below: Angus Scrimm and Guy Thorpe with the Warren art.
*(The Poe photo was preserved from an original
daguerreotype in 1904 by a C.T. Talman. Coincidence?)*
(Warren photo courtesy Guy Thorpe)

The first indication of *Phantasm*'s potential came with its first test screening on January 9, 1978, one month after the Dunsmuir shoot. With no controlling investor or studio watchdog, Coscarelli was free to interpret and act upon audience reaction as he saw fit. The crucial feedback received at this formative event provided him the guidance necessary to re-edit *Phantasm* into the film it is today. Cast were forbidden from attending the screening lest the audience recognize them, though Scrimm managed to find an inconspicuous seat.

In a journal dated 1/9/78, Angus Scrimm wrote:

> Screening at Fox of a rough cut of the movie. For several nights Don and Paul have approached young people in ticket lines at L.A. and Valley theaters inviting them. I'm the only actor allowed to attend on condition I slip into the projectionist's booth after the lights go down. The first hour is exhilarating, plays like a house afire with the audience loving it, laughing heartily, screaming at my appearances... but then the remainder plays less well.

In recent years, attempts have been made to recreate this early cut of the film, most notably by fan-editor Russell Wagus. While interesting as novelty items, these fan-cuts are still incomplete and serve to remind us that the majority of *Phantasm*'s cut scenes have never reached fans, making the print from the January test screening all the more elusive and rare.

THE METAMORPHISIS PHANTASMIC

January's test screening confirmed what Don Coscarelli already suspected; his film was still too long. Although the bank scenes had already been deleted, more cuts were in order. First written

Don Coscarelli, Angus Scrimm and Michael Baldwin reflect on *Phantasm*.
(Photo courtesy Scott Pensa)

"It wasn't fun losing that stuff, but - like Don - we eventually embraced the bigger picture."
Daryn Okada on deleted scenes

as an ensemble piece, *Phantasm* would instead focus on Mike, relegating Jody and Reggie to supporting roles. As Coscarelli tightened his film, nearly every performance lost screen time, from Mike and the Tall Man all the way down to the bartender and Myrtle the Maid. Among the few performances untouched by this re-edit were Tommy, Toby and the Morningside caretaker.

Angus Scrimm recalls the reflective day after January's showing: "Don and his co-producer Paul Pepperman phoned me the day after the Fox screening and said, '*We've come up with a list of things that have to be cut, and you're really going to hate this...*' I said, '*Number one on my own list is that the hanging scene has to go.*' They said, '*We didn't know how to tell you!*' I said, '*Well, obviously, I lose my Academy Award but we'll have a better chance at Best Picture.*' It was an eerily wonderful sequence but it stopped the picture cold."

"We lost a handful of scenes that I personally thought were pretty cool," Daryn Okada says. "It taught me an important lesson which was as a filmmaker you've got to pay attention to the film as a whole. You should keep from becoming too protective of scenes you think are precious as individual pieces because they might not serve the whole experience in the end. That's what you've got to focus on, the whole and not the pieces. It's not at all easy to let go of those scenes sometimes, especially with material like the hanging tree stuff. A lot of us felt like we had worked so hard on the film that we had actually left a little of our own blood in each and every scene. It wasn't fun losing that stuff but, like Don, we eventually embraced the bigger picture."

In addition to making new cuts, Coscarelli would also adjust the sequence of scenes that remained, steering *Phantasm* away from its linear narrative toward something more like a dream. Jody's chat with Toby and Mike's initial cemetery visit would now be told in flashback. Jody's mausoleum nightmare would be pushed from the middle to the third act. Answers would also be less forthcoming in the new version. How could Tommy's death be misconstrued as suicide? Why did the fortuneteller's granddaughter visit Morningside in the first place? What was the strange effect of the mist from Reggie's truck on the Tall Man? And finally, was it all just a dream? While the original film answered this last question, the new version would forever leave audiences guessing.

A revised conclusion was filmed on Sunday, January 29 at the Coscarelli home in Long Beach. Reggie, seemingly resurrected from the dead, may never even have died if audiences considered the film a dream. Instead, a plot twist reveals that Jody died in a car accident, leaving Reggie to adopt a grieving Mike. After a tender fireside chat, a grieving Mike heads upstairs and is startled to find the Tall Man waiting in the shadows. With the memorably chilling final line, "Booooooy!!!" the teen is pulled through a bedroom mirror as the film cuts to black.

Set inside the main character's bedroom from *Kenny & Company*, the final shot saw Michael Baldwin performing his own stunt as dwarf-double John Zumpano yanks him backwards through a mirror. Shirley Coscarelli's petite dog, Foxy, makes an appearance in the photo of Jody that Mike longingly views moments before his capture.

"We did so much of that stunt glass stuff that we all got used to it," Zumpano says. "I wasn't worried at all about doing my scene as the dwarf at the end. In fact, I was pretty excited about it. You've just got to remember with that glass not to hesitate when you burst through it. You go through completely and don't stop halfway because that's when you're most likely to get cut."

"I'd been yearning for months for the day when I could rid myself of the Tall Man's abysmal long hair," Scrimm says. "When the day arrived that I was told I was a wrap, I lost no time in getting to the barber. But then, of course, a better ending to the film was devised and hair extensions just didn't work. So we winged it with the short hair and hoped, in that final shock appearance, nobody would notice. Remarkably few did until *Phantasm* came out on home video with its endless replays."

Upon completion of the final cut, Coscarelli was ready to test *Phantasm* once again before an audience. This took place on Friday, November 3, 1978 at the Hollywood Pacific Theater on a double bill with *Cheech and Chong's Up In Smoke*. A full-page ad was taken out in <u>Variety</u> to announce the preview and featured the Jim Warren poster. Located on Hollywood Boulevard, the historic Pacific Theater would later host the premiere of *Phantasm II* before closing permanently due to the Northridge Quake of 1994. With its new ending and far leaner runtime, *Phantasm* fared significantly better this second time around. It was all the reassurance anyone needed that the film was ready.

AN AVCO EMBASSY RELEASE

Following November's successful preview, *Phantasm* was screened in France at the Festival international du film fantastique d'Avoriaz 1979 where it took home the Special Jury Award, besting both *Halloween* and *Invasion of the Body Snatchers*. Domestic distribution rights were soon sold to AVCO Embassy Pictures, beating out rival bidder New Line Cinema. Up until this point, AVCO Embassy was not known for its horror output, something that would change after *Phantasm*. An initial two hundred print run was announced for the Los Angeles and San Antonio markets beginning Wednesday, March 28 with additional locations opening on Friday, March 30, 1979.

"I had a guy working for me named Lenny Shapiro," former AVCO Embassy President and CEO Robert Rehme says. "He was in charge of acquisitions for Embassy and knew the business very well. He's the one who originally found *Phantasm* for us. He saw it and he liked it. Then he called me. We screened it. We loved it. We bought it. It happened as quickly as that. We recognized that it was a very unusual picture with a lot going on. We recognized it as having potential."

On Sunday, February 12, 1979, AVCO Embassy booked a double-page spread in <u>Variety</u> to announce their acquisition. The advertisement included artwork of a hand bursting from the ground. The studio would soon commission a new poster by famed *Ben Hur* illustrator Joseph Smith. Though the Jim Warren painting of the Tall Man would also be used in overseas territories, it was dropped from the domestic run. The Smith painting ultimately became part of the vast science fiction collection of genre historian Forrest J Ackerman before being gifted to an anonymous collector in November 2002.

"I was disappointed over that," Warren says. "But I know that my paintings are very artsy and not taken from the movie exactly, which is what they wanted and I understand that. I don't think I knew where it was used after it was picked up by a movie company. I would expect Europe and Japan to like my more improvised, surreal style as they take more artistic license there." Speaking of the film itself, Warren still holds it in high esteem. "I always liked it. I saw the rough cut before I did the painting and I loved the surreal 'anything goes' attitude."

On Saturday, March 3, AVCO Embassy previewed their new acquisition for the first time before a packed house in Westwood. The screening was a de facto premiere for the cast and crew. By all accounts, the screening was an uproarious triumph, eliciting laughter and screams from audience members at precisely the right moments. The night was so successful that AVCO Embassy added another preview on March 6. And yet another on March 19. By March 20, <u>Variety</u> announced an additional twelve previews for the Los Angeles area. And these would not be the last.

The <u>Los Angeles Herald Examiner</u> Ad from March 5, 1979:

> *Response to the sneak preview of PHANTASM was so PHANTASTIC that we're having another sneak… but they haven't yet cleared away the dead bodies from last week's screening so we've moved to another theatre. Look for us tomorrow at the UA Cinema Center in Westwood. If this one doesn't scare you, you're already dead!*

"We had a lot of enthusiasm for *Phantasm*," Rehme says. "It was a film that we had good projections for and thought would do good business. We certainly had our share of hits years earlier with *The Graduate* and *Lion In Winter*, but we couldn't keep it up. *Phantasm* came in at the right time. It wound up doing fifteen million at the domestic box office, which astounded all of us. Embassy hadn't done that kind of gross in years!"

"Just before the film was supposed to come out," Bruce Chudacoff says, "I remember a phone conversation I had with Don. He had been testing the film with audiences and it was doing well, but he continued to be nervous about its release. *'I'm really concerned about this,'* he would tell me. I asked him about what and he said, *'Well you're only allowed three failures in Hollywood.'* He didn't consider *Jim The World's Greatest* or *Kenny & Company* to be successes and he really wanted *Phantasm* to be a hit. He wanted a big hit and certainly he got it. That conversation was a remarkable insight into Don and tells you how he was thinking in the days before the film came out."

Phantasm had one final hurdle to overcome during its final days before release, a hurdle that would also plague two of its three sequels. In a rash decision, the MPAA ratings board had assigned the film an X-rating due to the gruesome sphere drilling of Ken Jones. Don Coscarelli assertively appealed this. With the help of advocate Charles Champlin, Coscarelli was able to convince the MPAA's president to downgrade *Phantasm* to an R-rating. Seldom would another horror director win such a dispute against the organization.

Press releases created by the distributor attempted with little success to duplicate the kind of sensational hype that had surrounded *The Omen* years earlier. One blurb announced that Willard Green's designs for the silver sphere had vanished in the wake of his death and that "no one living knows exactly

Don Coscarelli with two of his stars - Reggie Bannister and the 'Cuda.
(Photo courtesy Guy Thorpe)

Above: Michael Baldwin after the film's release.
Left: Angus Scrimm looks over the domestic poster.
(Photos courtesy Kristen Deem)

how it works." Another told of "hill people" terrorizing the film with police having to dispatch helicopters to set. Yet another claimed a mudslide had washed bodies from a local graveyard into Michael Baldwin's neighborhood, trapping him indoors until he could be bulldozed out. One story with a modicum of truth involved a crewmember having his scarf sucked into a giant fan at the Dunsmuir Estate. The tale concludes with Baldwin dashing to save him by unplugging the fan.

"I really think that story is bullshit," Baldwin says with a laugh. "I wish that I could say it was true, but it's not. I know that it did happen, that his scarf got sucked into the fan and his face was pulled against the cage but I don't think his neck was at risk for breaking and I certainly don't think I leapt up to save the day."

IMPRESSIONS

For a majority of the cast and crew, the Westwood screening was their first exposure to the film in its final form. Their reactions were positive, greatly bolstered by the audience's response.

"I walked out of the theater shaking my head," Bill Thornbury says. "I couldn't believe how well it was received that night. It was a rowdy audience too. From that point on I realized that everything was going to be okay. The picture was going to do well. Not having a background in the business, I was just greatly relieved that no one booed me off the screen. That's a critical audience, the college crowd at a midnight screening. I knew it was going to be okay after that, though. I might not work ever again (laughs), but I knew that the character basically worked for what it was. I was able to relax and just enjoy what transpired thereafter."

"That screening I went to with my mother," Kathy Lester says. "That's when I first saw the entire film. When my scene came on at the beginning and I saw the shot of me from the shoulders up and then somebody else's boobs very neatly edited to look like mine, I freaked out and started screaming. Don and Paul were sitting behind me and they were laughing hysterically. I turned to my mother and said, *'They're not mine!'* And she said, *'I know, I know, you should've done it because yours are better. You should've done the scene!'*

"I definitely remember seeing it in Westwood," Michael Baldwin says. "It probably wasn't the first time I had seen it, but I remember the screening quite well. It was for sure the first sneak preview I saw with an audience. I went with a couple of friends and I remember being shocked that people were laughing at it. It turned out that there were parts of the film that were humorous that I never knew would be funny. I was actually annoyed that people were laughing back at the screen. I couldn't understand it. I totally get it now, though."

"I had told the kids in my neighborhood and their parents about the film," Ken Jones says. "I wound up taking a bunch of them with me to see it. I really had no idea what it was about. I thought it would mostly be a clean-cut deal like *Kenny*

& Company besides my stuff with the ball. So we get there and right out of the gate, here's a guy screwing a girl on a tombstone. I almost died! The kids were looking at me really strangely. I had to go and apologize to each of their parents. It embarrassed the living hell out of me. Loved the picture, though. Don really knocked it out of the ballpark."

"When it first came out in the theater," Bill Cone says, "I went to see it with all of my children. I had no idea what it was going to be like because I'd only seen some of my stuff and it never had an ending. The first thing my kids saw was their father with a naked woman (laughs). The movie theater was pretty full and my kids scream, *'Look! That's Daddy!'* and everyone turns and looks at me. It was really awkward! I thought it was a great movie, though."

"Having not read a script, my first impression upon seeing it was that Don had made a very strange movie," Ralph Richmond says. "But it was a well made strange movie. It came as a surprise to me how well it did with critics and how the public went for it. I mean, they went for it in a big way. When people find out that I'm an actor, a lot of times, they'll ask me what I've been in. And I'll tell them *Phantasm* and they'll know it right away. I sometimes meet people who weren't even born when the film came out that know it and love it. It's become a certifiable cult hit."

PHANTASM UNLEASHED

As AVCO Embassy screened the film for critics, a wellspring of positive notices poured in. Variety praised Angus Scrimm's Tall Man as "delightfully frightening" and made note of Don Coscarelli's "cinematic ingenuity." Robert Osbourne of Turner Classic Movies fame called *Phantasm* a "genuine spooker" in his glowing Hollywood Reporter assessment. AVCO Embassy reportedly treated Osbourne to a private screening of the film during which he became so frightened that he nearly fled the theatre. "It won't win Oscars," his review read, "but it will earn [Coscarelli] a mass of friends among those who enjoy having their blood run cold."

"*Phantasm* is, as it set out to be, a scream. A loud scream."

Charles Champlin in his review

"I actually ran into Robert Osbourne one evening at the Beachwood Market in Hollywood Hills," Bill Thornbury says. "This was right after *Phantasm* had come out. Much to my surprise, he recognized me from the film and had complimentary remarks to say about *Phantasm*. He even dug my performance! I always appreciated hearing that from him."

In the UCLA Daily Bruin, Michael Auerbach wrote that Scrimm's Tall Man was "infused with Shakespearean panache." In the Hollywood Press, William Mangold praised Michael Baldwin's "fine, wide-eyed believability." Although he'd rated *Jim the World's Greatest* with an F three years prior, Mangold hailed *Phantasm* as "the most nerve shattering movie since *Jaws*." In the Los Angeles Times, Charles Champlin famously dubbed the silver sphere the screen's first "digital vampire." He also appreciated its relationship between humor and horror, saying that while it "does not laugh at itself," it does "draw shrieking laughs" from the audience. Champlin concludes: "*Phantasm* is, as it set out to be, a scream. A loud scream."

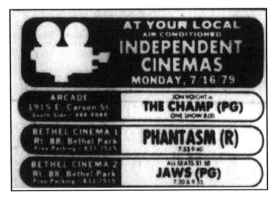

Air conditioned, you say?

The reviews weren't all positive, however. The film was periodically panned for what critics viewed as bad acting, a confusing storyline and poor direction, but such views were a minority. None seemed more scathing, however, than the official condemnation handed down by the United States Conference of Catholic Bishops, who classified *Phantasm* as "morally offensive." The clergymen staunchly objected to the film's exploitation of gore, nudity and violence, citing it as "a candidate for almost anyone's list of worst movies of all time." Such sharp disapproval might have been put to good use on the film's poster as a sure indication of quality.

More important than *Phantasm's* rave reviews was its impressive box office sum which topped $750,000 in its first five days of release, beating AVCO Embassy's own projection of $600,000. Two weeks later, *Phantasm* was racing toward the two million dollar mark in California and Texas theaters alone. By April 24, AVCO Embassy salesmen were dispatched to book *Phantasm* in every domestic market that would have the film. It would not only stand as AVCO's highest-grossing film of the year, but would also help usher in their biggest first quarter earnings since 1973. Elsewhere in America, *Phantasm* was just as successful, if not more so. It dominated the New York City box office in its opening week with more than one million dollars in ticket sales. By the end of *Phantasm's* domestic run, the film had earned more than fifteen million dollars. According to Robert Rehme these profits directly enabled AVCO Embassy to fund Joe Dante's *The Howling*.

Phantasm's returns were due in large part to AVCO's creative marketing. The distributor booked an entire week of sold-out previews at UCLA including a St. Patrick's Day "ghoul party." For that preview, the zealous AVCO held a hearse-stuffing contest on campus with the top prize being the hearse itself! The winning fraternity stuffed thirty-nine bodies into the coach, a feat that Rehme tried unsuccessfully to enter into the Guinness Book of World Records (the number would be broken by *Phantasm II*'s contest). In the spirit of William Castle's horror film gimmicks, AVCO trademarked a new process called Visurama, which saw an oversized sphere fly over the audience during a key scene in the film. Visurama was tested in California and Texas theaters but never widely implemented except in Japan. One significant part of AVCO's promotional campaign was a worldwide tour by Coscarelli and Scrimm that began in San Francisco and San Antonio just prior to the film's March opening. The following month found them jetting to Philadelphia, Kansas, Texas and finally Washington D.C. where they conducted dozens of interviews for radio, television and print media, often in the backs of hearses or in cemeteries.

"We were very aggressive in promotions and marketing," Rehme says. "*Phantasm* was unique and it lent itself to those kinds of gag promotions quite well. It seemed as though the promotions for that film were never-ending."

A BROADER HORIZON

After the success of AVCO's domestic release more than thirty distributors lined up to release the film in every corner of the globe. Roadshow gave the film a lavish run in Australia and New Zealand. Elan Films took it to Belgium. Aatrial Films handled the English Canadian release while Mutual Films took care of the French Canadian release. GTO Films released *Phantasm* in the United Kingdom. It went so far as the West Indies where International Film Distributors brought it to theaters. Eager to see Don Coscarelli and Michael Baldwin's follow-up to their hugely successful *Kenny & Company*, Toho-Towa secured Japanese distribution rights. Unlike *Kenny*, however, *Phantasm* was most successful on its home turf.

To avoid confusion with the Aussie sex-comedy *Fantasm*, Coscarelli's film was repackaged as *The Never Dead* for its Australian release. Coincidentally, Ralph Richmond

had launched his film acting career with 1975's *Video Vixens* alongside Con Covert, star of *Fantasm*. To promote *The Never Dead*, Coscarelli and Angus Scrimm embarked on a three-week promotional tour across Australia in June of 1979, after which the writer/director traveled elsewhere to promote the film. Though it enjoyed great success internationally, *Phantasm* was wildly popular in Paris where it debuted number one at the box office and remained there for the next five weeks.

BIRTH OF THE PHAN BASE

As *Phantasm* spread worldwide so was born an eclectic and enduring "phan" base. The film appealed to mainstream audiences and horror enthusiasts and even inspired a new generation of hearse collectors and funeral directors. Among the earliest phans were Guy Thorpe and Kristen Deem, both of whom would later crew on future *Phantasm* films. The earliest public declaration of phandom appears to have come from genre historian Forrest J Ackerman, longtime friend to Angus Scrimm, Thorpe and Deem. In the May 4, 1979 issue of The Hollywood Reporter, Ackerman ran an advertisement congratulating his tall friend.

"I first saw *Phantasm* at the Oceanside Valley Drive-in," Thorpe says. "I liked it the first time I saw it but the magic hadn't hit me yet. I thought about it a bit afterward and went back. Then I thought about it some more and went back again. By the third time, I was hooked. I must've seen it seven times

Forrest Ackerman's congratulatory ad

Rory Guy

~~531 So. Alexandria Avenue~~ · Los Angeles, Calif. 90020 · phone: ~~(213) 000-0000~~

April 30, 1979

Dear Mel,

Enclosed is the unused Braniff ticket from Houston to Dallas, remaining from the last "Phantasm" tour.

As you know, torrential rains and flooding in Houston made it impossible for us to reach the Braniff takeoff point, so the urbane and agile Al Guggenheim promptly switched me to another airline at an accessible airport. The only hitch was, there wasn't time to return to the hotel to remove costume and make-up. Can you imagine the consternation of the other passengers, having to fly out of Houston amid lightning and thunder, with the unholy apparition of the Tall Man occupying Row 1, Seat 1, on the aisle? I'm sure some of them thought it was a doomed flight.

My best to all the ladies and gents at AVco.

Angus Scrimm

Angus Scrimm

Letter from Angus Scrimm to AVCO Embassy concerning the promotional tour.
(Letter courtesy Angus Scrimm)

at the drive-in and another two or three times when it went to the walk-in theater. It's what made me want to buy a hearse, which I did that same year, which began my obsession. '*And so it begins,*' the Tall Man says."

"Seeing *Phantasm* at Rockaway Townsquare in New Jersey was a fortuitous accident," Deem recalls. "My father and I had just seen *Prophecy*, a horror flick about mutant bears, a real downer. Rather than going home, I begged to see the midnight screening of *Rocky Horror Picture Show* but we couldn't get in because my dad was out of cash. So we snuck into *Phantasm* instead. I was mesmerized by the lobby poster with the Tall Man's glowing red eyes and knowing smirk. Most movies you think about for a day and then forget, but *Phantasm*… I couldn't get it out of my mind!"

Concurrent with *Phantasm*'s release was the creation of genre heavyweight horror magazine <u>Fangoria</u>, which ran a story on the film in its first issue. A large cover feature followed in <u>Fangoria</u>'s second issue and again for each *Phantasm* sequel made since. The magazine's classifieds section united pen pals Deem and Thorpe, sparking a lifelong friendship.

SUCCESS & THE EVER AFTER

Upon the film's release, Stanley Eichelbaum wrote in the <u>San Francisco Examiner</u>, "The terror is so insanely overdone that the movie is bound to become the next cult classic, and I would not be surprised if it made *The Rocky Horror Picture Show* move over since it's ripe for the midnight trade." Indeed, *Phantasm* has gone down in history as existing on the top shelf of cult classic B movies, if such a distinction actually exists. *Phantasm*'s success finally gave Don Coscarelli the hit he desired and endeared Angus Scrimm, Michael Baldwin and Reggie Bannister to us. The cast and crew look back fondly on the experience, suggesting that *Phantasm* was just as much fun to make as it was to watch.

"The film's cult status didn't catch on with me at all," Baldwin says. "I thought it was just something that had been mildly successful. I figured that *Phantasm* had come and gone

and that there would be nothing long-term about it. I definitely didn't think we had a shot at doing a sequel one day, but it's very flattering to see that the film has taken on a life of its own. It's still going strong and probably will continue to long after we've all croaked."

"I am so proud to be a part of *Phantasm*," Kathy Lester says. "Knowing that this was a low-budget movie, I never thought in a million years that it would get the acclaim that it has. It wasn't like it was *Star Wars* or anything. But I've been blown away by how it's been received. It's reached cult status."

"When the movie came out, it wasn't like people knew me or anything," Bill Thornbury says. "But then I'd be in an elevator somewhere and someone would say, '*Hey, I saw you in Phantasm last night!*' so I got a taste of that and it made me appreciate what movie stars have to go through day in and day out on a much larger scale. I got the good part of it and then later got some of the not so good part of it. I got invited to do more things after that. I did an episode of *The Rockford Files* and did a couple of other things like a nighttime soap for a while. I worked quite a bit. It all worked out."

"I have been a part of over fifty movies in twenty-five years," Roberto Quezada says. "I truly hated most of them, including one of Don's – *Beastmaster*. The first *Phantasm* will always have a special place in my heart, but not only because it was my first movie ever. It's a way of making movies that we have wanted to duplicate ever since, but have never been able to after that. A big part of it is timing. It happened right on the cusp of being a bunch of kids who wanted to make a movie in someone's barn and of being adults knowledgeable and experienced enough to figure out how to make something that looked like a professional theatrical motion picture. But for the most part it was because a single group of friends just stuck it out. It was this randomly unique group of believers that made *Phantasm* so great to work on and why it was such a huge success: Don, Paul, Dave, Dena, George, Cory, John, Daryn, Michael, Dac, Shirley, and a handful of others along with Angus, Mike, Bill, and Reggie. Our collective lack of experience meant that we were too insecure to ever say to Don or to each other, '*You're crazy, that can't be done.*'"

tormentors. Each film results in a chase scene wherein the villain throws ahead challenges to slow their victim down. In each chase, the ground beneath the protagonists' feet turns to mush (Mike in the woods, Nancy on the stairs). Both pictures also end with a false sense of reality with the Tall Man and Freddy returning at the last moment in what appears to be a dream. In each film, a character is pulled backward through glass before cutting to credits.

These coincidences become all the more glaring when one considers that New Line Cinema, aka "the house that Freddy built," has long wanted a piece of the *Phantasm* franchise. The studio tried unsuccessfully to make or distribute *Phantasm*, *Phantasm III*, *Phantasm IV* and most recently a *Phantasm* remake in 2005. Not surprisingly, New Line originally offered *A Nightmare on Elm Street 2: Freddy's Revenge* to Don Coscarelli, who declined, before going with director Jack Sholder. Even *Elm Street*'s third offering features a Lavender-esque blonde nurse who turns out to be Freddy in disguise. This is not meant to imply that the *Elm Street* series is devoid of creative merit, but rather a clearly inspired work that took several *Phantasm* concepts and ran with them to great effect and box office return.

An inspired creation.
(New Line Cinema Publicity Photo)

A NIGHTMARE ON PHANTASM STREET

Of all the horror films *Phantasm* would inspire in its wake, none would borrow from it quite as successfully as Wes Craven's 1984 *A Nightmare on Elm Street*. Writing in <u>Wes Craven: The Art of Horror</u>, author John Kenneth Muir clearly points to *Phantasm* as a forerunner to *Elm Street*, albeit with less finite rules governing the distinctions between dreams and reality. Still, parallels between the two are striking and numerous.

Both Freddy Krueger and the Tall Man have unnaturally colored blood in order to emphasize their otherworldly qualities. Each villain loses four fingers that bleed unnaturally colored blood and soon regenerate. Both *Phantasm* and *Elm Street* feature scenes wherein the antagonist looms over the slumbering hero (the Tall Man over Mike in cemetery, Freddy over Nancy in wall). Both Mike and Nancy take a stand in the third act by rigging an elaborate trap to capture their

THE PHANTASM 2 THAT WASN'T

In the wake of Don Coscarelli's horror triumph, the demand for a *Phantasm* follow-up was strong. AVCO Embassy made public their desire for an immediate sequel, as did journalists and critics both domestic and foreign. Even Angus Scrimm spoke out in favor of reviving the Tall Man. It seemed as though everyone in town was ready for a sequel... everyone except Coscarelli. The writer/director voiced his apprehension while promotional touring abroad. In his eyes, following up a hugely successful horror film with another would forever label him a horror director.

"We at Embassy were very interested in getting Don to do a sequel to *Phantasm*," Robert Rehme says. "We were also interested in *The Beastmaster* but we weren't able to make a deal

Proposed logo for the *Phantasm 2* that wasn't.

with him at that time. With someone as new and as successful as Don was, we certainly would have liked to have stayed in business and made more pictures together. For whatever reason, it didn't happen."

Though her son was reluctant to start work on a sequel, Shirley Coscarelli was not and penned her own *Phantasm 2* script, which is not to be confused with the 1988 Universal Studios sequel *Phantasm II*. Her pitch, again to be produced by Dac Coscarelli, would have offered audiences a female-friendly adventure in contrast to her son's more masculine original. Child star Kristy McNichol, who bore an uncanny resemblance to Michael Baldwin, was rumored to star as Mike and Jody's cousin newly arrived in town to investigate the incident at Morningside. In fall 1979, a full-page ad announcing the sequel was published in <u>Variety</u> with a tagline that read, "It's everything you ever feared – and more!" The surprise announcement called for a January 1980 production start for a release later that year, none of which came to fruition.

On 10/2/80, Scrimm wrote in a letter to Kristen Deem:

To respond to your question, Phantasm II is quiescent just now, largely because Don Coscarelli Jr. is deeply involved in pre-production for The Beastmaster. He had strong feelings that he should follow Phantasm with a different kind of movie to avoid being typed as a horror director. There is a script already prepared for Phantasm II, however, in which the Tall Man figures prominently. My one suggestion for modifying the character next time is to develop a bit more the sardonic humor which was only hinted at in Phantasm I. How do you react to this idea?

"I remember liking Shirley's script, which had the wit and inventiveness of the bestselling novels she soon started writing," Scrimm says. "I must still have that script somewhere but haven't seen it decades. I seem to recall it was partly set in an abandoned old movie theater. Unhappily, the financing never fell into place, but if it had, who knows what changes it would

Angus Scrimm amassed a sizable following after *Phantasm*.
(Photo courtesy Kristen Deem)

have wrought in the *Phantasm* story arc as we know it today."

Following *Phantasm*'s success, the phamily branched out in different directions. Coscarelli forged ahead with 1982's *The Beastmaster* which marked Paul Pepperman's departure from filmmaking. Michael Baldwin made several television appearances before taking a break from screen acting. Bill Thornbury did the same before moving to Nashville to pursue a songwriting career. Reggie Bannister remained in California to focus on music and family. Angus Scrimm continued writing liner notes for Capitol Records and appeared in several films including 1985's *The Lost Empire* opposite Thornbury.

For this moment in time, *Phantasm* seemed to be a stand-alone hit, a brief phenomenon that had come and gone. Little could anyone have known that the Tall Man would stride into the nightmares of theatergoers once more nearly a decade after the original film's release.

Waiting for *Phantasm II.*
(Photo courtesy Guy Thorpe)

Chapter 2:
American Gothic

Announcement billboard on the Universal backlot.
(Photo courtesy Kristen Deem)

UNIVERSAL APPEAL

In the time since *Phantasm*, the horror genre had surged in popularity through powerhouse franchises like *Halloween, A Nightmare on Elm Street* and *Friday the 13th*. Box office returns on these properties were so robust that the decade saw only one year without at least one of them (1983) and two successive years with films from all three (1988 and 1989). Hungry for a lucrative piece of the horror pie, Universal Studios gladly aligned itself behind a new *Phantasm* sequel based largely on the enthusiasm of its Vice President of Acquisitions, Jim Jacks. That the sequel to Don Coscarelli's independent classic was being produced for one of the largest studios on the planet, the very one that had bungled the release of his debut film, might have spelled trouble.

"It was around 1987 when *Phantasm II* first came across my desk," Jacks says. "Don Coscarelli was wanting a bigger budget than he had on the first one. I met with Don and liked him right away. I thought it seemed like a good movie to make and we went into it with the hope that it would generate several sequels. We wanted to have our own horror franchise, our own *Friday the 13th* or *A Nightmare on Elm Street*. The head of Universal, Tom Pollock, was a big proponent of horror franchises and he liked the original *Phantasm* very much."

Rather than produce *Phantasm II* as a straight Universal production, Coscarelli negotiated an acquisition deal that would allow him to make the film on his own. Such an agreement charges that if a filmmaker will autonomously fund and produce a film by an agreed-upon date that a studio will purchase it upon completion for an agreed-upon amount. In this case, Universal's purchase price was around $3 million and the original release date August 19, 1988, which was coincidentally Angus Scrimm's birthday. When *A Nightmare on Elm Street 4: The Dream Master* later claimed this date, *Phantasm II* was moved up to July 8. For Coscarelli, this acquisition deal offered him a larger budget than he would have been able to raise independently. For Universal, it meant getting a genre picture on the cheap with an established horror icon in the Tall Man.

"I was temporarily back on the staff at Angel Records, holding down the job of Editorial Director for their Janice May who was out on sick leave," Scrimm says. "Don told me he had the money to do *Phantasm II*, had a script in the works, and would I please start letting my hair grow and start losing weight. The Tall Man is skeletal, and I think I was some thirty pounds over his *Phantasm* weight."

Negative pickups are not without their risks, however, most of which fell to Coscarelli. Had he not completed *Phantasm II* by the studio's deadline he could easily have found himself without a buyer for a completed picture. Likewise, had he surpassed the agreed-upon $3 million sum, the overage would have been his to pay as Universal's only obligation would have been to cover the original budget. Acting as distributor for the film, Universal would be able to make certain demands of *Phantasm II* concerning script and cast.

"They don't do negative pickups anymore," Casting Director Betsy Fels says. "At the time, you could make a movie for the studio that had nothing to do with the studio with the promise that they would pick it up. Now they're just

Don Coscarelli at the *Phantasm II* production office.
(Photo courtesy Kristen Deem)

independent films that studios buy. But this was a film that Universal knew they were going to buy so they had some say."

By way of Coscarelli's studio deal, *Phantasm* was being formally ushered into the Universal Monster Pantheon. This put Scrimm's Tall Man in league with the likes of Dracula, the Frankenstein monster and the Wolf Man. He would also figure nicely into Universal's then flourishing horror resurgence which included Norman Bates, Chucky the killer doll, Ash Williams and Michael Myers. Apart from timing, this new bunch had one thing in common: they were all acquired for sequelization after their preceding film(s) had done well elsewhere. Once the studio of home grown horror, Universal was now solidly in the business of horror acquisition.

SCRIPTING

Don Coscarelli would again handle writing duties on the new *Phantasm*, but this time with input from Universal via Jim Jacks. While the studio was keen for Coscarelli to include a female lead in the story, they outright requested that the story follow a more linear path than its predecessor. It was their opinion that post-*Nightmare on Elm Street* audiences would expect to be made aware of when characters were dreaming and when they were not. As a result, neither of Coscarelli's two originally scripted dream sequences made it into the film. The first dream was made into reality and the second removed entirely.

"Most of my involvement with *Phantasm II* was in the development of the screenplay," Jacks says. "Don and I both agreed early on as to what kind of a movie it was going to be. We wanted it to have several big scenes that would bring audiences to their feet. Once filming began, I mostly watched dailies and only visited the set occasionally when they were nearby. I wasn't hovering over them because I had my job as head of acquisitions to tend to. We certainly weren't going to tell Don how to make a *Phantasm* movie."

Picking up from *Phantasm*, Coscarelli's script finds Reggie thwarting the Tall Man's kidnapping of Mike by blowing up his own home. Ten years later, Mike is released from a psychiatric hospital to Reggie, who has since become a family man with no memory of *Phantasm*'s events. As the pair arrives home, the Tall Man vengefully recreates Reggie's gas explosion stunt from ten years ago, killing Reggie's entire family. The distraught father soon joins Mike in order to kill their common adversary. While following a trail of ghost towns, they meet up with a mysterious hitchhiking vixen, Alchemy, and a young telepath, Liz, with whom Mike shares a psychic bond. The heroes eventually catch up to the Tall Man and destroy him, only to have Alchemy morph into the mortician during the film's final moments. As their victory begins to ring hollow, Mike assures Liz that it's only a dream to which the Tall Man responds, "No, it's not!"

Coscarelli amps up both action and comedy in *Phantasm II* to great success. His script broadens the scope of the Tall Man's reach while retaining the qualities that made him memorable in the first film. Similarly, the script allows Reggie to become the pseudo-Ash underdog for which audiences would best remember him. Passing up the home-field advantage that most horror sequels count on, Coscarelli quickly moves his story away from *Phantasm*'s familiar stomping grounds. This not only makes for a firm tonal departure from the first film, it establishes the strong road-movie template to which future sequels would adhere.

If the script has any weakness, it is an incessant need to remind the audience of the original *Phantasm*. While Coscarelli injects *Phantasm II* with new ideas, he's ultimately retreading ground that prevents the story from concluding any differently than *Phantasm* did. His script is nowhere more successful than when it breaks free of this nostalgic bond to venture in new directions, such as a well-written sub-plot involving a haunted clergyman intent on stopping the Tall Man. Harmonious is the balance Coscarelli strikes between the plights of characters old and new, each hunting the Tall Man for their own reasons.

Still, the sequel is full of callbacks: The Tall Man again scares someone with his "funeral is about to begin" line. He also crashes through another window to abduct a lead character into his waiting hearse. Mike again dodges a charging

Shhhh! It's a secret!

sphere which then mistakenly dispatches a henchman. The third act again culminates in our heroes raiding the Tall Man's mausoleum before destroying it. Inside they rediscover the spacegate room where someone again falls through its open portal. A menacing bug again emerges from the Tall Man's wounded anatomy and in the film's final moments, a buxom babe reveals herself to be the Tall Man in disguise. Unseen dwarves pull the heroes backward through glass. Cut to black and cue Fred Myrow's theme.

In spite of being overly familiar at times, *Phantasm II* manages to reinvent itself as an action/horror film unique from its predecessor. Coscarelli's script is, just as he and Jacks had intended, full of memorable moments sure to remain in the minds of audiences long after they see the film. With elements including Reggie's chainsaw duel, the thrilling 'Cuda chase scene or the Tall Man's live embalming with acid, this *Phantasm II* was bound to be a riotous, bloody adventure.

THE PRODUCTION TEAM

Throughout the summer of 1987, Don Coscarelli worked to assemble his production team, a process over which he enjoyed complete control. In Paul Pepperman's absence, *Phantasm* Visual Consultant/Gaffer/Assistant Editor Roberto Quezada was promoted to Producer while Grip Daryn Okada took over as Director of Photography. Coscarelli also invited back Unit Production Manager Robert Del Valle in the same role as well as that of Associate Producer. Dac Coscarelli again helmed as Executive Producer.

"After *The Beastmaster*, Paul Pepperman decided to try another line of work," Quezada says. "That film nearly killed us. Our next project was *Survival Quest* and that meant that it was going to be just Don and me now. We both did everything to make this ambitious low budget movie and producer was the only title that made sense for all the shit I had to do. For the first couple of weeks, I was producer, first assistant director, and director of photography on *Survival Quest*. Daryn Okada, a personal friend of mine and today president of the ASC (the American Society of Cinematographers), stopped by to visit us on the set. He took one look at me and informed me that I looked like shit. I realized that I also felt like shit so I fired myself on the spot as director of photography and hired Daryn. By the time *Phantasm II* came along, Don, Daryn, and I were a pretty cool team so we didn't want to rock the boat. Daryn got my dream job, Don directed, and the only title that made sense for all the other shit that had to get done was co-producer."

"I enjoyed coming back for *Phantasm II* because of the friendships that Don, Roberto and myself had developed," Okada says. "By this point, we all knew would could rely on one another. It was different having all the responsibilities split up among other people this time around instead of us trying to take it all on like we did on the first *Phantasm*. We had to find people to crew the shoot that we could depend on to come back week after week."

Having a multi-million dollar budget meant that Coscarelli and Quezada would no longer have to self-assemble special effects nor work from a tiny contact paper mausoleum. They would hire qualified teams to improve upon *Phantasm* in both aspects. Friend and filmmaker Sam Raimi suggested Coscarelli hire Special Makeup Effects Creator Mark Shostrom, who in turn recommended Production Designer Philip Duffin. Both gentlemen had been key creative personnel on Raimi's own *Evil Dead II*.

"When Don called me," Shostrom says, "I'd just moved from a small shop into a larger, more equipped workshop which became Mark Shostrom Studio. Having just made that financial investment and putting my ass on the line, it was great to get a call for a film like this. When Don called, he told me it was called *American Gothic*. He said Universal would be distributing it. The fact that he had a major studio behind it gave me confidence. I kind of figured *American Gothic* meant a *Phantasm* sequel, but I wasn't completely sure. As soon as I read page one of the screenplay and it said The Tall Man, of course I knew what it was."

At the time of Shostrom's hiring, Coscarelli had yet to find someone to replace the late Willard Green as sphere effectsman. Whoever took the job would need to not only recreate Green's work but also to greatly expand upon it. Per Shostrom's recommendation, Coscarelli turned to effectsman Steve Patino to handle the on-set sphere effects with the trickier optical shots handed over to Dream Quest Images.

"When Don told me he had nobody lined up to do the silver sphere effects for *Phantasm II*, I told him I knew a guy he should meet," Shostrom says. "I was thinking of my friend Steve Patino. Steve and I had met a few years before when I hired him to do the rather complex fiberglass molds of the Pretorius monster for *From Beyond*. I told Don that Steve had just finished working on *Predator*, so this piqued his interest. Steve was really enthusiastic and a big fan of *Phantasm*. He dove in and gave it his all."

Patino associate James Vale recalls first hearing about the hush sequel from Shostrom. "He called the shop one night. He said, '*Listen, there's a movie coming up and believe me, you want to be involved. I can't tell you anything about it but you want to be involved. Clear what you have going on.*' And it was

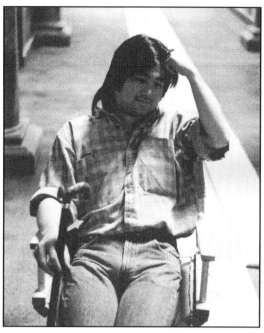

Returning Phantasmic Minds: Roberto Quezada (*left*) & Daryn Okada (*right*).
(*Photos courtesy Kristen Deem*)

Phantasm II and no one could talk about it. That was a big deal. You couldn't talk about it to your family, your girlfriend, your wife, no one."

More than any other film in the series, *Phantasm II*'s production was shrouded in a kind of secrecy ordinarily reserved only for *Star Wars* sequels. Script copies utilized a number of fake titles including *Morningside* and *The Dark* (both unused from the first film), *American Gothic, P2* and *Threadbare*. The project was so secretive that many cast and crew were oblivious to its actual title until after they were hired. Even twenty years later, the film's producer remains mum on the fake names. "There is a pressure to keep any Coscarelli project under a code name," Quezada says. "But if I told you why it would jeopardize the lives of loved ones – yours and mine."

"Secrecy on a film is fine, especially where the plot is concerned, but *Phantasm II* took it too far," Patino told <u>Fear Magazine</u> shortly after the film's release. "There was a lot of power play on that film. At first, the production got a lot of

people enthusiastic, but during the eight months of production, people started to hate one another. If you spoke out, you were threatened with loss of credit."

Opting for their own nickname, Vale, Patino and Shostrom chose an alias based on a popular Alison Moyet tune. "Whenever anyone heard us talking about *Love Resurrection* we were really talking about *Phantasm II*," Vale says. "That was *our* code name."

In a bold move, Coscarelli and Quezada hired a handful of qualified *Phantasm* fans as crewmembers. In addition to Patino, such fans included Production Assistant Guy Alford (watch for his cameo as the body embalmed by the Tall Man's henchman), Craft Serviceman Troy Fromin (watch for his cameo as the graver Mike and Reggie drive past) and Electrician Ralph Coon. Having befriended Angus Scrimm and Reggie Bannister years earlier, recent Stanford graduate Kristen Deem was a natural pick for crewmember and had a hand in everything from casting to hearse wrangling. Although hired as production assistant, her final credits were as Storyboard Artist and Unit Publicist.

"I was perpetually aglow," Deem says. "I was floating around the set, annoying some of the crew with my unabashed joy! They likely thought there was something wrong with me yet I couldn't have been happier. I woke each morning raring to get to set to see what new things awaited! I wasn't just watching *Phantasm*, I was living it!"

"Don has often welcomed dedicated fans who have something to contribute to the series and is always rewarded by doing so," Scrimm says. "They worked hard, made notable contributions, and accepted the modest recompense the series' budgets permit."

One perk for *Phantasm's* few returning cast members was that they would no longer be responsible for all their own stunts. *Phantasm II* would employ an entire troupe of stunt performers led by coordinators Solly Marx and John Michael Stewart. "My good friend Solly Marx was originally hired to be stunt coordinator on *Phantasm II*," Stewart says. "Solly then brought me in to meet Don and he hired me to coordinate as

The Tall Man and the perpetually aglow Kristen Deem.
(Photo courtesy Kristen Deem)

well. Don also cast me as one of the ghoul mortician characters because it was a stunt-heavy role. He does that a lot because it saves money to just let the stuntman do the acting if the part involves getting beaten or burned up in the end."

"I thought we had a really great crew on *Phantasm II*," Second Assistant Director Andrew Reeder says. "You could tell right away that Don surrounded himself with good people. Robert Del Valle was and still is one of the brightest guys working in film as a producer/production manager. Roberto, too. I also remember being continually impressed by what Mark Shostrom would come up with effects-wise. Though most were planned ahead, some of the makeup requests changed throughout filming and he was able to roll with it and deliver things with little notice. I had a lot of respect for those guys."

CASTING FOLLIES

In September 1987, *Phantasm II's* Lankershim Boulevard casting office opened in Universal City under Betsy Fels's leadership. Up until this moment there had been no reason to believe any *Phantasm* alumni were in danger of not returning. Both Michael Baldwin and Reggie Bannister counted on reprising their roles in the sequel. Universal's preference, however, was that Fels recast Mike and Reggie with working actors, which Baldwin and Bannister were not as neither had made a film appearance since *Phantasm*. As such, the studio was hesitant to headline a summer release with virtual unknowns. The situation reached a new level of grim when casting breakdowns went out to agents for every role in the script except the Tall Man. Hundreds of resumes answered back.

"I saw everyone," Fels says. "It seemed as though every bald guy and romantic lead in town was applying. I even had Brad Pitt on the list for Mike at one point because he wasn't really working then."

"It's too bad about Brad Pitt," Jim Jacks says. "Not that *Phantasm II* would've made him a star, but it would've been great to have established him there. I think we were hoping to find a young actor to play [Mike] that could blossom into something beyond these movies. The studio was always hoping to generate any number of new young stars with these pictures. We weren't at all insistent upon casting a name actor in that role because it was such a low-budget production."

The move to recast was not some malicious directive handed down by a domineering studio executive, but rather a request; one of only two made by Universal according to Don Coscarelli. Per the director's appeal, the studio agreed to let Baldwin and Bannister audition for their namesake roles in a desperate scenario. Following his first and last tryout for a Coscarelli film – ever – Bannister won back the part of Reggie, beating out rival applicant Jeffrey Tambor. Baldwin was less fortunate. Flying in from Colorado on Thursday, October 29 for a videotaped reading, he was ultimately rejected for the role of Mike. The degree to which Coscarelli challenged the studio on this has been contested over the years, unlike his candid and much-publicized regret over the recasting debacle. Had he completely stonewalled on Baldwin's behalf, *Phantasm II* might never have been made.

"If things in life had names that truly described what they are or do, filmmaking would be called compromise making and every job in the business would actually be called looking-for-work-again," Roberto Quezada explains. "You either cede control to the investors or to the fact that you don't have enough money to make the movie you really want to make. That's life and if it were easy everyone would be a director. Don is a master at this game and while most of the films he made required compromises, enough of his genius has always come through to make it a Don Coscarelli film and nobody else's."

"When you're working for a big studio, you have to toe the line," Andrew Reeder says. "If you're not taking hints the right way when the studio gives you these kinds of suggestions, it can get ugly. They could in turn take control from you in other places. I think Don played his hand well on *Phantasm II*. He succumbed to Universal in all the right places and rolled with the punches."

Exactly why Baldwin was rejected for his own role is a curious topic. One could argue that *Phantasm II's* characterization of Mike was at odds with Baldwin's more

The original Regman almost didn't return.
(Photo courtesy Kristen Deem)

sensitive portrayal in the first film, thus disqualifying him even before his audition. By pitting Mike as both action hero and romantic lead, Coscarelli perhaps unwittingly distanced the character from its *Phantasm* roots. No longer was the younger Pearson brother a spunky, inquisitive and vulnerable youth, but instead the dashing valiant type who gets the girl. In *that* version of the role Baldwin would seem a peculiar candidate at first. Considering that Mike had aged an entire decade in the sequel, Universal's move to recast the part did seem far more defensible than if the studio had succeeded in doing the same to Reggie. After ten years, a grown Mike could appear different in a way that Reggie would not.

"It was a drag," Baldwin says. "My pals were off making my movie. It was not fun, truly. But it's just part of the business and I've been a professional in this business my whole life. Sometimes you get the job and sometimes you don't, even when you think you should. I can't say it wasn't disappointing because it definitely was, but it was only a job. *Phantasm* wasn't and still isn't my whole life. I will say that I think Don Coscarelli regrets having to recast me in that show. It didn't do anything for anybody and it didn't help the movie. It just became a large inconsistency in an otherwise largely consistent franchise."

Shortly after Baldwin's audition, Fels brought in a new candidate for consideration, an up-and-coming actor named James LeGros. "I brought James in at the very last minute," Fels says. "I told him up front, '*I don't think you're gonna really want to do this*' but he needed work. Don was in the room when James walked in and read a few lines, and Don said, '*That's it. We don't need to see anymore.*' In a sense, Michael should be bitter about *Phantasm II*. All I know is that Universal wanted him to aesthetically look more like a romantic lead, which he wasn't."

In the years since, both fans and filmmakers alike have vilified the studio for Mike's recasting and for having attempted the same for Reggie. Universal's plan, however well intentioned, failed to account for the pair's contribution to *Phantasm*'s success. The casting fiasco also revealed just how little the studio knew about the creative property it had acquired. While LeGros' casting was an attempt to reach a more mainstream audience, it will forever remain a bane in the minds of both fans and *Phantasm*'s creator.

NEW BLOOD

As the casting drama over Mike and Reggie ensued, auditions for the other roles began in October on shaky ground, literally. Southern California experienced its worst tremor in years with the Whittier Narrows earthquake of 1987, which registered a 6.1 on the Richter scale. High-rise buildings across town were damaged beyond repair and the ground buckled to the point of cracking open. Production forged ahead, however, proving that it would take a far greater disaster to stop a *Phantasm* movie.

Actress Paula Irvine, who had appeared in Universal's *Bates Motel* television pilot in July 1987, was chosen for the series' new female lead, Elizabeth "Liz" Murphy. Newcomer and former model Samantha Phillips was cast as Alchemy, a role whose very name recalls the Lady in Lavender from *Phantasm*. "Paula Irvine was pretty easy to cast," Betsy Fels says. "Don really liked her a lot. She embodied everything about the normal American girl, which is what he was looking for. Samantha Phillips, on the other hand, nobody knew what to

Paula Irvine before a wardrobe test.
(Photo courtesy Kristen Deem)

do with her. I actually brought her in for Paula's role a bunch of times but she wasn't that sweet all-American girl, you know? She's Sam! I don't know how else to explain it. Don really wanted to make a place for her."

"On my way to the audition," Phillips says, "I had a car accident. So I arrived late and you're never supposed to walk in frantically apologizing and making excuses because no one wants to see that. I made every mistake you possibly could. I proceeded to sit down and tell Don Coscarelli that I had no idea why I was there because we both knew I wasn't going to get the role. He had me audition anyway and I did a passable to shitty job on it. I was more worried about how I was getting home that day. Then I got a callback for another audition and I thought, '*This guy hasn't had enough torture!*' I think I had one or two more after that one, including a reading with Reggie, before I was officially told I had the part."

Despite being written as "heavy set," normal-sized actor Kenneth Tigar was cast in the role of Father Franklin Meyers, beating out fellow contender John Astin of *The Addams Family* fame. "When I get a script and audition for something, I try and get as close to the part as I can," Tigar says. "I don't wait for what will happen in the movie. If a part is worth doing, it's

New Mike.
(Photo courtesy Kristen Deem)

worth working on even if I don't get a role. I just figure that I'll always get to play the role once and that's in the audition. So I may as well prepare for it and get as close as I can. After I got the part, I viewed the original *Phantasm* and was very impressed with what Don was able to do with a shoestring budget. I mean, he wrote it, he directed it, and he produced it. To come up with something as unique and as stylish as it was, I was impressed."

Among the Tall Man's undead army in *Phantasm II* would be two featured henchmen, silent and dressed in matching black suits. The more action-heavy of these two roles was assigned to Stunt Coordinator John Michael Stewart with the other going to actor Mark Anthony Major whom Coscarelli chose from a group audition.

"Don told us that we were going to be chased and pinned to a wall by something very frightening," Major says. "He wanted to see fear, terror and our vulnerability to break away from whatever was holding us back. I saw a few people do it and it looked okay, and when it was my turn I did basically the same thing. Don liked how I played it, so he had me do it a second time with more specific instructions. He told me that the

thing chasing me was this silver ball. I immediately thought of *Phantasm* and, of course, it was! I had no idea because the title was *Morningside*. I didn't make a connection with that being the name of the cemetery. I told Don that I was a *Phantasm* fan and a big horror buff and he goes, '*Oh, you know about horror movies?*' and I told him, '*More than you'll ever want to know.*' Later that day I got a call saying I had the job."

Although a handful of actors would appear as dwarves in *Phantasm II* such as Felix Silla (best known as Cousin Itt from *The Addams Family*) and Phil Fondacaro (a well-known Ewok performer on *Star Wars: Return of the Jedi*), it was Ed Gale whom Coscarelli cast as the film's featured dwarf player. Gale was best known for his work in the title role from *Howard the Duck* and would soon appear as Chucky in the original *Child's Play*.

"I think they were mainly looking for someone who could work inside of a restrictive costume," Gale says. "Don Coscarelli, who was surprisingly young, hired me on the spot when I met him. He sent me home with a script and told me to pay attention to the ending because that's where my big scene

Kenneth Tigar (*left*) and Mark Anthony Major (*right*) getting into character.
(*Photos courtesy Kristen Deem*)

was, where I met Reggie in the spacegate world. So I'm reading through it later on, enjoying it, and I get to the ending and the last ten pages are missing. It says '*Confidential Ending Withheld*'. I'm just like, '*What!?*' so I call Don right away. It turned out that he gave me the wrong script and immediately sent me over a full copy to read through. I loved it! I thought the whole thing was awesome. I was happy to be a part of it."

A PROPER PHANTASM

In stark contrast to the unencumbered creation of its predecessor, *Phantasm II* would be produced using, more or less, industry standard procedure. Dedicated departments would handle specialized tasks rather than the "everyone does everything" approach of the original. There would also be little time for Don Coscarelli to re-write or re-shoot ineffectual scenes due to the pace made necessary by Universal's release date. Frequent departmental meetings would be in order to ensure his vision was being realized properly and on time. Just as they'd done on *Phantasm*, the production secured another Chatsworth warehouse for filming, this one larger.

"*Phantasm II* was a really wild ten months of work," Robert Del Valle says. "Unlike the first film, we had a budget and we had a schedule, and we had to stick to both. The budget allowed us to have a larger mausoleum set this time around and we had a terrific production designer, Philip Duffin, to construct the new sets. He was really great in finding creative ways to stretch his budget. Having a budget also meant that we were able to have some new visual effects and considerably more elaborate makeup effects. These were all things that were going to make the film successful in the end but they also required a kind of preparation and management that we weren't worried about on the first film. It was a much more serious production."

"The biggest difference between *Phantasm* and *Phantasm II* for me was the expectation level," Daryn Okada says. "We didn't have that on the first one. We had to somehow be bigger and better than *Phantasm* but still retain some of the simple values from that film. We really did not want to let the audience down, either the old audience coming back or the new audience coming in for the first time. There was so much more at stake on *Phantasm II*."

Duffin pitched his upgraded mausoleum layout to Coscarelli using a scale model. His design depicted a T-shaped hallway with several rooms jutting off from the main corridor. Although the script called for Perigord Mausoleum to be another white marble structure à la Morningside, Duffin instead went in a gothic direction with dark hallways, large columns and bright red stained glass windows. The set was built in pieces throughout October, erected at the Chatsworth warehouse in November, painted in December and camera-ready by early January 1988. The shooting schedule was front-loaded with location work starting in December to accommodate set construction. Warehouse filming was slated to begin in January with most of the film's makeup effects staggered several months beyond that to allow Mark Shostrom and company time to complete Coscarelli's tall order of gags.

"The effects in *Phantasm II* required a lot of overlap between the departments," Shostrom says. "You had multiple effects departments working on scenes like when the sphere chops the priest's ear off or when Angus gets drilled. You can't have one department not cooperating with another

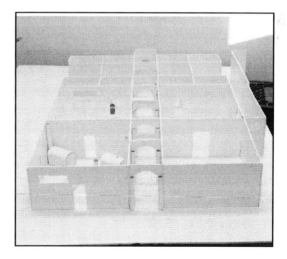

Philip Duffin's Perigord Mausoleum model.
(Photo courtesy Kristen Deem)

Above: Mark Shostrom photographs Angus Scrimm.
Right Middle & *Bottom*: Applying the alginate.
(Photos courtesy Kristen Deem)

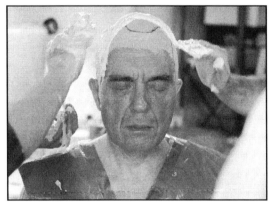

and, fortunately, we all got along really well on *Phantasm II*. If I remember correctly, the priest's death scene called for mechanical, optical and makeup effects. I collaborated a lot with Steve Patino in preproduction to pull some of those scenes off. He always delivered on the mechanical end."

Throughout the making of *Phantasm II*, almost everyone on the cast would find themselves in Shostrom's makeup chair at one point or another. For some, this meant having life casts taken. On October 16, Angus Scrimm ventured to Shostrom's studio for his turn. Molds of the actor were needed for the film's extravagantly messy finale in which the Tall Man is embalmed with hydrochloric acid. A strange and potentially frightening procedure, Scrimm's entire head was encased in prosthetic alginate. Kristen Deem went along for moral support and to document the procedure.

Left: Angus Scrimm looks over the freshly pulled mold.
Right: Mark Shostrom sculpts one of the Tall Man heads.
(Scrimm photo courtesy Kristen Deem)
(Sculpture photo courtesy Mark Shostrom)

In a journal dated 10/16/87, Deem wrote:

Anxious minutes pass as I watch them cover Angus' entire head with white alginate. The room goes very silent. None of us want to say or do anything to disturb his peace of mind. If he should startle and open his eyes or mouth... [...] Occasionally, Mark calls out, 'How ya doin', Angus?' One finger for good, two for not good. There is even a special hand signal for "HELP! Get me out of this NOW!" Luckily, Angus keeps lifting just one finger. He is a trooper. I can only imagine how claustrophobic this must be. Minutes later, Angus is prompted to bend forward and the mold is gently tugged from his face. He is smiling with relief, laughing. The cool air of the room must seem like heaven! Mark explains how he will create several face and hand "meltdown" appliances from these molds, and even a life-sized animatronic head of the Tall Man!

"Those classic heads," Scrimm says. "I knew at once that future generations would venerate them in the same way they hallow Michelangelo's David."

"For my scene as the barrel dwarf, I had a full body cast done, which was something I'd gone through once before," Ed Gale says. "First we did it without my head, then just my head, then my hands and feet. After the life casting, I went home for a couple of months while Mark Shostrom and his guys sculpted the suit. Then I was called back for fittings and producer approval and, shortly thereafter, it was time to start filming. I thought the dwarf suit Shostrom came up with was a work of art."

For Patino and company, this time was spent figuring out how to replicate and expand on the sphere effects from the first film. "We were able to get our hands on pieces of the original *Phantasm* sphere, which was really cool," James Vale says. "We took the exact blades from that ball to cast the new blades from. The originals were heavier, almost like solid metal. We were building the new spheres out of acrylic Plexiglas to be much lighter."

Recreating the spheres proved to be a much easier task than getting them to fly, however. Early flight tests included a wrist-rocket system that when wound too tightly would shatter the propelled ball on impact at the far end of the wire. For the sphere team, it was trial and error on a daily basis to figure out what was going to work. "Mostly error on that day," Vale adds.

"I was doodling in the casting office one night as we were wrapping things up," Deem says. "They'd just brought Paula Irvine on board to play Liz. She came bouncing out of the second office where they conducted the actual auditions. She saw me sketching and said, '*Wow, did you do these?*' Then grabbed up my pad. Before I could stop her, she ran into the next room and showed Don. I thought, '*Oh, no, I'm gonna get fired. They're going to see that I'm out here drawing instead of doing anything practical.*' They came out moments later. Paula had such a vibrant glow about her, and Don was following behind her. And he had this stunned expression on his face. He said, '*Kris, these are pretty good. How would you like to do storyboards with me?*' It was one of my best experiences on *Phantasm II.* I had such a blast working with Don on these. They had me doing so many other jobs each day that I could only use what few hours I had at night to work on storyboards, often over dinner. This usually meant dinner at Angus' home, with me sitting at the kitchen table while he was cooking spaghetti. I'd sit there, watching him at the stove, using his profile to create the panels for the hearse chase. Then I'd give Don the storyboards the next day with tomato sauce on the edges!"

PRODUCTION'S START

Phantasm II's cameras rolled at sundown on Wednesday, December 9. The first several nights were spent in Highland Park, a suburb of Los Angeles, where scenes of Perigord Manor would be staged. Amongst the first footage shot was the steamy encounter between Reggie and Alchemy. "I've gotta tell you," Reggie Bannister says, "I agree with all those actors who say that a sex scene is probably one of the hardest to shoot. That

Closed? Better try the Bates Motel.
(Photo courtesy Troy Fromin)

"I remember joking that the only thing we didn't shoot that first day was a car crash."

Daryn Okada on the hectic first day schedule.

particular scene, though, was a lot of fun. To see Reggie in that situation, it was just funny."

"It was definitely funny," Samantha Phillips says. "*Phantasm II* turned out to be the only love scene I've ever done where I kept my underwear on. I had never done one before that so I was really shy about showing skin. What really made it strange was that Reggie's wife was outside in his trailer while we were filming, so that kind of made me a little more reserved that day. With Alchemy, I remember feeling that I needed to understand the character's motivation so I asked Don, '*Why am I all hot for a bald dude? Why don't I want to bang Mike instead?*' which I was actually doing in real life, and he was like, '*I don't know. You have a fetish for bald guys,*' and I got to thinking about that. If you have a fetish for bald guys, you must really love bald heads! That was something I could really get into for the scene, so I did a whole bunch of playing with his head, smacking it and kissing it. (laughs)"

"Our first day of filming had us all over the place," Daryn Okada says. "We were slated for both day exteriors and night interiors, one of which was a love scene. I remember joking that the only thing we didn't shoot that first day was a car crash. But it turned out that our assistant director had scheduled it that way on purpose so that we would look good in our first batch of dalies. After that, he scheduled us more logically. It was a new experience for all of us, having outsiders watching our dailies. The Universal people were essentially judging the film before it was even done, which is how studio films often work. It definitely added pressure to what we were doing, even though we only ever heard back positive things from them."

As originally filmed, the Perigord Manor section of the film was to feature another love scene, this one of the psychic variety between Mike and Liz. The young couple first dream of lovemaking atop a tree in a vast forest, then on the shore of a desolate beach and finally while falling through clouds before waking in their bed fully clothed. The scene concluded with Liz telling Mike, "That was the safest sex we'll ever have."

"Even though we were well covered up it was shot in such a way that we appeared to be naked," Paula Irvine told Femme Fatales magazine. "It ended up on the cutting room floor because of technical reasons so we did our lovemaking by having a telepathic dialogue. I wasn't sorry about that either. The reason I was reluctant to do that scene as originally planned is I have a weird quirk about nude scenes and nudity in general. If in order to get a role I had to agree to be nude, I would change my entire profession. To me, nudity should not be a prerequisite

James LeGros and Reggie Bannister strike a silly pose.
(Photo courtesy Troy Fromin)

for obtaining a role. Something would be ethically wrong with an industry that requires that. Of course, there are some roles that do require nudity and those roles should be reserved for the people who don't have a problem with it."

In the film, the upstairs lovefest is interrupted when a grenade trap is triggered downstairs. Hearing the explosion, Mike and Reggie abandon their dates to investigate. In another deleted bit, Alchemy pulls away a large chunk of hair from her scalp as Reggie runs out, foreshadowing her later transformation into the Tall Man during the film's ending.

In a journal dated 12/9/87, Kristen Deem wrote:

> *The first shot is in the can. We are on our way to making another Phantasm! We decide the occasion deserves something truly celebratory in a "Phantasm" vein. I find myself running up the street to a liquor store and buying a six-pack of Dos Equis amber beer. The cold brew delights Reggie and his wife, Gayle, plus a few crewmembers that come to give Reg a heads up on the timing for his upcoming scene. [...] The hearse is now parked in front of the manor. The lighting crew is having a difficult time prepping the shot because the polished black surface of the hearse reflects EVERYTHING, even the crowds across the street. The hearse can only mean one thing. [...] I watch Reggie and James tear out the front door of the manor, then down the sidewalk. Angus guns the hearse to life and peels out down the street before they can catch up. On another take the hearse suddenly stalls. Reggie and James race all the way to the driver's door, throw it open and begin to drag a very surprised Angus out! We're all laughing. "Cut!" They won't print this take, of course. But Reggie is beaming! It is like a small victory for him!*

Production continued the following night with additional interiors, including the kidnapping of Liz by the Tall Man. In a scene that heavily recalls the first *Phantasm*, the alien mortician crashes through a window at his unsuspecting prey. It was here that the company incurred its first mishap when a shard of candy-glass cut Angus Scrimm across the cheek, proving once and for all that the performer's blood was indeed red and

not the speculated yellow. Speaking further to <u>Femme Fatales</u> magazine, Irvine warmly reminisced about her towering co-star: "In the films, he's the personification of evil, but in real life he's the most charming, caring man. When he threw me into the hearse, he was terribly worried that I might be hurt or uncomfortable. He was very sensitive to how I felt and still is to this day."

Although such overnight shoots proved taxing on all involved, they were perhaps hardest on Scrimm, who maintained his post at Capitol Records by day, sometimes leaving that job to attend night filming. "Let me recite you a list of names," Scrimm says. "Brown Meggs, Marvin Schwartz, John Patrick, Renny Martini, Raoul Montano, Janice May, Patti Laursen, George Sponhaltz, Brad Engel, Tom Evered, Barry Golin, Harry Pack. These were all my closest associates at Capitol/Angel Records and they were all much bemused

Reggie Bannister rehearsing.
(Photo courtesy Troy Fromin)

that their mild-mannered colleague who wrote liner notes for them was gaining a modest reputation around the world as a fearsome figure to be dreaded and feared. They did all in their power to accommodate my occasional absences from the office to film and I, in turn, never missed an editorial deadline — or at least not by much."

A GRAVE DISCOVERY

On Monday, December 14, the company moved north to Valencia for one of *Phantasm II*'s more striking landscapes, the pillaged graveyard of Mariton County. In the film, an armed Mike and Reggie traverse the exhumed cemetery in order to reach its decrepit mausoleum. Previously an abandoned oil property, the Mariton locale was hastily converted for use in the film. Its exterior was a mere lightweight façade prone to toppling over, which it did in the middle of a take before a visiting Sam Raimi.

"Sam came over as we were trying to push the mausoleum set back upright," Philip Duffin says. "We had a good laugh because we both were remembering that this exact same thing had happened to us on *Evil Dead II*. We had built a castle façade atop a sixty-foot cliff for the ending and, of course, a big wind came and blew it over too. It happens. I remember that we were really under the gun on time with that graveyard location. I only had one guy with a bulldozer to make the uprooted cemetery happen. I just showed him on a piece of paper how I wanted the holes dug and I left for the afternoon. When I came back, amazingly, he had made dozens upon dozens of empty burial plots. It looked stunning in person and even more so in the film."

Close examination of the scene outside Mariton Mausoleum reveals a brief, unscripted nod by James LeGros to Michael Baldwin's *Phantasm* performance. "As craft services, I had regular interactions with the cast," Troy Fromin says. "And as a fan, I was really disappointed that Michael Baldwin wasn't in our film and didn't mind saying so, even to James LeGros.

After Twin Peaks but before Silent Hill.
(Photo courtesy Troy Fromin)

He apparently listened to me and came back the following day to say, 'Troy, I want you to know I've watched the first movie carefully and in the scene outside the graveyard in our film I'm going to have a red lollipop just like Michael did when he saw the Tall Man walking down the street in that film.' And he did it. You can see it in the film right as they're gearing up. I thought it was a nice tribute to Michael's performance."

"James was bright, likable, professional and a very good actor," Angus Scrimm says. "He and Reggie had a great time off camera playing darts — with a large photo of the Tall Man as their dartboard. I don't think James had any idea of the conflict the rest of us were feeling at the rather murky absence of Michael."

"No one really talked much about Michael being replaced by James LeGros," set regular Guy Thorpe recalls. "That's not to say that Michael wasn't missed - he certainly was. There was simply nothing anyone could do about it, so I think everyone just forged ahead with filming and made the movie they could. I don't think too many people on the crew even gave it much thought, come to think of it. The only people

November 27, 1987

Mr. James Jacks
100 Universal City Plaza
Bldg. 65, Room 10
Universal City, CA 91608

Dear Mr. Jacks:

As per our telephone conversation on Wednesday, November 25, this
letter shall confirm your approval of Reggie Bannister for the role
of Reggie and Samantha Phillips for the role of Kemy.

Kindest regards,

Betsy Fels,
Casting Director

BF/kd

Above: The long awaited confirmation of Reggie Bannister's
return as well as Samantha Phillip's casting.

Right: The dartboard photo from Reggie Bannister and James
LeGros' dressing room.

(*Letter/photo courtesy Kristen Deem*)

Top: Paula Irvine with Ruth C. Engel
Bottom: Paula Irvine and Angus Scrimm on the Perigord set.
(Liz/Grandma photo courtesy Troy Fromin)
(Liz/Tall Man photo courtesy Kristen Deem)

who would have been aware of it were the ones who were fans or who knew Michael personally like Don, Roberto, Angus, Reggie, and of course Kristen and myself."

Four days later, the company moved filming to a real graveyard, Sunnyside Cemetery in Long Beach. Here they staged two scenes inside an actual burial plot, the first of which was deleted from the film. As Mike stakes out Perigord Cemetery he is soon discovered by one of the Tall Man's gravediggers and saved only when a massive headstone falls onto the attacking goon, crushing him. This excised scuffle would have explained where Mike had acquired the gas mask he is later wearing when Liz discovers him in the same empty grave. As for the actual burial plot, multiple crewmembers recall a mysterious substance that oozed from within. Later, it was suggested to be rust-induced.

The vacant leaky grave.
(Photo courtesy Troy Fromin)

"Whenever you're shooting a horror movie, strange things happen that you can't always explain," Andrew Reeder says. "After one of the graves had been dug up at the Long Beach cemetery, an orange-colored ooze began seeping out from the dirt walls inside. Everyone freaked and bolted out of the grave. No one wanted to go back in it after that but Paula Irvine was a real trooper. She was very brave and went back into the grave a number of times to do her scene. At the time, no one really thought of it as being rust-driven. Being in a graveyard surrounded by coffins at night, your first thought is that a neighboring body is leaking out. I'm sure we wrapped filming on that hole very quickly after that incident."

"I had a cameo in that scene as a gravedigger in the cemetery when Mike and Reggie drive past," Fromin says. "I might be the first graver you see in the movie. That happened pretty quickly. They said they needed someone. Knowing that I was a big fan, they asked me and I said, '*Hell yeah.*' I was immediately outfitted and given a rubber pickaxe. By the time the scene was over, the prop rental was demolished. I think they wound up having to buy it. The props guy, Will Blount, was the gravedigger later on inside the mausoleum pushing the gurney."

In a journal dated 12/18/87, Kristen Deem wrote:

> *Late in the evening there is a visitor at the cemetery. Don's mood brightens considerably and he rushes over to greet the man. I gasp as I recognize the visage of Paul Pepperman, another veteran from the original Phantasm. He and Don go back to their freshman days as roommates at UCLA. What must Paul be feeling returning to a Phantasm set this night? As much as I want to discuss his experiences, I sense that he is a private person and keep my distance.*

PRELUDE TO AN EXPLOSION

Don Coscarelli's sequel script was perhaps nowhere more ambitious than in its opening which picked up exactly where *Phantasm* left off. Turning the clock back nine years, however, was something far easier said than done. Not only was the production team without access to Michael Baldwin (who no longer resembled his teenage self), they were without access to the original location used for Reggie's home. Stuntwoman Lori Lynn Ross was used to double Baldwin while a nearby Chatsworth residence served as Reggie's downstairs interior. Mike's 1978 bedroom was recreated inside the Chatsworth warehouse. The finished sequence, the first part of which was filmed at the warehouse on Wednesday, December 16, bridges the two films seamlessly.

"Don and I were constantly looking back and forth between this movie and the first one," Daryn Okada recalls. "We discussed in-depth how we could extend the ending of the original and expand upon it. We wanted to make it as if our movie was evolving from the first movie. We paid close attention to the lighting and camera work so that we would know exactly what shots would cut well against one another, new against old. We felt by being loyal to the first *Phantasm* right away we might earn the audience's respect."

While Coscarelli used newly filmed material to correct the *Phantasm* gaffe of Angus Scrimm having noticeably shorter hair in Mike's bedroom, he accidentally created an even bigger blunder with Reggie's magically disappearing guitar. The instrument, which was left propped against the fireplace, disappears between shots before re-appearing in a different spot. The director had originally envisioned having Reggie's ice cream truck parked outside when the Tall Man arrives, icy mist billowing from its freezer. This vehicular cameo was nixed, however, when the company failed to secure a matching replacement truck, the original having long since vanished. Although scripted as an immediate continuation of *Phantasm*'s ending, the theatrical cut of *Phantasm II* would see it narrated in pseudo-flashback by Paula Irvine's Liz as she explains her psychic connection to Mike.

The opening sequence is quick to unleash Mark Shostrom's redesigned dwarves for the Tall Man's assault on Reggie's home. Ed Gale, no stranger to stunt work, plays the minion that bursts from a kitchen cupboard onto an unsuspecting Reggie. He reappears moments later upstairs as the dwarf dragging Mike from his bedroom, which is actually

Left and *Right*: Mark Shostrom's redesigned dwarves.
(Photos courtesy Mark Shostrom)

a redressed Chatsworth warehouse hallway filmed later on January 13. Close-ups of Shostrom's mechanized dwarf puppet fighting with Reggie were captured even later on March 28. After wrapping the Chatsworth residence in the early morning hours of December 24, the production adjourned for holiday break.

"One of the first things I did after getting hired was to design the dwarves," Shostrom says. "They weren't really seen much in the original *Phantasm*. In fact, I think they were just little kids with hoods on. Don had specific requests for them this time around, like the snarling dwarf, the full body canister dwarf and the Grandma dwarf, so the dwarves were meant to be seen quite a lot more in *Phantasm II*. Nailing the designs for Don was the first order of business. As I recall, Angus was still in contract negotiations and we were not able to get him for life casting early on, so we started on the dwarves first. Between my sketches and the ones Bryant Tausek did, I think altogether we had around six or seven. Once funds started rolling in, Bob Kurtzman sculpted the snarling dwarf from my sketch, Everett Burrell sculpted Grandma and we all did a background dwarf. David Barton made the eyes and did an amazing job mechanizing the snarling dwarf. Except for Ed Gale and the snarling dwarf - which were foam latex - all the others were slip cast high quality latex masks with hands."

"It wasn't much of a drag when I found out that the dwarf role required a full body costume," Gale says. "Up until that point in my career, all I had ever done were costumed roles. I actually found it a lot easier because I'm introverted myself and somewhat shy to a degree. By putting on a costume and mask, I could be whatever I wanted to be with it. It's not like I had any lines to memorize. On the other hand, I did have to create an entire performance out of just the way I move, which is always a challenge."

Following the Tall Man's foiled kidnapping in 1978, *Phantasm II* skips ahead ten years to find an adult Mike hospitalized at Morningside Psychiatric Clinic. Sharp-eyed viewers can spot a cameo by Roberto Quezada as a patient in the bed adjacent to Mike's. The subject of Mike's questionable mental state is a missed opportunity for the plot, which instead picks up just as Mike is being discharged into Reggie's care. The psychiatric ward angle would later be explored to greater effect in the unproduced *Phantasm Forever* where a committed Mike would be haunted by visions of the Tall Man. As it stands, Mike's hospitalization is a mere footnote in the *Phantasm* story.

Troy Fromin's nixed cameo as a Morningside orderly.
(Photo courtesy Troy Fromin)

"I was originally going to have two cameos in the movie," Troy Fromin says. "In addition to being a graver, I was going to be in a second unit shot outside the Morningside hospital just before they interview Mike to let him go, but the shot was never done. An assistant director had forgotten an important cable for the camera, so we couldn't film it that day and just wound up getting it later on. I would've been seen dressed as an orderly walking past the front door."

ON LOCATION

Upon return from holiday break, the production reconvened at Wolze Ace Hardware in Highland Park on Tuesday, January 5. Per the script, Mike and Reggie had to amass a wide arsenal of homemade weaponry before they could begin their hunt for the Tall Man. This pilfering yields them a chainsaw, an electric drill, a custom-built flamethrower and Reggie's now famous four-barrel shotgun. The actual construction of these memorable props fell to Wayne Beauchamp.

"The four-barrel shotgun really is as simple as it looks," Beauchamp says. "We just welded two shotguns to one another, double-cut them and brought them together with a single wood stock. I'd never want to shoot that thing with a real load in it, though. I don't know that it would stay in one piece because in certain places it's only being held together with pipe strapping."

In a journal dated 1/5/88, Kristen Deem wrote:

> *The hardware store is a reminder of earlier decades long before the advent of Home Depot. On this stormy day, I spend awhile quietly wandering the murky shop. There is a layer of dust on almost everything, which I realize is due to the store's upkeep, not some fancy set dressing. At the front of the store, Roberto signs for checks and contracts. Mission accomplished. I study the antique cash register, oddly propped open. Upon the counter lays a chainsaw, a drill, a wad of fake money, a face shield, and a strange looking flamethrower. I sense these items are significant, perhaps the very props that will be used during today's filming.*

Shop Smart. Shop S-Mart.
(Photo courtesy Kristen Deem)

Kenneth Tigar between takes.
(Photo courtesy Kristen Deem)

The following day the production moved to the Pines Campground in Angeles Crest National Forest for another scene later omitted, one that rendered the Mariton County Mausoleum raid only a dream per the original script. That Mike had only dreamt of the exhumed cemetery, the decrepit mausoleum and the Liz creature was to have been revealed when the blaze of Reggie's flamethrower cross-faded into a campfire near Mike's sleeping bag. Upon waking, he explains to Reggie that his nightmare means they're getting closer and that Liz is in danger. With this scene's deletion, the events at Mariton became part of the film's reality and the Liz creature became a true calling card of the Tall Man.

That evening and much of the following day were spent capturing scenes set inside Father Meyers' home. In the film, the fearful clergyman is seen drinking heavily before an unexpected visit from the grotesquely embalmed corpse of Liz's grandfather. In a *Phantasm* throwback, Father Meyers blames the chilling sound outside on the wind to keep from confronting the true source. The scene abruptly cuts away when the priest finally gazes through the front door peephole to find the grandfather's ghastly face staring back at him.

"I remember one particular shot in Father Meyers' home that was almost impossible to get right," Kenneth Tigar says. "It's the one where I open the little window in the door and the camera rushes in tight on my face. That was difficult to do going forward at that speed because the camera kept hitting the door. So Don figured out that we could shoot it backwards, starting at the door and quickly moving away from it. So basically, I acted that scene out in reverse, looking terrified through the peephole. I thought it was a very clever solution. It was one of several moviemaking tricks I learned on *Phantasm II*."

The material set inside Father Meyers' home stands among the most heavily trimmed in all of *Phantasm II* with footage removed both before and after the arrival of Liz's undead grandfather. Originally, the scene was to open with the priest desperately phoning a colleague, Father Dom Luchese, to request his help in performing an exorcism on Perigord Mortuary. Father Luchese accuses his friend of drinking again and promises to enroll him in a local parish's rehab program. After seeing the corpse outside, the scene would have continued with a terrified Father Meyers locking himself inside a closet (the script has him using the *Phantasm*-screwdriver method), whimpering in fear with the barrel of a revolver resting in his mouth. Outside, his rotting assailant claws at its stitched-up lips in a vain attempt to speak.

"I really liked the part and felt very sympathetic toward Father Meyers," Tigar says. "I remember going into filming and being as compassionate as I could because I believed that's what the role was all about. He didn't even have to be a priest, really. He's just someone who wants to help others and was willing to lay down his life to do so, not that he isn't afraid. He's very afraid. That struck a chord with me."

3, 2, 1.... EXPLOSION!

On Friday, January 8, the production converged on a Hawthorne neighborhood where several houses were slated for demolition to make way for a new freeway overpass. The producers had reserved one of these homes to destroy in the film. Although the script specifically called for two separate house explosions (one to conclude *Phantasm*'s ending and another to kill Reggie's family), a more cost-effective plan was to destroy one house and then split the resulting footage between the two scenes. Philip Duffin's crew descended upon the house in advance of filming to install a false second story to make for an even greater explosion.

In order to fool the audience into thinking two separate structures were being destroyed, the filmmakers strategically stationed multiple cameras on opposite sides of the property, none of which could be in view of the others. In the backyard, Mike (stuntwoman Lori Lynn Ross) and Reggie (Reggie Bannister) from 1978 were to be scurrying away as their house blows. Over by the garage, the Tall Man from 1978 (Angus Scrimm) was to be waiting by his hearse. In front of the house, Mike (James LeGros) and Reggie (stuntman Bobby Brown) from 1988 were to be arriving in the 'Cuda as the house explodes. Coscarelli's script had originally called for flaming dwarves to land near Mike and Reggie on the front lawn following the 1978 blast, but this detail was omitted prior to filming.

"The location was on a flight pattern to LAX," Roberto Quezada says. "We had to get clearance from Washington, D.C. on the phone and then only had a five minute window when we could blow the house up between planes landing. Just getting a normal shot off under circumstances like that would traumatize anybody, but we had three units with actors that had to act on two of them and one unit in a moving car that had to get a clear shot of the damned thing. The safety fireman assigned to us by the city to keep the size of the blast down turned out to be a *Phantasm* fan and turned his head after telling our pyrotechnic effects guy to 'blow the shit out of it!'"

If Scrimm was worried about the impending stunt going awry, he wasn't letting it show outwardly, though he did complete his will just prior to the night's filming. "Things are always exploding around me," Scrimm says. "I looked forward to the warmth. It was a coolish night."

In a journal dated 1/8/88, Kristen Deem wrote:

Guy and I found James and Angus within one of the trailers, the warmth of which was a relief from the bitter cold. When Guy complimented Angus on his Tall Man makeup, James quipped, "It's remarkable how little he needs." Angus' eyes went wide, blinking in astonishment at the insult, and then he shook his head, chuckling, "A wit! We have a wit!" James laughed and clapped Angus jokingly across the shoulders. The night was getting colder with each passing minute. I watched, at first in awe, then in boredom, as they continuously rehearsed Angus' pulling up and stepping out of the hearse [...] An anxious crowd stood in the distance, eager for us to blow the house. An even more anxious fire chief gave us an ultimatum: Do the explosion by 1 AM or filming is cancelled. I could see panic in Allan and Roberto's eyes. We were down to the wire. Then the final countdown began. Three... Two... One... EXPLOSION! What a blinding burst! And the noise! I blinked back tears and squinted into the heat, desperate to see if Angus was still there, still moving. He was! Proud and rigid as ever, he hadn't even winced! Slowly, eerily, I watched him turn and glance back at the orange inferno.

"Although my camera was a good hundred and fifty feet away from the house," Quezada says, "I remember my face feeling sunburned for about a minute after the explosion. I can't believe the blast didn't affect Angus' performance in that shot. Study his face. That guy is a professional to the marrow of his bones, a true actor in the best sense of the word."

"Now don't get me wrong," Andrew Reeder says, "it was a very safe work environment that night and they had plenty of precautions in place, but I think the guys who rigged the explosives might have underestimated their work just a little bit. (laughs) I say that because the explosion was a lot bigger

Perigord Mausoleum takes shape.

(Photos courtesy Kristen Deem)

"At the end of a seventeen-hour day in front of the cameras, he's pure slapstick, and there's nothing I can do to contain him."

Angus Scrimm on the Tall Man

than most of us had anticipated. I was just amazed that the garage door didn't take Angus out when it blew off. I'm not at all surprised to hear that we blew out some of the neighbors' windows. We're lucky that's all we did."

"I can still vividly remember the night they blew up the house," Guy Thorpe says. "I had brought my video camera to set in order to capture it for posterity. The funny thing is that while the initial flash and fireball were huge, it only lasted a few seconds and it was gone. When you see it in the film, it's exaggerated into this long, horrific explosion that destroys the house. In real life, it was over so quickly that it was kind of anticlimactic considering how long we all stood around waiting for them to get it ready. But I suppose that's the magic of film editing!"

The night of the house explosion saw yet another deleted scene, this one set immediately after the blast in 1988 that kills Reggie's wife and child. As the distraught family man runs from the 'Cuda toward the burning house, Mike tackles him, yelling that it's too late for him to save his loved ones inside. Abruptly shifting his demeanor from hysterical to calm, Reggie realizes that Mike's foreknowledge of the blast must mean that the Tall Man is real. As the two friends vow to band together in pursuit of the Tall Man, they embrace before the giant flames.

Why this scene was removed is obvious. It was dramatically unrealistic, even for a *Phantasm* film. Reggie's hasty transition from grieving patriarch to collected vigilante in the moments following his family's murder suggests either a hyper-accelerated grieving or a psychotic break from reality. The scene's dialogue, which was vitally important to show

Reggie's newfound bond with Mike, was later rewritten into a short funeral scene staged during post-production.

PERIGORD MAUSOLEUM

Thursday, January 14, marked the final day of mausoleum construction, which allowed warehouse filming to begin the following morning. In a humorous touch, Don Coscarelli had crewmember names inscribed upon the brass nameplates adorning each crypt. These began to disappear just prior to wrapping the film, becoming crew souvenirs, which hampered further set-up shots of the corridor.

Among the first scenes filmed on the Perigord set was the confrontation between Father Meyers and the Tall Man. The mortician warns, "They have no need for your services." Father Meyers responds, "Who are you to question the words of God's servants?" Although the Tall Man had no scripted reply, Angus Scrimm improvised a number of responses. In one take, he jokingly retorted, "I'll let you see my resume."

The scene continues as the Tall Man telepathically lifts the priest by his rosary, then delivers a deleted line from the first *Phantasm*, "You think that when you die, you go to Heaven. You come to us!" As he releases the choke hold, the clergyman drops to the ground and exclaims that he is dealing with the Devil himself. Once again, the Tall Man had no scripted response, but that didn't discourage Scrimm from offering a few suggestions of his own. Unused lines included: "Ah, a figure from your mythology," "A poor relation, we never talk about that side of the family," and "You underestimate me, priest."

Angus Scrimm stops to smell the (fake) flowers.
(Photos courtesy Kristen Deem)

"The longer the shooting goes, the funnier the Tall Man gets," Scrimm says. "At the end of a seventeen-hour day in front of the cameras, he's pure slapstick, and there's nothing I can do to contain him."

On the topic of his fellow actor, Kenneth Tigar remarks that Scrimm was "a gentleman and a gentle man. There's a softness and an intelligence to him that I found compelling. Of course, he's a very wonderful performer. He's like Boris Karloff, a very scary guy on screen but a sweet guy off screen." While flattered, an all-too-humble Scrimm shrugged off any such comparison at the film's Pacific Theater premiere: "Mr. Karloff must be turning over in his grave at the very thought. Having been a longtime fan of his, I absolutely reject the suggestion but I'm honored to even be mentioned in the same sentence. He's a legend."

"While the camera crew was setting up the next shot, Angus decided to stroll around the set," Kristen Deem writes. "I followed him over, he didn't know, and he was studying the crypt that my name plate was on. When he realized I was next to him, he turned and said, 'And there you are...' and I felt this chill because he was there in makeup and costume. He keeps in character between shots, so it was partly the Tall Man that was saying that to me. Angus also has this very comic side where he likes to ham it up. He would go to from crypt to crypt, smelling the plastic flowers. Quite silly. When I asked if he would strike a more serious pose, he transformed. He drew in his energy and became solemn and still. There was a hardness, a gleam in his eyes as he became the Tall Man. That photo was just us joking around. I had no idea it would become such an iconic photograph years later. While working with Don's parents on publicity, I was told that the set photographer was intimidated by Angus and typically shot him only with other cast members. Since we needed a stand alone picture of the Tall Man for the press kit, I submitted the photo I'd taken."

The next several days were spent capturing Father Meyers' fatal clash with the silver sphere. Rather than simply

Kenneth Tigar uses his good ear to make a phone call.
(Photo courtesy Kristen Deem)

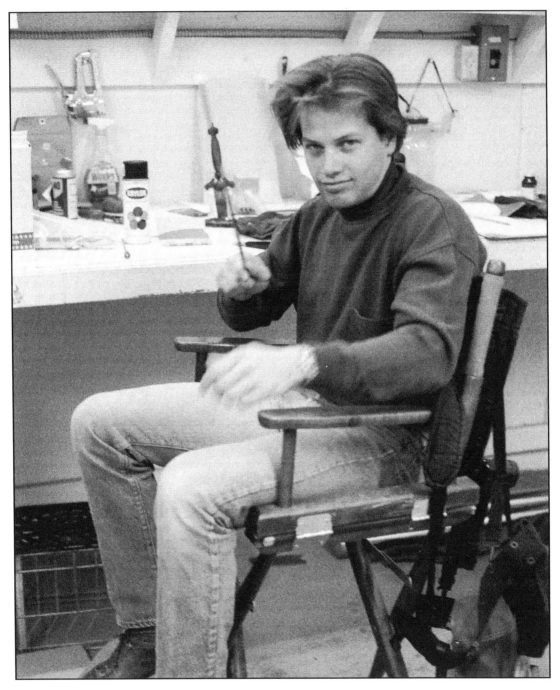

James LeGros before a scene.
(Photo courtesy Kristen Deem)

A lighthearted moment between takes.
(Photo courtesy Kristen Deem)

Between takes with the Tall Man.
(Photo courtesy Kristen Deem)

drill its victim per *Phantasm*, the upgraded sphere of *Phantasm II* first toys with its prey by slicing off the clergyman's ear. Coscarelli had originally written for the sphere to make a return trip and slice off Father Meyers' remaining ear before the kill-pass, but this was pared down. The task of removing Tigar's ear fell to makeup artist Robert Kurtzman under Mark Shostrom's supervision. Kurtzman would later reuse the same technique for the infamous ear-mutilation scene in *Reservoir Dogs*.

"We started by first taking small, detailed life casts of Ken's ears," Shostrom says. "Then we glued his ears flat to his head and did a second series of life casts of each ear - only now including a larger portion of his surrounding head area. The idea was to use the first casts to make perfect clay replicas of Ken's ears. These were placed onto plaster replicas of the larger versions with the glued-flat ears. To make this easier to understand, you must realize that whenever you have an effect where you have to remove a protruding body part like a nose or ear, you cannot actually take it away. Prosthetic makeup is an additive process. You have to create an illusion of something being removed. You hide or push down, glue down, the existing body part as best you can and go from there."

The effects crew ran into trouble, however, when it came time to remove Tigar's ear prosthetic on camera. The challenge was how to make Steve Patino's silver sphere fly past the actor's head in a perfectly straight line while directly in front of the camera. Throwing it would not produce the necessary precision and wire-propulsion would be visible at such close proximity. The solution, which came from Shostrom, was to utilize gravity by tilting the actor, camera and set 90 degrees clockwise. By dropping the ball straight down past a horizontal Tigar, the effects team achieved a straight line of flight.

"Sometimes on these seemingly complicated effects the simplest solution works the best," Shostrom says. "All Steve Patino had to do was drop the sphere and it would fall straight. The ear coming off was done just as Dick Smith had done in *Taxi Driver* for Robert DeNiro's bullet hit in the neck. Bob and I stuck the ear in place with gel blood, blended off the edge with makeup and pulled the ear off with a five pound fishing line

Robert Del Valle and Angus Scrimm on set.
(Photo courtesy Kristen Deem)

shots, Tigar simply held the ball in place as blood shot out from it. In *Phantasm*, this shot could only be filmed from certain angles with Ken Jones' hands firmly planted around the sphere lest the camera reveal the blood tubing. On *Phantasm II*, Patino improved the effect so that the tube could be better concealed within Tigar's wardrobe, allowing him to grip the sphere with only one hand. The tube therefore ran down his shirtsleeve, pants leg and across set to a fifty-five gallon drum of blood, nearly all of which was used that day.

"It was fun watching those scenes play out," Beauchamp says, "but you never think about what happens after they yell '*Cut*'. Then you've gotta clean it up! Everyone had to grab a mop at some point and pitch in. It was a huge mess."

"The blood you see coming from the priest's head [as opposed to the sphere] was actually squirted out from inside the ball," Patino assistant Steve Cotroneo says. "As soon as the fake plastic drill-bit hit, we would push a syringe to trigger the blood. On one take, we didn't push hard enough, and instead of squirting out, the blood just dripped out a hole in the sphere. Patino was bummed about that because you can actually see some of that take in the final version of the film. Then to make matters worse, <u>Fangoria</u> did a big article on *Phantasm II* and what photo did they run? A great big still grab from the movie showing the priest being drilled and the blood is just pouring from the ball. Patino was pissed! He had wanted it to look like the blood was coming from inside the priest's forehead."

SPACEGATE SHOWDOWN

By early February, the crew had moved on to the spacegate room set for part of the film's ending, an almost exact replica of its *Phantasm* forerunner, which had been unwittingly destroyed by Reggie in the initial film's climax. Amusingly, the Tall Man of *Phantasm II* has upgraded the room's security to include a high-tech lock requiring a sphere-key to open. Despite this safeguard, the heroes still manage to infiltrate his chamber. "The idea for that lock came from one of the casts we had done of the spheres," James Vale says. "We were sitting around the

- practically invisible on camera. There was a shot later where Ken turns and puts his hand to his head. I made sure Don shot that at only a 3/4 angle, which still worked. Any straight to face shots would have revealed the buildup on Ken's head."

The next day involved Tigar doing a scene to which few actors can lay claim. He was drilled by a silver sphere, the sanguinary baptism of the *Phantasm* franchise. "Shooting that moment was really one of the most interesting things I've ever done in my entire career," Tigar says. "The effects technology was not that advanced at that time and if it was that advanced, we certainly didn't have the money to do it. So to get that ball to hit me at the right moment, we had to try some interesting things. I remember that for one shot, I was in a corridor and they were actually throwing balls at me."

Father Meyers' drilling scene in *Phantasm II* was achieved in much the same way as the caretaker's drilling in the original film. For close-ups, a large rig was constructed with a sphere that featured a working drill bit. For medium and long

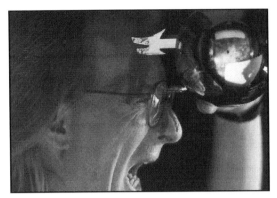

Mark Shostrom loses an argument with Steve Patino.
(Photo courtesy Mark Shostrom)

shop and Steve was looking at this inside-out cast and noticing that it's the perfect dimensions of a ball. So he goes, '*You know we could rig this up so that you have to insert a sphere-key to open the doorway.*' He pitched it to Don and he liked it and just like that, it became part of the movie."

In the film, the Tall Man appears suddenly just as Mike, Reggie and Liz begin to torch the spacegate. Tossing Reggie into the portal (filmed Monday, February 1), the mortician prepares to embalm Liz alive (filmed Friday, February 5). Mike saves Reggie and unleashes the sphere-key upon its creator just in time to save Liz. After a moment of yellow bloodshed, the Tall Man effortlessly crushes the offending sphere and tosses it aside (filmed Wednesday, February 3).

This scene marked the first time James LeGros and Angus Scrimm appear onscreen together in *Phantasm II*. It was only the second time Reggie Bannister and Scrimm appeared together. Spacegate room protocol on the sequel mirrored that of its predecessor. The pristine white floor was covered in protective cardboard between shots and crewmembers were required to wear hospital slippers over their footwear. The scene where Mike demonstrates the gate's pull to Liz reuses Paul Pepperman's mirror effect from the original film. Moments later, Mike unleashes one of the spheres upon its master, quipping, "Suck on this!" An unused alternate line would have had Mike say, "Let's play ball!"

"One gag I always liked was the sphere the Tall Man crushes, the one that drills him," Vale says. "That was a Mylar balloon, turned inside out, then wrapped around a sponge. They mixed in a great sound effect as he crushes the Mylar and then it cuts away to a piece of metal being thrown on the floor. It comes together great because I think the audience is fairly convinced he actually crushed a sphere."

After discarding the traitorous sphere, the Tall Man grabs Mike. Within moments a grotesque insect bursts from the mortician's forehead, recalling the finger bug from *Phantasm*. Don Coscarelli achieved this effect by alternating between Scrimm and an animatronic Tall Man created by Mark Shostrom's team. "I did not envy James LeGros in that scene," Shostrom says. "So much of it was him working with a rubber dummy right in his face while an insect crawls out of it covered in yellow blood, the recipe of which included smelly corn syrup and milk. Don shot that thing for hours. I know James had to be getting tired of it, but I think both he and the dummy look great in the scene."

"Angus was one of the nicest guys you'd ever want to meet," Vale says. "I remember one day going up to him and asking, '*So Angus, what's the deal with the Tall Man? Why doesn't he just kill them and get it over with?*' And staying perfectly in character, he answered, '*My boy, the Tall Man is... bored. He's bored. He's been doing the same job for so long. And here comes a*

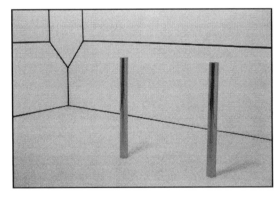

The upgraded spacegate room.
(Photo courtesy Kristen Deem)

boy who will play a fun game. And that's all it is to him, a game. He's having fun. He thinks they're playing with him. He doesn't think he's killing people. He doesn't get it. There's no life and death to him, really.' I don't know if he made that up on the spot or had already thought about it, but it sounded good to me!"

EMBALMING THE PHANTASM WAY

The second week of February saw filming continue on the mortuary prep room set with the Tall Man's messy demise. As Mike rips out the cranial insect attacking him, Liz buries a trocar deep into the mortician's back. Reggie stumbles to the embalming machine and engages it, injecting the Tall Man with hydrochloric acid that promptly dissolves his skin. Although most of the Tall Man's meltdown was captured during this time, Don Coscarelli re-staged the scene twice more for additional coverage, re-subjecting Angus Scrimm each time to Mark Shostrom's gruesome makeup. The Tall Man's hideous demise would feature prominently on the cover of Fangoria's seventy-fifth issue.

   "They all took great delight in disfiguring me," Scrimm told <u>Worlds of Horror</u> magazine while promoting the film. "Shostrom was the worst. In the course of doing the Tall Man's meltdown sequence, Mark applied to my face or body, in various combinations, jello, cream, apple juice, food coloring, mustard, yogurt, raw chicken skin and God knows what else. I think of him as the Julia Child of special-effects makeup. Every time I emerged from a session with Mark, I felt like I'd been in a junior-high-school cafeteria food fight. Most maddening of all, Mark has a habit of humming gleefully while he's working, and all the time wearing the most bedeviling grin."

   "That makeup was incredible," Troy Fromin says. "I remember one day Mark Shostrom sent me to the market to get him chicken pieces. He was using the skin and fat from them as part of Angus' makeup for the meltdown. He took the actual chicken, the good part, and threw it in the garbage. I couldn't even afford chicken to feed the crew with and here he

The Tall Man mourns a fallen comrade.
(Photo courtesy Troy Fromin)

was tossing it out! I said, '*Dude, that's good food! Why would you throw it away?*' and he goes, "*Well, if you want it, there it is. Eat it.*' I took one look at Angus' face and decided to leave it alone."

   Of all the makeups in the *Phantasm* franchise, the Tall Man's meltdown stands paramount as employing the most effects techniques. Not only did Shostrom - who co-directed the scene with Coscarelli - apply several makeup stages to Scrimm's face, his team also provided an eye-bursting Tall Man head, melt-away gelatin hands and a life-sized melted Tall Man dummy. This last prop was only utilized in a cut scene where a new Tall Man emerges from the spacegate to retrieve the previous Tall Man's melted corpse. This re-appearance was removed at the suggestion of Jim Jacks, who felt it lessened the shock value of Scrimm's surprise appearance in the final seconds of the sequel. The deleted scene, which was captured on Tuesday, February 2, would later be recycled to greater effect during the opening sequence of *Phantasm III*.

   On Wednesday, February 10, the company made its first pass at the finale of *Phantasm II*. Coscarelli's story concluded with the twist development of Alchemy changing into the Tall Man. The mortician attacks Reggie, then – in answer to Mike and Liz' assertion that it's only a dream – snaps "No, it's not!' Cut to black. Per the shooting script, Alchemy's

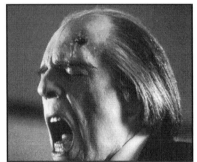

Top: Angus Scrimm grabs hold of James LeGros.
Left and *Right*: The makeup effects crew manipulates the Tall Man animatronic puppet.
(Photos courtesy Mark Shostrom)

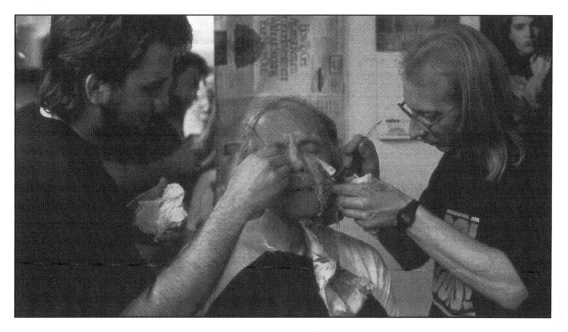

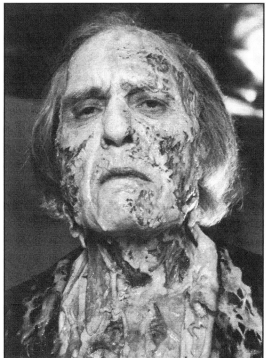 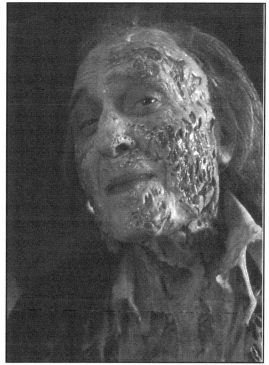

Top: Bob Kurtzman and Mark Shostrom removing Angus Scrimm's meltdown makeup.
Bottom Left and *Right*: Their gory, gruesome and grotesque makeup.

(Photos courtesy Mark Shostrom)

transformation was to be communicated to the audience empirically; one moment Samantha Phillips would be driving the hearse and the next moment Scrimm would be in her place. This twist reveal of the Tall Man led to much speculation about the Alchemy character throughout the film. Was she the Tall Man all along or had she been taken at some point? For Phillips, the answer is clear.

"Oh, I was definitely the Tall Man right from the start," Phillips says. "I played her that way so that there was always this sense of mischievousness about her. I was really green at the time so I didn't know how to subtly portray that. I might've overplayed it, honestly."

CREMATORIUM DAYS

Beginning in mid-February, the production shot in the southwest corner of the warehouse which was redressed by the art department to become three different sets. It is first seen as the abandoned Mariton County crematorium where the hideous Liz apparition appears, then as Perigord Mausoleum's basement where Reggie chainsaw duels a graver, and finally as Perigord's working crematory where Liz escapes live incineration. On the other side of the room's ceiling-level windows, which are viewable in all three scenes, stood the Perigord Mausoleum set. The first scene to utilize this area was the Mariton County scene, which began filming on Friday, February 12.

As previously mentioned, Coscarelli first envisioned the Mariton scene as a dream inside Mike's head. When it became part of the film's reality, the Liz creature shifted from nightmare vision to monstrous doppelgänger, one that Reggie swiftly torches. The scene utilizes makeup effects by Mark Shostrom's team and fire effects by Wayne Beauchamp. The creature emerging from Liz's back was an animatronic puppet mechanized by David Barton and puppeteered by Everett Burrell. A mold was fitted to Paula Irvine's back, from which the creature rose. A wigged mannequin was used for close-ups since the back-creature setup required Irvine to assume an

Creating the back-creature scene.
(Photos courtesy Mark Shostrom)

uncomfortable crouching position for grueling hours.

"This was something Pepperman pretty much handled all by himself on *Phantasm*," Roberto Quezada says. "By that I mean he built the effects, manipulated them just outside of the camera's view while they were being shot, and coordinated when everything was going to be completed, shot and so forth. As a producer I was lucky to have a good budget and phenomenal special effects guys like Mark Shostrom, Greg Nicotero and Robert Kurtzman on *Phantasm II* so that all I had to do was make sure everything worked on schedule and to show up the day we had to shoot. The main work was in the weeks and weeks of planning, and the meetings Don had with each of us describing what he wanted, the special effects guys coming up with other far out ideas for what Don would like, and them all figuring out how they would deliver what was planned and promised. As I said previously, Don is an extremely difficult taskmaster. An important part of his talent is his ability to motivate people to walk through fire to do the best they possibly can for his movies. I just needed to make sure they did it on time."

"We had a funny nickname for the creature that comes out of Paula's back in the movie," Shostrom says. "We called it Skylar Knobloch. Don't ask me how that came about, but during the 80's there were people in L.A. that collected movie props. They couldn't have a second piece generated from the same mold or a replica. It had to be the same one used in the movie. These rubber props just sit on a shelf and rot away because they're foam rubber so I sold Skylar to a fellow and that's the last I heard of him."

Several years later, Shostrom had a bizarre reunion with the prop during a visit to Planet Hollywood in Dallas, Texas. "I walk by one of the displays and see Skylar in all his glory with cables sticking out of him. And there's a photograph in the case of Kevin Yahger's giant Freddy snake from *A Nightmare on Elm Street 3*. Now Skylar was just a small prop that would fit on your arm, but the Freddy creature was three or four feet tall at the head. So I pulled the manager over and said, 'Excuse me, you've got this wrong,' and he had a really bad attitude about it. He said, 'Well, how the hell do you know?' and

Skylar Knobloch, a handsome devil.
(Photo courtesy Mark Shostrom)

I said, '*Because I made the Phantasm prop and my friend, Kevin, made the Freddy snake.*' You can clearly look at them and see that they were two different creatures. I just got kind of pissed off about it and my girlfriend convinced me to give up on trying to convince him and we just continued with lunch."

The warehouse was next converted from Mariton County's abandoned crematory into Perigord's functioning crematorium where Liz does battle with the henchman played by John Michael Stewart. Crewmembers kept careful watch over the oven as the wooden chamber was prone to catching fire. For the shot where Liz narrowly misses diving head first into the flames, Solly Marx delegated personnel on either side of the oven in case Irvine failed to bail out in time. Marx himself eventually crawled inside the furnace for a harrowing shot of the henchman's charred hand desperately slapping the glass.

"I think we had two days to shoot the stuff in the crematorium," Stewart says. "Paula was great in the scene

Above: Mark Anthony Major and John Michael Stewart.
Below: Ed Gale crawls across the rocky terrain.
(Henchmen photo courtesy Troy Fromin)
(Gale photo courtesy Mark Shostrom)

where we struggle with each other. I, however, was not great. I had a tooth let go in the middle of that and was in screaming, agonizing pain. I had to have an emergency root canal. I think we brought a dentist or someone to the set after hours just to get me some relief because I couldn't function. After we finished filming, I went to an actual dentist. All I can think about when I watch that stuff is how horrible I felt during it."

The crematory scene prior to Irvine and Stewart's struggle together contains a nod by Coscarelli to Sam Raimi. The *Evil Dead* director had originally asked to be sphere-drilled in the sequel, a request Coscarelli was unable to accommodate. As consolation, he filmed a scene of Stewart's mortician pouring ashes into a bag labeled with Raimi's name, ashes also being a clever reference to Bruce Campbell's most famous role.

"I wasn't there when Sam Raimi visited us on set," Troy Fromin says. "I was there, however, when Rob Tapert, the producer of the Evil Dead films, stopped by the Chatsworth set. He and Don were apparently friends. Rob and I got to talking

on set and we hit it off. In fact, he immediately gave me a small part to play in Sam's *Darkman* because I'm also an actor. If you watch the beginning of *Darkman*, I'm one of the tough guys on the dock in San Pedro. I remember Sam Raimi having all of us lined up on set and asking us as characters, '*What's on your mind in this scene?*' I answered back that I would like to have a part in *Evil Dead III*. He said, '*No, no. Don't focus on that movie. Focus on this movie.*'

The final redressing for this warehouse area was a transformation into the basement of Perigord Mausoleum for Reggie's infamous chainsaw duel. The scene required that Reggie Bannister choreograph all the action before filming with Bobby Brown, the stuntman under the graver mask. Stewart praises Bannister for acting out the entire fight, except for the shot where his character jumps over a chainsaw blade that narrowly misses his crotch.

"Reggie Bannister is one of the nicest guys," Troy Fromin says. "I kind of dreaded going to locations that were an hour and a half from my home because I'd have to drive home at night and come right back in the morning. It was a lot of driving on very little sleep. For the locations that were near Reggie's house, he would let me crash on his couch, which I always appreciated. On another night, I wound up sleeping on the floor of the office at the cemetery we shot at. I was probably too tired to care where I was laying my head."

"As filming started, workdays stretched from twelve to sixteen, even eighteen, hours during some brutally cold, wet nights," Deem says. "The Valley roads became so flooded from torrential rains that I could barely navigate my old Pinto back over the hill towards home. Angus and his family became my guardian angels, often allowing me to collapse for evenings in their home. Hot soup, a warm blanket, Angus' wonderful humor, and a good night's rest; those were some of my sweetest memories. Their kindness and caring truly kept me going."

Stories circulated by Universal at the time of *Phantasm II*'s release told of one exhausted crewmember who didn't even try to make it home, be it his own or someone else's. Production resumed the following morning to find him asleep in a prop coffin, earning him a reputation as a vampire.

RETURN TO THE RED PLANET

Tuesday, February 23 saw *Phantasm* return to the Santa Fe dam in Irwindale, which would again serve as the Tall Man's mysterious Red Planet. The sequel's sole excursion here provided audiences with a fleeting glimpse of the alien landscape as yet another hapless hero, this time Reggie, accidentally falls through the spacegate and then needs rescue. Strangely, Don Coscarelli's script provides no explanation why the portal has relocated from high in the sky per the first film to a fixed point on the ground in *Phantasm II*. As Reggie struggles on the planet's rocky terrain, a mangled dwarf played by Ed Gale emerges from a slime-filled barrel and crawls menacingly towards him.

"That design was based on the Bog People of Europe," Mark Shostrom says. "I had seen one at the British Museum a few months prior. He'd just been discovered two years before and was named Lindow Man. I recall studying him for hours at the museum and I suppose I must have wondered if I could ever use his inspiration for a film character. Lo and behold, when Don told me canister dwarf was, in effect, pickled, I showed him my book on Lindow Man and said, '*I want to do something like this*.' I really got into the sculpting process, making areas of his face smashed and flattened but with skin texture, as if his head had been leaning on the side of the canister for a long time. I painted him by hand in the same way, lots of detail, using the British Museum book as my guide."

Restrictive under any conditions, the discomfort of the dwarf suit was compounded by the location. "In my twenty years in the business," Gale says, "I've learned that location people are basically evil. They always pick the worst location for the actors. If I'm shirtless, we'll be shooting in Alaska. If I'm in a huge suit, it'll be in Arizona. But in the end, it always looks beautiful and I suppose that's why they're location people. *Phantasm II* was hell. They had to carry me around because I couldn't walk in the costume across the jagged rocks. Once I was inside the barrel waiting for the scene to start, I would hear things like this: 'Wait, this is wrong. Fix the lighting. Wait for the airplane to pass over. Non-actors please clear the set. Someone fix that shadow.' All the while I'm baking in that dark canister. A good way to lose weight."

The canister dwarf-suit fared even worse in the sun than its inhabitant, becoming stuck to an AD chair and remaining attached to the seatback even as the actor walked away. The time lapse photography that would become the Red Planet sky was filmed on March 31.

"I would've liked to have seen more of the Tall Man's planet," Troy Fromin says. "I said to Don one day, 'Why can't they just go there and see more of what goes on?' and he tells me, 'They wouldn't be able to breathe there, Troy.' I didn't really buy that so I told him, 'You're the genius, you can make it happen. Just write some explanation into the movie.' He heard that and just sort of walked away. I guess it would've been too expensive with all the effects to show a lot of the Tall Man's planet, but it would've been nice."

BURNT OFFERINGS

The first week of March saw filming return to Valencia in an attempt to kill one of *Phantasm*'s most beloved stars, the Hemi 'Cuda. A nasty brush with the Tall Man's hearse finds Reggie trapped inside the wrecked muscle car. A stream of gasoline courses downhill toward flaming debris, which is sure to ignite back towards the 'Cuda. Mike has mere seconds to rescue Reg from the car before it explodes. One of the collaborators behind this dangerous sequence was Wayne Beauchamp who recalls its fiery ending with a laugh, "It looked like a tanker truck going off, didn't it? That fireball shot up fifty feet into the air! It was incredible! Coscarelli always did like over the top explosions."

The scene was meticulously choreographed so that James LeGros and Reggie Bannister would appear perilously close to the flaming gasoline trail and subsequent explosion. Somewhat nervously, both actors agreed to perform the stunt

Reggie Bannister and James LeGros on the Motel set. Notice the gravel at bottom left.
(Photo courtesy Troy Fromin)

The hero 'Cuda and its wrecked sibling alongside it.
(Photo courtesy Kristen Deem)

themselves rather than use doubles. "I love it when Mike is running up the hill to the car and there's a flaming tailpipe embedded in a tree, like the undercarriage had been ripped out," Beauchamp says. "That whole scene worked really well. These days, you'd probably use a special camera lens to compress the shot and spare your actors the danger, but back then James and Reggie were literally running down the hill right beside the flame as it shot past them back uphill to the car."

"All these types of memories end similarly," Roberto Quezada says. "With a bunch of idiots frantically trying to undo some line of dominoes heading towards disaster. Half the crew is frantically trying to blow out the fire at the bottom of the hill, while the other half is clawing at dirt with their fingernails to try to divert the course of a flammable river that is also invisible because it's so dark. Did I mention this is a night scene?"

Years later, television horror host Joe Bob Briggs would lament the destroyed car while hosting a TBS presentation of *Phantasm II*. "This movie contains the most terrifying scene I've ever witnessed. A perfectly decent 1971 Hemi 'Cuda flips over, lands on its roof and bursts into flame. I cried for two hours. It's amazing what they'll let these people do for the sake of a goldang movie. A Hemi 'Cuda, greatest muscle car ever made! So many horses you couldn't get insurance for

it and they use it for a stupid movie stunt. That's like cutting up the Mona Lisa, you know? Or destroying the original Poker Playing Dogs."

A short while later, the production executed a second fire effect with Reggie climactically setting fire to Perigord Mausoleum. Rather than burn down Philip Duffin's Chatsworth warehouse set, the production team recreated the mortuary prep room in a vacant parking lot, which accounts for its sudden asphalt flooring. This also accounts for what is obviously accelerant fluid on the walls and cabinets before Reggie torches them with the flamethrower. "I think we knew early on that we couldn't do that scene inside or else we'd be burning down the warehouse," Robert Del Valle says. "Giant flames inside, you can see how that's a bad idea. I think we had the fire department come by to supervise it. As I remember, it went down great."

The construction of the flamethrower prop was also entrusted to Beauchamp, who describes it as a self-lighting BernzOmatic torch equipped with three butane tanks strapped together. The giant flames seen in the film came not from the butane tanks, but from a gas line that ran from the prop down Bannister's shirtsleeve, pants leg and across the room to a propane tank. "The same kinds of torches are used

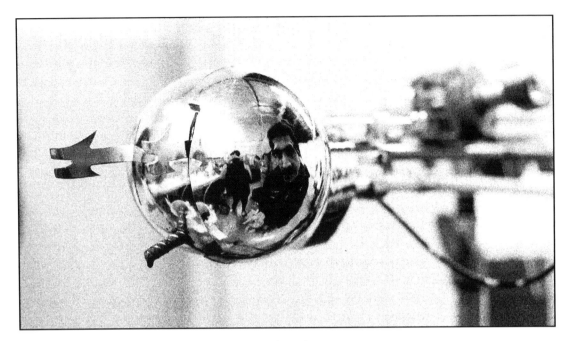

Drip... drip... drip...
(Photo courtesy Kristen Deem)

in agriculture for bush burning," Beauchamp says. "Ordinarily, we'd have a stunt person doing that but Reggie was great about doing it himself. We made extra sure that our propane lines were secure because the last thing we wanted was for a line to break in his pants and cook him from the waist down."

The burning mausoleum set wasn't the only one created on top of a parking lot. The production built another outdoor set for the brief scene in which Mike and Reggie stop at a motel for rest. The motel set, while sporting a breathtaking mountain view, was actually only two walls.

FLIGHT OF THE SILVER SPHERE

There was perhaps no sphere effect more challenging on *Phantasm II* than that of flight, which begged for an upgrade keeping with the orb's other enhancements. To achieve a more

impressive aerial sphere, Don Coscarelli turned to Dream Quest Images for the company's unique experience in motion control photography. The FX team sought to mobilize a lightweight camera around a stationary sphere rather than the other way around, the same technique that made spaceships fly in the original *Star Wars* trilogy. This allowed the ball to remain in focus, closer to camera, and helped better prevent both equipment and crew from being reflected in its chrome surface.

"We were called in for the trickier sphere shots," effectsman James Balsam says. "Some things you just can't do practically on set. Flying around a corner in close-up while rotating is one of those times, one of several times, where fishing wire just doesn't get the job done."

Dream Quest began motion control filming of the spheres in early March. Numerous takes were needed to comprise any given shot in the film, each one capturing a different element. One pass might only record the sphere's outline while another would capture the protruding blades. At least one pass would be needed for the ball itself and another for moving images reflected on its chrome surface. Further passes would include shadows, blood splatter and other moving parts such as drill bits.

"Being that it was a precision process, sphere photography took a long time," Balsam says. "In order to get the right depth of field, we sometimes had to use long exposure times. It might take you an hour to capture a pass of something that's only on-screen for a few seconds. It's a slow process for sure, especially when you consider that a single composite shot might consist of five or six motion control passes."

Although such optical effects weren't completed until late in production (the film's workprint and a rough trailer edit borrowed *Phantasm* sphere footage), they were much touted upon completion by Universal in promotional materials as an impressive display of the film's effects prowess. "Motion control has one big advantage when it comes to shooting any object," Balsam says. "It's real. There are very subtle visual cues that real things have that digital simulations don't get right. They're very, very, very good at the digital stuff, but your brain is usually able to pick out the little nuances a real object has. Even now, shooting a model still looks better than digital. It would certainly be easier to make the chrome spheres digitally today but they'll never look as good as the real thing and that's what we gave people on *Phantasm II*."

BURROWING

March 1988 concluded with the sphere burrowing of Mark Anthony Major's mortician. The scene continues the orb's bad habit of turning against its own teammates – the Tall Man and *Phantasm*'s caretaker having already faced its directionally challenged fury. Mark Shostrom suggested to Don Coscarelli that the sphere enter through the mortician's back, burst from his head and then lodge itself in the ceiling, trailing brains behind it. Dreading how the MPAA would judge such a spectacle, Coscarelli instead had the ball ensnare itself while attempting to exit the mortician's mouth. In a line filmed but

later deleted, Mike observes, "It doesn't stop until it tastes blood." Major's mouth appliance was sculpted by Robert Kurtzman and applied by Everett Burrell under Shostrom's supervision. The casket showroom where the scene unfolds was previously young Mike's 1978 bedroom.

"That was my first time having a heavy-duty head mold taken of my head," Major says. "That's an experience I've had four or five times since, nothing I ever look forward to. Regarding the makeup, as long as I was able to see and talk through it, I was fine. The sphere that covered my mouth was removable so that I was even able to eat with the appliance on. I usually had to eat lunch alone, however, because no one wanted to sit across the table from me. Something about seeing me stuff food into a gaping bloody face wound turned them off. I can't imagine why…"

Strangely, neither of the Tall Man's silent henchmen in *Phantasm II* appear onscreen with their master, unlike *Phantasm*'s caretaker. They do appear to take fashion tips from him, however. "The no dialogue thing didn't bother me," Major says. "It sort of made sense for John Stewart and me to be silent. Our relationship to the Tall Man was hinted at, a

Mark Anthony Major today next to his Borg character.
(Photo courtesy Kristen Deem)

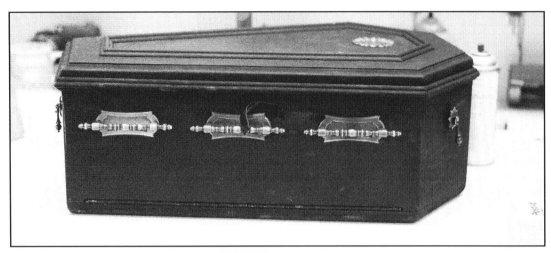

Above and *Left*: Some boxes are best left unopened...
(Photos courtesy Kristen Deem)

subtle suggestion of what was there, maybe even telepathic. Most people forget that we never appear together with the Tall Man. My role is very isolated. It's almost as if I'm in my own film within a bigger film. It was actually much to my regret that none of my scenes were with Angus. It would've been nice if he could've just pointed for John and me to go do something."

"Mark Anthony Major really went all out filming the sphere sequences," Kristen Deem says. "He was so intense, so jazzed! The physicality of it made my jaw drop! He would throw himself at the corner wall and then slam himself around in circles. The guy must've gone home with dozens of bruises but he was so into that character and the opportunity to be working on a *Phantasm* film! I really admired him. Part of his zeal was that he was promised a SAG card at the end of production. Mark sure earned it!"

"There was one sphere I really liked and wanted badly to be in the movie," James Vale says. "It actually started out as a mistake. We were doing a liquid casting of the sphere and the resin formed down at the bottom of the ball. So when you roll it along the floor, it wobbles around uneven like it's drunk. Remember the sphere that goes through the mortician's back and gets stuck trying to come out his mouth? Steve Patino and I originally wanted it to come out all the way and roll around on the floor drunk with blood. They didn't go for it, but we thought it was a great idea!"

April brought a transition to post-production with a strong focus on editing. A skeleton crew remained in Chatsworth to capture various "pick-up" shots. On Thursday, April 7, this entailed dollying the camera past the Tall Man to a miniature coffin from which several spheres emerge, a product of Patino's creative involvement. Later that day, it meant having grip and future cinematographer Shane Hurlbut pitch two dozen spheres down a mausoleum corridor, each one shattering upon impact. This attempt to recreate the *Phantasm* sphere-in-flight effect was for naught, however. Such shots would eventually go to Dream Quest.

"Think back to the little coffin the spheres were kept

in," Vale says. "Steve and I went around town trying to find a child's coffin to use in that scene, which we never found. Oh, the reactions we got from the different mortuaries! We found out that children's coffins are mostly made out of cardboard, not like an ordinary adult coffin. We told this one funeral director what we wanted to do with the coffin, that we wanted to take it apart and put silver spheres in it and have them come flying out to attack people and he freaked out. He totally lost it and kicked us out of his place, yelling at us the whole time. I guess he just didn't understand what *Phantasm* was all about. Someone finally just built the smaller coffin from scratch."

MUSIC

In addition to pick-up shots and editing, April saw Fred Myrow and Christopher Stone hard at work on the film's score, which received an overhaul to match the sequel's faster pace. Stone's music contributions were in addition to his sound design duties, which again included the dwarves, spheres and spacegate.

"It all goes back to that great theme Fred made for the first film," Stone says. "It's a versatile piece of music, which made it really easy for me to explore different renditions of it. For the sequels, we were able to include tiny pieces of Fred's theme amid more atmospheric sounding music and still have the audience recognize it. On a musical level, we worked like producer-artists back and forth. Since my keyboard chops were a little ahead of his, I spent most of the time playing and Fred spent most of the time producing."

"Don is much more sensitive to music than most film directors," Fred Myrow told GASP Magazine. "Especially if you've seen *Phantasm II* or *III*, it's almost wall-to-wall music and the music is literally part of the way the film works. Some directors do a film that is basically completed and the music just adds a few elements but Don is there the whole time. He really cares and has a great sensitivity to music. He's probably one of the most exacting directors to work for because every split-second of that thing has to make him happy. So Don is very much involved, not in the writing of the music, but certainly in

supervising the way it comes out and that's one of the reasons I've tended to stay with him. He's really happy when you nail it."

"I don't think having a bigger budget affected us much on the second film," Stone says. "Certainly it made our lives easier, but it didn't change the tone of the music which we had already established as being electronic in nature on the first film. I think it was important for us to continue that and to continue blending the music with Don's style of direction. Whether we had a million dollar music budget or only a tiny fraction of that, it wouldn't have made a difference artistically."

EARLY SCREENINGS

The film was first previewed before a test audience on Monday, May 2. With the exception of Angus Scrimm, cast and crew were not allowed to attend, though an enthusiastic Kristen Deem and Guy Thorpe did buy their way into the screening by offering ticketholders $20 for their seats.

"Kristen and I were lucky enough to get into the first test screening," Thorpe says. "It was up at Universal's eighteen theater complex. We barely got in because it was a limited capacity deal where they invited more people than they had seats for. I guess someone tipped us off that they were having it there. It was fun getting to see the full cut of the film before Don started taking things out. I remember it had the longer version of Father Meyers' drilling and the dream sex scene was intact. It was basically the workprint version of the film."

"I remember us standing gleefully in line, then seeing Don, Dac, Angus, Betsy and Roberto off to the side, and I remember Don's jaw falling," Deem grins. "He looked so flabbergasted! That screening was such a trip for us. To be there, seeing the first rough cut, the very first audience reactions. And the theatre was packed! We loved it! Of course, there were some minor problems with the film, mainly with pacing in the middle, and we were more than honest about writing these down at the end. They had handed out these cards so that you could write down what you thought of the film. I looked over my shoulder and there was Don in the seat right behind

"I feel I must have done something right if I grossed out the MPAA. I have no love for that organization."

Mark Anthony Major on the ratings situation.

us reading everything we were writing and looking none too pleased! It was hysterical!"

"During the research screenings, the audiences would go absolutely crazy when the sphere burrowing scene came up with the mortician," Jim Jacks says. "This was a film that played well to its audience and we felt that if we could get people into the theater they would like it. We screened the film for Universal executives. They burst out laughing during the sphere scenes. They just weren't used to seeing anything gory like that. When the film was over, they went, '*Oh my God. This is one of OUR movies?*' You have to understand that Universal wasn't making those kinds of films back then."

In preparation for promoting the film, Universal's marketing department screened *Phantasm II* again on Sunday, May 15 and immediately sought to include the climactic "It's only a dream," "No, it's not," exchange in trailers and television spots. Rather than spoil the film's conclusion in advertising, Coscarelli re-filmed the exchange on Wednesday, May 18 exclusively for the preview, this time using the mausoleum set instead of the Tall Man's hearse. The film's trailer began by defining the word phantasm, seemingly in answer to the original film's trailer, which repeatedly asked the viewer, "What is *Phantasm*?"

As May came to a close, Scrimm, Tigar and Phillips were busy recording dialogue in ADR sessions at Disney Studios. Tigar and Scrimm were mainly recording painful screams for their death scenes, while Phillips had to re-record entire scenes. "That's the only thing that bums me out about *Phantasm II*," Phillips says. "A chunk of my audio somehow got destroyed and I had to loop a large part of my role. I had never

looped anything before so I was trying to match my mouth and say the same words again the same way. I can watch the movie and tell exactly where it's all looped. It's annoying. It feels like it's not me speaking."

THE MPAA STRIKES BACK

On Tuesday, May 31, news hit that the MPAA had reached a verdict on *Phantasm II*. Deeming it too gory for an R-rating, it was given the dreaded "X" much to the dismay of all involved. "Studios won't release a movie with an X-rating," Jacks says. "We faced a big fight trying to get that rating down to an R. We eventually got Tom Pollack, the head of the studio, involved and he hadn't even seen the film at that point. He didn't actually see it until the research screening and when the scene came up where the sphere burrows through the guy's body, he turned to me and said, '*You got me to fight to get an R-rating for this?! Even I would've given this an X if I were the MPAA!*' But he was very pleased with how the film turned out. We all were."

"As you probably know, they had originally given Phantasm an X-rating because of the scene where the caretaker is struck by the silver ball," Angus Scrimm says. "And Charles Champlin had a heart-to-heart talk with the head of the thing and said, you know, this is really funny, the audiences laugh at the end of this scene. So they left it in, and they evidently got criticism from some of the parent groups, so they were all prepared with their scissors when *Phantasm II* came out, and they were vindictive about it. Obviously many much more gruesome and cinematically vivid things had been allowed to

Phantasm's creator and his star.
(Photo courtesy Kristen Deem)

go through. But they were determined to get their own way, and they demanded cuts."

"It was my understanding that the film had five strikes against it to earn it an X-rating," Mark Anthony Major says. "Three of those were for my scenes. I feel I must have done something right if I grossed out the MPAA. I have no love for that organization."

The ratings board was troubled not by the sphere burrowing or even by the live embalming of the Tall Man with acid, but mainly by the sphere drilling of Father Meyers. Coscarelli in turn argued that he timed the scene to match the drilling of the caretaker in the original *Phantasm* (which the MPAA had originally allowed under an R-rating). They responded that rating standards had become "more stringent" since then and that it would not be permitted this time around. The battle continued. The actor on the business end of the sphere sided with Coscarelli and Universal, not wishing the censorship of his character's grisly demise.

"I don't believe in censorship," Kenneth Tigar says. "I don't believe in the ratings board. I believe that the entire country is crazy when we try and dictate what people should see and what they should not see. I remember when I was a kid, I used to love horror movies. I went to them all the time. Now that I'm older, they scare me and I don't go! So if I don't go, I don't go, and that's my form of censorship. That doesn't mean that the artistic form shouldn't exist for those who love it."

"I really didn't expect that scene to be a problem on *Phantasm II*," Daryn Okada says. "I was looking at it as belonging in the world of a horror movie, like it fit in perfectly there. When they told us we had to cut it, I took it as sort of a backhanded compliment as if we'd done this scene really well, maybe too well. It apparently came off so well that it affected the MPAA to the point where they couldn't give us an R-rating for it. If it was totally hokey, I imagine it would've been fine with them."

FACE-OFF

On Thursday, June 2, Don Coscarelli, Angus Scrimm, Mark Shostrom and Bob Kurtzman convened a meeting at Shostrom's studio to explore possibilities for modifying *Phantasm II*'s conclusion. The goal was now to show Alchemy's transformation into the Tall Man onscreen rather than to only suggest it per the script. More filming was scheduled the following Monday, June 6, so that a revised ending could immediately be cut into the film for Universal to witness the following day.

"We came up with Angus peeling away Sam's rotted face to reveal his own," Shostrom says. "I very quickly did a painted mask of Sam from a life cast we had, wigged it and showed it to Don and he approved. Keep in mind, however, that Angus has quite a large head and Sam has a very petite head. So you're going to run into trouble when you try and fit a mask of Alchemy over the Tall Man. There's just no way to make that look right. The reverse would probably be okay, Angus' face over Sam's, but that didn't fit the scene. We shot it many ways and many times, but it never worked out."

In a journal dated 6/6/88, Kristen Deem wrote:

The divider window slammed down (John Duffin was working this) and Angus snapped, "No, it's not!" In the meantime, Mark Shostrom, also in the driver's seat, let the half-face Kemy appliance slide off of Angus' face to reveal a fully transformed Tall Man. There was a gooey ooze/slime all over the left side of Angus' face and hair. It didn't look at all convincing. Mark Major and I both agreed it looked more like the Tall Man had scalped Kemy and was holding the scalp up, then letting it fall off, revealing a seemingly very sweaty left side of his face. [...] Pizza arrived and the crew took a break from filming. It was amusing to see Angus eat his pizza because the slime was still oozing down his face and dripping all over his jacket and food. It was hideous to watch!

"That day went on for hours and hours," Shostrom recalls. "I think we wrapped after midnight. The little divider between the rear and cab of the hearse kept falling at an angle and sticking to the point of frustration for all. Hearing Angus say 'No, it's not!' repeatedly got my friend Greg and I chiming in with 'No, it's snot!' each time the divider screwed up. Angus and the crew found this quite amusing and giggles all around made shooting more difficult."

As the shoot continued into the night, it became apparent that the Alchemy gag wasn't going to pay off as hoped. A decision was made to make one final pass at the original ending. Footage captured in early February included the Tall Man's reveal and final line from a fixed point in the back of the hearse. This new take would find the camera dynamically moving past Mike and Liz to the Tall Man's reveal, his final line spoken in close-up. It was a vast improvement.

As originally scripted, the Tall Man's "No, it's not!" was to follow with a hard cut to black. This ending was then expanded with a shot of dwarves pulling Mike and Liz backward through a hearse window, further likening the sequel to its predecessor. This idea was suggested to Coscarelli by Jim Jacks who felt the movie needed one final scare following the Tall Man's surprise reveal. Among the ravenous dwarves was stuntwoman Lori Lynn Ross, who had doubled young Michael Pearson in the film's opening flashback.

PRODUCTION'S END

On Wednesday, June 10, Angus Scrimm received an afternoon call requesting that he be on the *Phantasm II* set within an hour. With the release date less than a month away, the battle with the MPAA had to be conceded and the sphere-drilling scene altered. The only way Coscarelli could maintain the suspense while trimming the gore was to insert reaction shots of Liz and the Tall Man. This reveal finally indicated that the mortician was responsible for and enjoying the gory spectacle. Scrimm performed several reactions that ranged from straight-faced to malicious enjoyment, though he refused a request that the Tall Man laugh while observing the drilling.

"I am a firm believer in the need of an independent movie censorship board to moderate the worst excesses of unrestraint in pursuit of the shock dollar," Scrimm says. "I just don't like it when they meddle with my films."

Post-production continued until June 21 when the final piece fell into place with Scrimm's additional dialogue

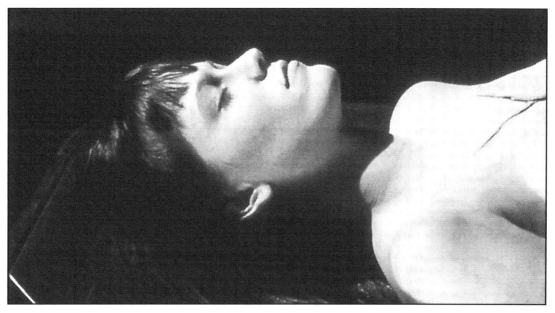

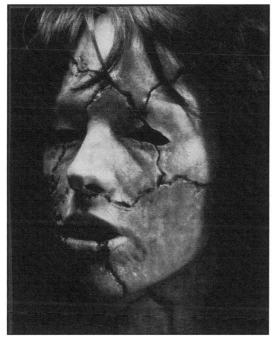

Top: Samantha Phillips sporting an autopsy "Y-incision" makeup.
Bottom Left: The nixed breakaway Alchemy mask.
Bottom Right: Angus Scrimm with Alchemy-hair-pull makeup in the hearse.
(Alchemy Photos courtesy Mark Shostrom)
(Scrimm photo courtesy Kristen Deem)

Press screening ticket at Universal Studios.

recording at Disney Studios. *Phantasm II* was now officially complete. Two days later, Scrimm would tape host segments as the Tall Man for Channel 5's July 2 broadcast of *Phantasm* to promote the upcoming sequel.

CAST & CREW IMPRESSIONS

On Wednesday, July 6, *Phantasm II* was previewed for cast, crew and studio executives at the Alfred Hitchcock Theater on the Universal lot. For most who attended the three screenings that day, it would be their first viewing of the finished film.

On 7/6/1988, Kristen Deem wrote:

> I watched all the arriving guests and made a great effort to greet everyone with whom I was familiar. Most of the film's actors showed up: Ruben, Ed Gale, Mark Anthony Major, Reggie (with his wife, Gayle, and his agent, Terrance Hines), Paula, James, Angus and Samantha. Kathy Lester from the original *Phantasm* was even there, dressed in a deep purple silk blouse and a black skirt. I watched Angus greet Kathy with a warm embrace. There was a fondness in his expression

as though she was a much needed relief and reminder of his past associations. [...] At the conclusion of the film, as my name appeared on screen during the closing credits, Angus made an obvious effort to turn around in his seat and quietly applaud me. James did also and then leaned back and gave me a helluva warm, strong handshake! I felt a great surge of relief. "Thank you for the support, fellows," I thought gratefully. I quietly congratulated them also and watched as James' father proudly gave his son a huge hug.

"I thought it was fantastic, that we'd really done justice to the original *Phantasm*," Mark Shostrom says. "I think I first saw our film at a special screening Universal held. It was during the daytime and I can remember Sam Raimi being there. In fact, he sat next to me and I remember him laughing out loud when he saw where Don had put his name on a bag of ashes.

"My initial reaction to the movie was absolute horror," Kenneth Tigar says. "Not because of the movie, but because I can't stand watching myself! When I watch myself, it makes me go crazy. So I don't think I have an objective view of the movie, though looking at it now, it's a much better picture than I remembered it being. When I did it, I thought of it as a B-movie at best but it's really held up over time as something quite good. I'm flattered for the opportunity to still be talking about it twenty years after the fact."

"I was a little disappointed by how much footage didn't make the film," Andrew Reeder says. "I personally know that Don left a lot on the cutting room floor. The first cut of *Phantasm II* was considerably longer than what we have now. I thought there were some good scenes, some dream material that really tied it all together, that didn't make the cut. Of course I really liked the movie overall. It was fun to make and fun to watch. I just wish we had been able to get more of it in there."

"It was so weird seeing the movie," Samantha Phillips says. "I didn't understand it when I read it. I didn't understand it when I filmed it. And I didn't understand it when I saw it. In fact, I still don't understand it. But people really seem to love it. I still get fan letters to this day from people for that film. There's a whole subculture of people that love those movies."

Tall Man about town.
(Photo courtesy Kristen Deem)

WORLD PREMIERE

On Thursday, July 7, Universal Studios and radio station KCAL held *Phantasm II*'s world premiere at the historic Pacific Theater in Los Angeles. Attendees included Don, Dac and Kate Coscarelli, Samantha Phillips, Guy Thorpe and Angus Scrimm in full Tall Man costume and makeup. In costume, the actor greeted the gathering – and very excited – crowd outside. As the Tall Man, Scrimm hosted a hearse-stuffing contest on a red carpet decorated with dozens of posters. Forty-seven fans proceeded to cram into the funeral coach, assisted by Scrimm. News reports at the time erroneously claimed the event as a Guinness World Record.

Scrimm spoke to the press from inside the hearse, switching between his own identity and that of the Tall Man. When asked by Movie Time's Christopher Chisholm if he was

Angus Scrimm, the Tall Man replied, "You're not confusing me with that pallid, nondescript, perfunctory actor! He's merely the medium through which I manifest myself!" Moments later, the Tall Man angrily cut in, "Down, hambone! This is *my* evening and *my* performance!" Later in the interview, Scrimm came to the defense of his other half: "He's a sweet, loving man, a charming man, who is here to obtain dead bodies, however he may, to take back to his planet to use as slaves. Now there are some here who would find in that something to object, but he's only doing his job."

"It was nothing short of awesome," Thorpe remarks. "It was an event like the big movie premieres of the old days. KCAL was there to host it and Angus mingled with fans as the Tall Man. They had a big Velcro poster out front and anyone who could land a ping-pong sphere on the Tall Man's face won a *Phantasm II* T-shirt. It was a blast! After the festivities outside, we all piled into the theater and watched the movie in a packed house. Let me tell you, they all loved it – every single person in that theater!"

"I'll never forget seeing it for the first time that day," Phillips says. "At this point, I was dating Robert Carradine from *Revenge of the Nerds*. He came with his twelve-year-old daughter as my guests. As I'm sitting there in the theater for the big premiere for the first movie I've ever done, it comes to the embalming room scene and there's the overhead shot of my entire body naked, crotch hair and all. I scream out loud, '*Oh my God!*' and I could hear people around me laughing because my voice is very recognizable. I don't know if I ever saw Don after that, but I know that he probably didn't want to see me because I was very specific about not showing crotch hair and there it was. I wasn't nearly as comfortable with my body then as I became shortly after that."

PHANTASM II RELEASED

On Friday, July 8, *Phantasm II* opened on 1,227 theater screens against sequels to *Short Circuit*, *Crocodile Dundee* and *Arthur*, all of which would sadly best it (*Who Framed Roger Rabbit* would ultimately win the weekend). The horror sequel would open in ninth place at the box office and vanish from the top ten by the following weekend, an even worse debut than the

Phantasm II - not the only sequel the summer of 1988.

franchise-ending *Poltergeist III* had recently suffered. Although it turned a modest profit, Don Coscarelli's follow-up was seen as an underperformer by the studio. The middling box office take might have stung less had the reviews been not quite so bad.

On 7/8/1988, Kristen Deem wrote:

Seven years ago today, I met Angus for the first time over lunch at the Ambassador Hotel. Rather fittingly, today was also the opening day for Phantasm II. The big day. Angus phoned while I was asleep to tell me that the photo I'd taken of him (used in Universal's press kit) was now being used in today's issue of the New York Times. At 12:30 PM, the phone rang again. Sure enough, it was Angus. He was phoning to thank me for the roses. The flowers had just arrived a few minutes before. He was really grateful – particularly about my praise for his work on P2. He sounded really modest as he half-joked, "That's a nice compliment coming from a New York Times photographer." He wanted to discuss today's newspaper articles regarding Phantasm II. He and Don were quite upset about the review Variety had done. Don had warned Angus not to read it. Of course, this had only piqued his curiosity. Angus immediately went out to get a copy.

Variety's review, which called the film "utterly unredeeming," would be the first of many blistering reviews. There was perhaps none more scathing, however, than that of Gene Siskel and Roger Ebert. Siskel began his assessment by ranking *Phantasm II* as "one of the worst movies of all time" while dismissing the original as "disgusting but popular." Ebert charged that Coscarelli had been "too lazy to write characters or a plot" and wrote the film off as "an exercise in the ego of special effects people." He would later include the film in his review compilation book I Hated, Hated, Hated This Movie.

"Siskel and Ebert almost seemed angry at the film," Mark Anthony Major says. "They gave it two thumbs down and what clip did they show on *At the Movies*? The scene where I chop off my hand! That made me laugh and still does. After a certain point, you just have to shrug off bad reviews like that.

When they're that awful, they almost become better publicity for the film than if they were to have done a good review. I never let the bad reviews bother me. Either you get this film or you don't, and those guys clearly didn't. Fortunately, there's been plenty of people throughout the years who do get this film."

The film was most reviled for the story which led The San Francisco Chronicle to title their review "*Phantasm Sequel – Brainless.*" Another headline by The Orange County Register read, "Including a Storyline is the Death of *Phantasm II*" while The Seattle Times' review joked that "*Phantasm II* Buries Its Plot." The denouncement printed in The Watertown Daily Times charged in bold letters, "Sequel Copies *Phantasm,*" and began its stinging assessment with "If you saw *Phantasm,* you've seen *Phantasm II*." Not unexpectedly, the United States Conference of Catholic Bishops once again condemned the series, calling *Phantasm II* "morally reprehensible" and without any "redeeming qualities."

One of the kinder reviews came from The Chicago Tribune which dubbed *Phantasm II* "the only movie of much real interest [this summer] with a roman numeral attached to its title." Yet even this good review pointed out that Coscarelli hadn't "extended his 1979 original as much as he's remade it." The reviewer went on to praise the sequel's nightmarish

Universal gave the film a strong marketing push.
(Photo courtesy Kristen Deem)

imagery and suggest that moviegoers give it a second look.

"After the preview screening, the studio really thought they had a hit," Jim Jacks says. "We expected the bad reviews that came in, but what we didn't expect was how the film opened. It didn't open as strongly as we'd hoped, but we had a lot of fun in the preview screenings. It really pleased the audience. We gave it a big marketing push because we felt if we could just get people into the theater, they would like it."

"At first, the audiences were about fifty percent packed," Kristen Deem says. "But over the next two weeks, I went to theatres to watch the film and there would be almost no one there, at most maybe fifteen people in the audience. This was so sad for me, having put almost a year of my life into this film then watching it fizzle out within the first week or so. It was so frustrating. Maybe it was never intended to be a mainstream movie. Maybe it was always just a cult movie. We had no idea of the scope of the *Phantasm* audience at that time. We went at it thinking it would be like a *Halloween* sequel."

BLUE BALLS

Though buzz on *Phantasm II* grew quiet following the film's release, one controversy did rear its head when Steve Patino took his quarrel with the sequel's producers public. Unhappy with his experience on the film and his absence on the poster's credit block, Patino went so far as to tell Fear Magazine that he felt Don Coscarelli should relinquish control of the franchise to someone else. Though the effectsman made clear his desire to return on *Phantasm III*, he was not asked back by that production. In the same Fear Magazine interview, Patino joked there would be a silver sphere on his grave when he died since he was now the keeper of *Phantasm*'s silver sphere. He passed away in 1994 with no such adornment.

"I feel badly that Patino never got the recognition he deserved on *Phantasm II*," Steve Cotroneo says. "I know this was something that upset him a lot. I don't know about his relationship with the producers and the director of *Phantasm II*. I knew that something had happened between them, but I was young and I don't think Patino cared to share a lot of these stories with me. All I know is that he barely got credit on the movie, and that in most of the articles that appeared in <u>Fangoria</u> and other magazines, he was almost never mentioned. Or if he was mentioned, he was just called the 'Ball Wrangler.' I now know how upsetting that is."

"I loved the movie but seeing it was bittersweet," James Vale says. "Steve had it in his head that he was going to be doing *Phantasm III* and when I said I wanted to stay on the East Coast he got mad. We had a huge argument about it and it wasn't until years later that I realized he had died. I thought he was just still mad all those years and not returning any of my phone calls. I didn't find out about it until 1998. I was at a HauntCon in Illinois and from around the corner came Tony Timpone. One of the first things he said was, '*Shame what happened to Steve.*' I thought that maybe he'd pissed someone off or gotten himself blacklisted. But turns out he'd been dead. It changed my life learning about it that way. I'll never forget it."

"He dived into doing these effects heart and soul," Mark Shostrom says. "I thought he really did a great job with the spheres. Some people had a problem with Steve's personality being a little too forward but Steve was a showman. At the end of the day, when it came to the actual effects, Steve had everything worked out to the T. A lot of his sphere work overlapped into my work and the mechanical effects he came up with worked like a charm. Steve was really proud to be the guy doing the spheres for a *Phantasm* sequel. Sure, he probably flaunted his position. In those days, we all did. Many of us makeup effects guys from the 80's thought we were rock stars. I wish Steve were alive today. He was a good friend and I miss him."

If nothing else, Patino was rightly proud of his involvement with the series. A true *Phantasm* fan long before the sequel, he frequented horror conventions afterward for an opportunity to mingle with his fan brethren. He gladly signed 8x10s of his spheres, manufactured a garage model kit and often displayed *Phantasm II* items in his traveling prop collection. He would later lend his talents to Full Moon's *Phantasm*-inspired *Netherworld*, a film on which Shostrom also worked. In place

The sphere man of *Phantasm II*, Steve Patino.
(Photo courtesy Kristen Deem)

of a flying orb, *Netherworld* featured another Patino creation - a flying hand that lethally attaches to the foreheads of its victims.

"I think for the most part Steve had a great time working on *Phantasm II*," Vale says. "He sold a bunch of the silver spheres after filming. It's so weird because Steve actually sold one off to Kirk Cameron before he became born again, religion-wise. I can't imagine what Kirk's done with it since then, but back then he was a huge *Phantasm* fan."

LEGACY

Regardless of the critical disdain and mediocre box office return it garnered, *Phantasm II* has become one of the genre's most well-liked sequels. The sequel boasts some of the best production designs, scariest makeup effects and thrilling action sequences. Reggie Bannister and Angus Scrimm were most iconic in their respective roles; both quipping some of their most quoted lines. Many fans would even claim this as

their favorite Phantasm chapter. In 2009, it made *The AV Club* website's "23 Great Movies Not Available on Region-1 DVD" list alongside such classics as *The African Queen.*

Time has been kind to this sequel. Although *Phantasm II* was the last to arrive on DVD format in North America, it was the first to be given special edition Blu-Ray treatment. *Phantasm II* is still regularly celebrated with special filmmaker-attended screenings, indicating a far longer shelf life than the now dusty *Arthur 2: On the Rocks, Crocodile Dundee 2* and *Short Circuit 2.* The sequel also introduced *Phantasm* to a whole new generation of fans unaware of its predecessor. Even a cursory glance at footage from the Pacific Theater premiere reveals a teenage crowd too young to have seen Don Coscarelli's original film during its initial run nine years earlier.

Phantasm II also bolstered the careers of its cast and certainly their recognizability. "I probably shouldn't confess to this, but I groove on being recognized," Scrimm says. "But it seldom happens, possibly because I rarely go anywhere dressed in a tight-fitting black suit and boots with two-inch lifts. [...]

Despite angry critics and lackluster box office, *Phantasm* was not dead.
(Photo courtesy Kristen Deem)

While *Phantasm II* was still in the theaters, I went one midnight into the Pavilions market on Ventura Boulevard. I'd asked my sister Lucille if there was anything I could bring her. She said, '*Twinkies.*' I looked throughout the store for Twinkies and could find no Twinkies. A young clerk was stocking the shelves, so I asked, '*Are there Twinkies anywhere?*' He said, '*Aisle seven.*' I thanked him and started off, and he called out, '*Sir! Aren't you the guy in Phantasm?*' I said, '*You have a keen eye.*' He said, '*Would you say 'Boy' for me?*' I looked nervously up and down the aisle and, seeing no other customers about who might assume an insane man was loose in the store, I said, '*Boyyy!*' The young clerk said, '*You are him! Wait till I tell my friends the Tall Man was in here asking for Twinkies!*'

Shortly after *Phantasm II*'s release, Scrimm was asked to parody his most famous role in Jim Wynorski's horror-comedy *Transylvania Twist*, which also starred Robert Vaughn, Terri Copley and Boris Karloff in a posthumous cameo appearance. In one scene, Scrimm ominously rounds a corner as a variation of Fred Myrow's theme begins: "You play a good game, boy, but now your time has come." Scrimm then produces a silver sphere only to pitch it like a baseball at the heroes who are suddenly and inexplicably decked out in baseball attire. The scene finishes with the Tall Man playing ball. "I thought Don Coscarelli might not want me to do the scene," Scrimm says. "He was delighted, so I did it with relish. *Transylvania Twist* is one of my favorite films, not just of my own work but of the genre. I wish Jim Wynorski would do a sequel. There's that great Wynorski humor in every one of his films, but *Twist* is non-stop gags and many of them are terrific, off-the-wall comedy."

The *Phantasm* world would become quiescent for years following its first sequel. Filmmakers and fans were immediately ready for another chapter, even if the studio was not. Unbeknownst at the time, the next installment would be but a few short years away.

"When we finished *Phantasm II*, my thoughts went right away to whether or not there would be a *Phantasm III*," Mark Anthony Major says. "Of course I wanted to be in it, even though my character met his end in part two. I figured out a way to resurrect him from the dead and wrote story ideas and even did some sketches that I gave to Don and Roberto. They liked what I had done, but obviously wound up not using it. I was very ambitious at that time in my career."

"I had such a good experience working with Don on *Phantasm II*," Ed Gale says. "I would've liked to have returned for *Phantasm III*, absolutely. I would've done it for him for nothing just to be part of another one of his films."

"I didn't understand it when I read it.
I didn't understand it when I filmed it.
And I didn't understand it when I saw it.
In fact, I still don't understand it.
But people really seem to love it."

Samantha Phillips on *Phantasm II*'s legacy.

Pondering *Phantasm III.*
(Photo courtesy Kristen Deem)

Chapter 3:
Lord of the Dead

Reggie Bannister at the Fangoria Weekend of Horrors.
(Photo courtesy Kristen Deem)

PHAMILY REUNION

In the wake of *Phantasm II*'s commercial underperformance, neither filmmaker nor fan knew exactly when it would be time for another sequel, assuming one was even warranted. Several years passed with no sign of life in the franchise until a June 1992 convention appearance by Reggie Bannister. Fielding audience questions at the Fangoria Weekend of Horrors, the actor regaled fans with stories about the making of the first two films. Of course, the burning question was asked: would there be a *Phantasm III?* Much to everyone's surprise, Bannister not only confirmed that there would be a sequel but also revealed that Don Coscarelli intended to return Michael Baldwin to his namesake role. The audience roared with applause.

"I was surprised," Baldwin says. "It totally came out of the blue. When someone calls you and says they want to cast

you in a film that you don't even have to audition for, that's pretty great!" This marked not only the performer's return to the series but also his return to film acting which he had left following the first *Phantasm*. Though he topped the cast list of the original *Phantasm*, Baldwin would now receive second billing behind lead Reggie Bannister. "I think Don was probably unsure about me as an actor, having not worked together in so many years," Baldwin says. "So he wound up writing the script of *Phantasm III* for Reggie, which is fine. Reggie certainly deserved to have a bigger part in these movies."

Even more surprising was Bill Thornbury's return as Mike's dead brother, Jody. Having also left the film industry following *Phantasm*, Thornbury spent several years in Nashville where he enjoyed a successful career as a songwriter. "Like with Michael," Thornbury says, "I think Don was concerned in bringing me back because I hadn't done anything in a long time

A NEW DIRECTION

Not so scary...
(Photo courtesy Kristen Deem)

and because I also had a contemporary Christian CD coming out. He didn't know if *Phantasm III* was going to be congruent with that. It was totally congruent and I told him that."

Early word of Bannister's return helped dispel speculation that his character was left for dead at the end of *Phantasm II*. "No, Reggie wasn't killed by Alchemy," Bannister told GASP Magazine. "But he does continue to get the crap beat out of him in part three. Every other page it seemed like, *'Reggie's face smashes into the floor of the mausoleum'* or *'Reggie does a home-plate slide into a wall.'* We didn't finish shooting any given night until I was on the ground somewhere."

On Friday, June 19, 1992, Angus Scrimm wrote:

Don Coscarelli phones: "Get out the Tall Man suit and polish the boots!" New Line has offered to partially finance two new Phantasm pictures to be shot back-to-back starting this winter, with Don to raise the rest of the money from foreign investors.

Phantasm III's tangled roots stretch far back, before *Phantasm II* had even begun filming in the fall of 1987. Despite telling Fangoria that he had no plans for a third film, a forty-page treatment bearing Don Coscarelli's name circulated behind the scenes. This pitch bore no resemblance to the eventual 1994 film, nor did it much acknowledge the events of *Phantasm II*. If anything, this original *Phantasm III* had much more in common with the later scripted *Phantasm: 1999* project. The story involved Reggie being kidnapped by the Tall Man and used as bait to lure Mike Pearson. Our young hero rides a motorcycle deep into the desert to find his friend and destroy the alien mortician. On the road, he recruits a monkey companion and a love interest when he visits a witches coven. As for the Tall Man, he was now operating out of an industrial mausoleum capable of processing scores of bodies every day. This direction had been abandoned by the time Coscarelli re-partnered the franchise with Universal Studios for *Phantasm III*. New Line Cinema, the studio that had been outbid by AVCO Embassy on the original *Phantasm*, had missed out yet again.

On Friday, September 4, 1992, Angus Scrimm wrote:

Don is scripting Phantasm III, but feels that to come up with a Phantasm IV script as well would overwhelm a winter start date. Moreover, MCA Universal's savvy hands-on head man, Robert Blattner, has bettered New Line's PIII offer by a substantial amount, so Don has signed with MCA Universal.

The first draft of Coscarelli's new *Phantasm III* script was unveiled on October 1, 1992. Continuing on the heels of *Phantasm II*, this draft finds Mike being kidnapped by the Tall Man and groomed for a mysterious transformation. Jody returns as a ghostly, spherical apparition to aid Mike and Reggie, though his loyalty is often called into question. In order to rescue Mike, Reggie teams up with ex-military femme fatale, Rocky, and streetwise orphan, Tim. While the trio does eventually find and destroy the Tall Man, they learn that Mike is tragically beyond their salvation. He has become a creature much like the Tall Man himself. As Jody chases after his evolving brother in the final moments of the script, Reggie accuses Jody of knowing it all along. In response, Jody warns Reg not to follow because Mike is "lost to you." The film concludes with an arctic burial of the Tall Man's cranial gold sphere. Just before the camera cuts to black, we see an inscription on the icy marble tombstone: "The Tall Man, R.I.P."

Where one might argue that *Phantasm II*'s script was light on story, *Phantasm III*'s pages are bursting with content. Coscarelli packs his threequel full of twists, thrills and laughs while successfully venturing deeper into sci-fi territory. The film is decidedly campier than its predecessor including madcap zombies and a hot pink hearse. If there's a flaw in Coscarelli's tale, it's that no sooner does he stage a touching reunion between Mike, Jody and Reggie then he frustratingly disbands them for most of the film. Fortunately, new characters Tim, Rocky and the trio of zombie looters are fun and invigorating additions to

the series. The film fittingly preserves the Tall Man's mysterious, enigmatic nature in a handful of memorable scenes.

Coscarelli continues to draw inspiration from the original *Phantasm,* particularly with Tim whose story (and even wardrobe) mirrors that of young Mike. Both are presented as orphans, their late parents now in the shrunken company of the Tall Man. Both stumble onto the Tall Man's scheme following a funeral, then set out to battle the otherworldly mortician. As originally written, Tim would survive the last moments of *Phantasm III* to become Reggie's surrogate kid brother just as Mike had once become. When viewed as the closing chapter of a trilogy, this exchange would have brought the franchise full-circle. As Tim became the new Mike, Mike would become the Tall Man, and *Phantasm* would seemingly continue on this way.

"I thought it was a direction we needed to go," Michael Baldwin says. "What direction are the characters going in *Phantasm II*? They're not going anywhere. They're just trying to kill the Tall Man. I think the critics were right in that it was

The original cast... still "hot as love!"
(Photo courtesy Guy Thorpe)

basically just a remake of the first film. At least in *Phantasm III* the characters are going to new places and transforming. That was important."

Recalling her continuity doctoring of *Phantasm II*, Coscarelli immediately sent the first draft of *Eternity* (the working title) to Kristen Deem for more of the same. Four days later, on October 5, she faxed him a thirty-five page critique that outlined its strengths and weaknesses, and offered suggestions, several of which were incorporated into the next draft. Among those used were the Lady in Lavender's cameo, the liquid nitrogen dipping of Rocky's crematory poker, and the design of the Tall Man's surgical device.

"What I found so intriguing was the new direction Don was taking with Mike Pearson and the Tall Man; the concept of Mike evolving and the Tall Man grooming him as a replacement," Deem says. "I also loved that the original trio was back—Michael, Jody and Reggie—so that this sequel was a return to its roots. The downside was that *P3* then went way off tangent, becoming two movies in one. So much screen time was devoted to the zombies, Rocky and Tim. True, this new material added much humor and hinted at Don's desire – with Tim – to attract a whole new generation of fans. Yet all this distilled and compromised the film. Though the two stories do eventually merge, I would have preferred if *P3* had focused solely and in depth on the Pearson brothers."

BACK IN BUSINESS

Rather than another return to Chatsworth, Don Coscarelli set up shop inside a former egg hatchery on Radford and Sherman Way in North Hollywood. To assemble the production team, he brought back a dozen *Phantasm II* crewmembers. Roberto

Michael Baldwin and Reggie Bannister outside the North Hollywood warehouse.
(Photo courtesy Guy Thorpe)

Don Coscarelli back in the director's chair.
(Photo courtesy Kristen Deem)

Quezada was chief among those to return, this time as unit production manager. He suggested that colleague Seth Blair replace him as co-producer. "One day I got a call from Roberto asking me if I was interested in producing a movie for Don Coscarelli," Blair says. "I guess Roberto either really liked or really hated me! We'll never know! The three of us met poolside at Don's office, which were these bungalows in the back of a hotel on Hollywood Blvd. I think my belief in myself that I had enough experience came through in the interview, because I got the job right away."

"When someone makes a sequel to something, it's because the prequel made money," returning makeup effects artist Mark Shostrom says. "And a lot of times on the second film, you have a bigger budget than the first. So on the third film, you often have even more money to work with. That happened to me on the *Nightmare on Elm Street* series. It didn't quite happen on the *Phantasm* series. On *Phantasm III*, when Don called me for it, I assumed like anyone that we had more money to work with. Imagine my surprise when I found out that we had a lot less. But the upside was that Don was able to

give my partner, Dean Gates, and I a really long lead time since we didn't have a crew."

"I was excited to work with Mark on *Phantasm III* because I thought he was doing something different than most other shows at that time," Gates says. "With effects departments getting bigger and bigger, it was common in those days to have an assembly line approach. You had a guy that did molds, a guy that did sculpting, a guy that did fabrication, a guy that did hair work and so on. On *Phantasm III*, Mark and I helped each other out with life casting and then divided up the effects between ourselves to handle from beginning to end, which I liked."

One crewmember who didn't carry over from *Phantasm II* was outspoken sphere effects artist Steve Patino, despite his very much wanting to return. Patino's absence was likely due to his very public bashing of Coscarelli and Quezada in print media. He was replaced on the threequel by Kerry Prior of Dream Quest Images, who had also worked on *Phantasm II*'s sphere optical effects.

Although cinematographer Daryn Okada did return for *Phantasm III*, it was for second unit shooting. The lead cinematographer – also recommended by Quezada – was up-and-coming DP Christopher Chomyn, who took time to study the look of the previous two *Phantasm*s before filming began. "Most of the flying spheres in the first two films were done as post-effects," Chomyn says. "They were cutaways that were not seamlessly integrated into the tapestry of the films. Don and I spoke about it and we both wanted to make the spheres part of the environment. Don in particular wanted more balls. He hired me in December and we planned to start in January. Over the Christmas holidays, I spent countless hours staring into Christmas ornaments wondering, '*How in the world will I hide my reflection?*'"

"I was doing another movie between *Phantasm II* and *Phantasm III* called *Witchboard*," returning stunt coordinator John Michael Stewart says. "Don came to visit our set the day I was going to pipe-ramp a Suburban through a boat. I told him that I wanted to do the biggest pipe-ramp ever for the next *Phantasm*. He liked the idea so he let me add in the pink hearse stunt. Then he came to me and said, '*Here's*

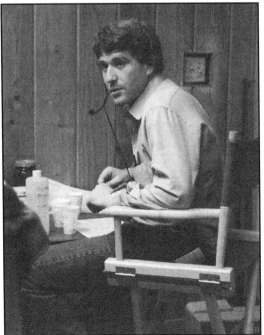

Top: Cinematographer Chistopher Chomyn
Bottom: First Assistant Director Jeff Shiffman.
(Photos courtesy Kristen Deem)

the script. What else do you want to write in that will work and we can afford?' So I came up with some ideas. He let me write, coordinate and direct all of the action scenes for that one. This meant that I was also second unit director for some of the stunts. Don gave me a lot of freedom and I liked that. *III* was definitely a much more stunt-heavy film than the previous one. I remember we threw someone out of a car and ran them over, tossed people over railings, all kinds of stuff."

"*Phantasm* was released when I was a teenager and it was rather big," First Assistant Director Jeff Shiffman says. "I saw it and liked it, but I never saw number two. I was very excited to be working on number three, though. There weren't a lot of people asking me to be their first assistant director at this point in my career. A mutual friend set up a meeting between Don and myself. He interviewed me and I didn't think much of it. I did two other movies and the day after wrapping the second movie, I got the call that I was hired. It came as quite a surprise."

One *Phantasm II* crewmember invited back but unable to return was production designer Philip Duffin. Duffin's absence may have contributed to the decision to bypass constructing a mausoleum set. Instead, the crew worked inside two real-life mausoleums, both on the grounds of the picturesque Angeles Abbey in Compton. The main sprawling mausoleum was modeled after India's Taj Mahal and would serve as the Holtsville and Bolton mausoleums. A modern mausoleum next door served as the Tall Man's futuristic prison mausoleum. Years later, Angeles Abbey would reappear in *Terminator 3: Rise of the Machines*, *Constantine* and also an episode of *Alias*.

More than ever before, *Phantasm III* called for hearses – and in mass quantity. To manage this peculiar necessity, Coscarelli created the position of hearse coordinator and entrusted this duty to series follower Guy Thorpe. "As far as I know, there's never been a movie credit before mine called hearse coordinator or hearse wrangler," Thorpe says. "I think I've wrangled more hearses than anyone else before in Hollywood, to tell you the truth! Between the two films, I wrangled about twenty-five altogether." Now known to fans as 'the hearse man of *Phantasm*,' Thorpe first heard about the new film directly from Coscarelli in late 1992. "I got a call from Don asking if I still had the hearse from part two," he continues. "I said, '*Yeah. Why?*' and he said, '*Well, we're going to need it for the beginning of part three!*'"

As fall turned to winter, turbulent salary negotiations were underway to secure the return of *Phantasm*'s original cast with the production pleading poor. As compromises were being brokered, a tragedy befell Universal Studios that nearly derailed the sequel altogether. On Saturday, November 2, company President Robert Blattner was killed in a plane crash in Colorado. Blattner had been the film's biggest advocate at the studio and with his passing came a temporary freeze on all projects green-lit under his watch.

"The very next day Don called me," Kristen Deem says. "He sounded quite depressed. His voicemail said, '*Kris, Phantasm III is not looking too good. Universal may back out,*' and he explained what had transpired and that preproduction was on hold. It was an awful week for us all. The next phone call from Don a week later was far more positive. He was too busy to talk, but cheerfully told me everything was again a go. This made me realize how precarious, how fragile, bringing a film to life can be. Nothing is ever certain."

On Monday, November 9, 1992, Scrimm wrote:

> New MCA Universal head Louis Feola has greenlighted the Blattner films. Though I've been growing the Tall Man's long hair since June, he has remained elusive. I've welcomed his reticence; once he moves in on me for a film, he lingers long after it's finished, an obnoxious guest who won't depart till he's ready. The Tall Man's got intriguing dialogue. I need him with me to figure out how we're going to play these scenes.

NEW CASTING

With *Phantasm III* back on track, Don Coscarelli and casting director Jacklynn Briskey began auditioning for new roles in the script. Despite the return of four lead actors, there were more than a dozen roles left to be cast including two new leads.

Phantasm's new booooooy.
(Photo courtesy Kristen Deem)

First among the new leads was Tim, described in the script as being '*Holtsville's only survivor, a scruffy eleven year-old*'. This would be newcomer Kevin Connors' first film role. "At that time, I was going to three auditions per week," Connors says. "I remember being really excited about the script, knowing I was going to shoot a gun and drive a car. These are things that any twelve year old would be excited about doing, movie or not! I remember it being a very physical interview and running around a lot. It wasn't really a sitting in a chair, reading lines kind of thing." Following his casting, Connors' parents rented the first *Phantasm* to give him a better idea of his involvement. The young thespian quickly recognized his character's inspiration. "I'm very much the replacement for Michael in our film," he says. "In a way, my character was a tribute to his character from the first film."

The second new lead was Rocky (full name Roxanne Veray), described in the script as being '*slim, muscular and having an attitude*'. For Gloria Lynne-Henry it was a perfect fit. The struggling actress had recently trimmed her long hair short

Phantasm III's bold new leading lady.
(Photo courtesy Kristen Deem)

to stand out in auditions and had begun an exercise routine after losing a *Star Trek* role because producers thought her butt was too big. "*But I'm a black woman*," Lynne-Henry laughingly exclaims, "*we have big behinds!*" By late 1992, Lynne-Henry was out of work, broke and facing the reality of moving back home to Michigan. That's when she got the call to audition for an untitled sci-fi movie. As she entered the lobby, she noticed something about the other actresses auditioning for Rocky.

"Every girl in that office had long hair like I used to have," Lynne-Henry says. "I was the only one with a butch haircut. I was perfect for Rocky. I walked into the audition like '*I'm going to get this part!*' That confidence definitely paid off." Five callbacks later including one videotape reading with Reggie Bannister, she was given the role. "It was right after my last audition and I was given the role that I had to file for unemployment for the first time in my life to hold

me over in California until we started filming in January." Other roles in the script were being cast with just as much careful scrutiny as Rocky. Chuck Butto was chosen to play a doctor that examines Mike early in the film. "It was just the normal casting process for the most part," he says. "My agent submitted me and I got the audition. But I was called back three times before I was actually cast, which is unusual for a small character like that. The director was pretty picky. I was aware of the *Phantasm* reputation at that point because I was a fan. I remember seeing the first film when it came out and being creeped out (laughs). It was cool to be cast in one of the sequels."

Irene Roseen was cast as the nurse who cares for Mike before turning demonic, a most atypical role for the veteran actress of stage and screen. "I had heard of *Phantasm* before I got the role," she says. "It had a certain legitimacy to it. Had it been any other horror film, I would've thought twice about doing it. The closest thing I've ever done to the demon nurse has to be any one of the Shakespearean villains. I've done many different Shakespeare festivals on both coasts and I don't think you get much more villainess than Regan from *King Lear* without the help of some special effects. Fortunately or unfortunately, I had those to work with on the film."

Sarah Scott Davis was chosen to play Rocky's ill-fated partner, Tanesha, who quickly learns that a silver sphere is no object to stand in the direct path of. Rounding out the cast as the looter (later zombie) trio, Henry, Rufus and Edna, were actors John Davis Chandler, Brooks Gardner and Cindy Ambuehl.

CALM BEFORE THE SHOOT

On Saturday, December 5, Angus Scrimm traveled to Mark Shostrom's Pasadena studio for another torturous round of life casting. Shostrom needed several molds of the actor's body for *Phantasm III*'s icy conclusion wherein the Tall Man is frozen alive. As with *Phantasm II*, Kristen Deem was on hand for support. "For the head cast, Angus called Don at home to discuss what expression the Tall Man should have while he's

Top: The Pearson Brothers reunited!
Bottom: Kristen Deem and a Tall Friend.
(Photos courtesy Kristen Deem)

Together again: Angus Scrimm and Mark Shostrom.
(Photo courtesy Kristen Deem)

impaled and pushed into the freezer," Deem says. "We decided the expression should be subtle, like the ice cream truck scene in *Phantasm*, not one of agony."

On Saturday, December 5, 1992, Scrimm wrote:

> With Kristen Deem along to assist, and the little five-year-old West Highland terrier Cappy who just joined my family, I drive to Mark Shostrom's Pasadena studio for a lifecasting session. With wicked zest, Mark and his associate Dean Gates slap alginate all over my face, head, arms, chest and hands. While unobserved, Cap shows his new allegiance to me by chewing bits out of an old Freddy Krueger cast he finds on a low shelf.

Not everyone on the *Phantasm III* cast was as seasoned as Scrimm when it came to makeup effects. For Irene Roseen, the life casting process was an uneasy one. In the film, her turn as the Demon Nurse entails a silver sphere bursting from her cranium. "The process was long and frightening," Roseen says. "I went out to this studio where Mark Shostrom and Dean Gates had their makeup shop. They were a team and I'd heard that they had an amazing reputation for this sort of work and were quite well known in the business. After working with

them, I thought they were brilliant. They explained to me that my face was going to be entirely covered and that if I was at all claustrophobic, it would be difficult. I don't even like crowded elevators so I told them that this was probably going to be difficult and it was. I think the whole ordeal would've been much easier if they could've sedated me. That would've been a marvelous idea! Like at the dentist!"

As filming neared, the production team began to realize the incredible scope of Don Coscarelli's vision, particularly as it related to the budget. Despite being produced for less money, *Phantasm III* was bigger than its predecessor in almost every way imaginable. A lesser director might have attempted to scale back the film until it more comfortably fit the budget, but not Coscarelli, who still held dearly to the mind-over-money formula that made his shoestring budget on *Phantasm* work so well. *Phantasm III*'s limited budget also resulted in the tightest shooting schedule the series would yet experience.

"The first order of business was getting the budget and schedule in order so we'd have a foundation to work with," Seth Blair says. "I knew this was going to be a real big challenge for me because of the number of shooting days, locations, special effects and second unit work that were required on this film. That's when the tension begins between the director and producer. Don's job is to get his vision on film and mine is to deliver it on time and on budget. Kind of like oil and water!"

"I think Seth Blair had a lot of pressure working on him during filming," Christopher Chomyn says. "Most of the people on his crew did not have a lot of experience. Don and Roberto had the most experience. Our schedule was set up in a way that, had it worked, would have accommodated the crew's lack of experience. So the plan, and I'm not sure it was a good one though it was well intentioned, was to schedule two weeks of exterior filming so we could get the crew up and running and working together. It would also give the art department time to build the sets. Then we would move inside the warehouse two weeks into filming and the crew would have become a finely oiled machine that was two weeks more experienced than when they were hired. None of this worked out as we had hoped."

The days before Christmas brought forth a final shooting script and schedule along with an end to contract negotiations. Costumer Carla Gibbons was busy outfitting the cast with their wardrobe selections. "None of us knew what had become of the Tall Man's elegant, tailored black suit from *Phantasm II*," Deem says. "It might have been a rental from Western Costume. So Carla needed to start again from scratch for this film. Eventually we got to discussing the Tall Man's bizarre, alien tie pin. For me, this was always the crown jewel of his costume. I proudly loaned Carla an exact replica I had created back in 1987. The oval bead was made of red Czechoslovakian glass with an AB iridescent finish. We didn't want anything to befall the original piece from *Phantasm* that Shirley Coscarelli had created back in 1977." (The original Tall Man suit and tie pin remain with Scrimm to this day.)

FORWARD ON ALL FRONTS

Production of *Phantasm III* began on Thursday, January 7, 1993 and was met with a torrential downpour of rain, spoiling the scheduled exterior shoot. A backup plan to work indoors was quickly devised but nixed when filming was unexpectedly cancelled due to permit issues. "It was a horrible start," Seth Blair says. "Getting shut down on your first day of shooting, that's something no one expects to happen."

"We got rained out of our location on the first day," Christopher Chomyn says. "All of a sudden, our exterior filming was out the window. They asked me, '*What can we shoot inside?*' and I asked what cover sets were available to us. We still had to unpack the trucks but the day didn't have to be a wash. We could film *something*. Turns out, none of the sets were camera ready. So we decided to just shoot 'Cuda interiors using poor man's process. All we needed was to hang some lights and put black drapes behind the car. We start rolling and what happens? The Fire Marshal comes in and shuts us down because we didn't have a permit to shoot there that day. At that point, we were done. There was a lot of speculation as to who tipped them off that day. I won't say who I thought it was."

On Tuesday, January 12, Angus Scrimm wrote:

A call from Santa Paula, where heavy rains are making shooting impossible. Don, who must be anxious over the costly delays, only says, "Instead of making a movie, I should be building an ark!"

Unexpected rain forced the production indoors again on a subsequent day. Instead of filming highway sequences with the 'Cuda, the decision was made to move to the recently completed motel room set where Reggie was to make love to Rocky in a dream sequence. The intimate on-camera moment was a first for Lynne-Henry and only a second for Bannister. "I was so nervous," Lynne-Henry says. "Don wanted me to rehearse it and I told him, '*I can't rehearse this scene. I know how to have sex and if you just roll cameras, you'll get what you want.*' So Don calls '*Action!*' and I start getting into the scene. '*Oh, Reggie. Oh, yeah. Oh, you're so big!*' And then I hear this huge laugh and I turn around and Don is cracking up! But he apologized and was much more serious the next time. It was all right though because I knew I could trust Reggie in that scene. He had a wonderful spirit about him and he took care of me and I liked that. He was very professional."

Wednesday, January 13, marked Angus Scrimm's first day of filming as the Tall Man for the white light dream that brings Mike out of his coma. This scene was the first time that

Cruising in the 'Cuda.
(Photo courtesy Guy Thorpe)

Top: Don Coscarelli and Kevin Connors.
Bottom: Not a fan of the cold.
(Photos courtesy Kristen Deem)

Michael Baldwin, Bill Thornbury and Scrimm had performed together since the original *Phantasm*. "I seem to remember that we didn't rehearse any of those scenes before we shot them," Thornbury says. "We just jumped in cold, which was fine with me. I still felt like Mike and I shared that old chemistry together despite all the years that had passed. No matter what stage of his life he's been in, I've always found that Mike was really easy to work with and just puts you at ease. And Angus, he was just as scary and solid an actor as he's always been."

This dream tunnel sequence was a cover set for the day's originally planned location, which was to be the orphanage scene where Reggie attempts to ditch Tim. Filmed later in production, the scene featured cameos by both Coscarelli children, Chloe and Andy, and Thornbury's son, Ben.

"I've always wanted to be a good parent and introduce my son to different things," Thornbury says. "I thought Ben would enjoy being near or around a movie that was being made with me in it. It would make it more of a possibility that he could do that some day. So even at that young age when he was still just a baby, we put him in *Phantasm III*. It's fun to look back on."

CEMETERY SHOOTING

On Friday, January 22, the production traveled south to Sunnyside Cemetery in Long Beach to film day exteriors of the funeral for Tim's father, the Sheriff of Holtsville. Cemetery photography resumed the following evening with the Tall Man stealing the Sheriff's corpse and abducting his widow while Tim watches. *Phantasm* co-producer Paul Pepperman dropped by set this night for a surprise reunion.

"Instead of isolating themselves in their trailers to rest or read a book until they were needed, Michael and Reggie were quite enthusiastic about the film and remained on set," Kristen Deem recalls. "They'd even pitch in and help the crew. They both had this light of enthusiasm in their eyes to see all this coming to life once more. We were all a family again."

"Over the course of the first two movies, the cast and crew did become a family and despite that, I never felt like I was outside of it," Kevin Connors says. "I became part of that family and being the only kid on the set of an adult oriented movie, I was embraced and at the same time protected. I think everybody felt like I was their own kid." The actor shrugs off his first encounter with the film's gory makeup effects that night. "The makeups didn't bother me, not that I had seen a lot of that before. Horror movies just were never really my thing. My parents sheltered me appropriately growing up, but not on the film; one of the things I definitely give them credit for. I think they knew once the movie was done, I was going to see it all anyway. I think at one point, within about three minutes, I shoot one zombie, I Frisbee the second and I hatchet the third. It was all just part of the job."

Since many of Connors' scenes were filmed during school hours or very late at night, the production hired an on set teacher to keep him up on his schooling. "We had an unusual shooting schedule, Tuesday through Saturday," he says. "I would go to school on Monday and meet with the teachers and get my packets of homework. I had three hours, legally, set aside each day for homework. And because there's a lot of

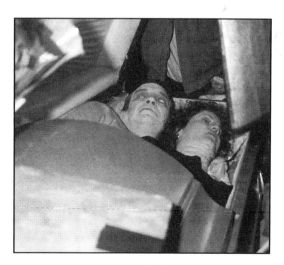

Beau Lotterman and Claire Benedek
(Photo courtesy Guy Thorpe)

downtime on a set, I was able to catch up on it when I wasn't shooting." For the rest of Connors' downtime on set once the homework was completed, Coscarelli bought his leading lad a gift to occupy his time. "He bought me my first TV, which I still have. He really didn't have to do that and it gave me a little extra something to do on the set when I was done with my homework and waiting for a scene to be shot."

STORMS OVER ANGELES ABBEY

On Saturday, January 30, production moved to Compton's Angeles Abbey for several weeks of location work. For the *Phantasm III* team, it was an unpleasant locale fraught with strange happenings. The first incident occurred when Don Coscarelli and several crewmembers were mysteriously locked inside while scouting the facility. They were released once the groundskeeper realized they hadn't returned from their tour.

"We were in the lamest, crappiest, oldest, smelliest, rundown mausoleum in America," Michael Baldwin says. "It was awful. It was the kind of place where you figure that somewhere, someone is breaking the law. You would walk down the hallway at three in the morning and it would stink like rotting flesh. It was putrid, literally." Baldwin was more right than he realized as the Angeles Abbey Memorial Park was successfully sued in 1995 for $5 million for staging fake graveside services and burying bodies in the shoulder of a nearby roadway.

"We were there for two weeks or more," Jeff Shiffman recalls. "I do distinctly remember the night we began smelling one of the bodies. It was either fresh or they didn't process it right but you could definitely smell it. Certain people couldn't handle it and wouldn't even go into the mausoleum. Try filming when your crew won't enter the set. It's tough."

On Saturday, January 30, Angus Scrimm wrote:

Suddenly, the skies outside, which have threatened all day, go berserk: Thunder crashes, lightning splits the heavens and smites the earth. The dressing room trailer lights blink off, and all at once there's a deafening drumming on the roof as though evil gods were pounding to be let in. Hailstones! Mopping the fog from my window, I peer out. A turbulent river washes over my front steps - and nowhere in all the great outdoors is a living soul to be seen. I'm alone in a primordial world. After a seeming century, the storm stops. Brave little costume assistant Lisa Dyehouse has come for me: "They wanted you an hour ago. Don kept asking, 'Who's going to go get Angus?' and nobody volunteered."

Kristen Deem's journal recounts other peculiar episodes that night. At one point, a rooftop crewmember accidentally kicked in a stained glass window, which rained down upon Deem, Coscarelli and the actors during a scene discussion. Later on, overworked generators had to be shut down for a period, plunging the crew into darkness inside the mausoleum with the Tall Man in their midst. Following the storm, cameras rolled on the chilling moment when Mike is entombed and taunted by the Tall Man. This required Baldwin to wedge himself inside an actual crypt and have a glass wall bolted on behind him.

"That was my least favorite scene in all of *Phantasm*," Baldwin says. "I beg Angus to let me out and he says to me,

> ## "We were in the lamest, crappiest, oldest, smelliest, rundown mausoleum in America."
> Michael Baldwin on Angeles Abbey

Top: Guy Thorpe with Coscarelli and cast.
Bottom: The picturesque hallways of Angeles Abbey.
(Group photo courtesy Guy Thorpe)
(Abbey photo courtesy Kristen Deem)

'Use your brain' and I go 'I don't know what you meeeean!' It was horrible. I hate how I say it and, unfortunately, the director was not there to coach me for that scene. He was off dealing with a technical issue of which there were many that night. Because anybody would've heard me read that line and gone, "Oh, no. We're going to change this." I just wanted to get out of that crypt so bad that I didn't care and the scene stayed that way. Thornbury still makes fun of me for it."

On Saturday, January 30, Kristen Deem wrote:

Between breaks, I discussed this scene with Michael, Reggie and Angus. Each of them felt that there was a real bond between Mike and the Tall Man. That, in fact, there was almost an affection. Mike was an alien who had somehow "forgotten" his roots. Perhaps he was even the Tall Man's prodigal son – now returned home – refusing to "remember" who and what he was. The way Michael and Angus played the scene, it really made you wonder!

Baldwin was re-imprisoned in the crypt for his character's rescue scene later that night. In the film, Jody appears to Reggie in a dream and guides him on a rescue mission to the Tall Man's mausoleum prison, location unknown. Unearthly green lasers scan the dark corridor. Morphing back into a sphere, Jody blasts open Mike's cell with a laser of his own. Suddenly, the hallway glows red; the Tall Man has arrived to thwart Mike's escape.

"I really liked the transition we did in the mausoleum with Jody going from human to sphere," Christopher Chomyn says. "If you pay attention, we don't actually show it happening. We do earlier in the film with an optical effect, but here it takes place off camera. There's a point where Bill Thornbury moves out of frame past Reggie and as Reggie backs up, the Jody sphere hovers in behind him. You only hear the transformation, but you're sold on it because it's quick and effective. We knew we didn't want to transition Jody with a cut. We knew it would be more powerful if we didn't cut away. The challenge was in how to communicate what's happening to the audience without

Between takes at the Abbey.
(Photo courtesy Guy Thorpe)

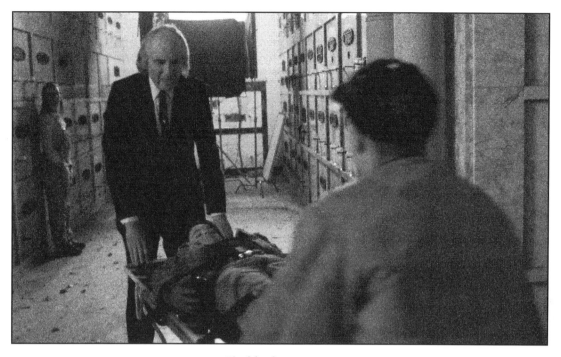

The deleted gurney scene.
(Photo courtesy Kristen Deem)

directly showing them what's happening. It worked wonderfully and it didn't cost a thing."

"The lasers in that scene were fantastic," Shiffman says. "We had a specialist come in just to operate them. It was the first time I'd ever seen lasers that powerful. We had several safety meetings about the lasers because if someone had caught one of them in the eye, it would've meant big trouble. The beauty of it was that they were practical effects."

Mausoleum shooting continued throughout early February when things began to veer off-schedule due to a flurry of circumstances, one of which was the unexpected rain. Blair notes that principal photography was originally slated to shoot for just forty days. "I knew this was going to be a problem from the beginning," he says. "I had enough experience to know this was a very ambitious schedule for the amount of work we needed to shoot, given all the effects and stunts and locations that were in the script. The budget, in my opinion, didn't

support it. We ended up shooting forty-six days, which was no surprise. Not to me anyway." Such bumps in filming proved to be a headache for many of the major players including a frustrated Scrimm. On February 3 and 4, he spent all night in Tall Man costume and makeup without ever actually going before camera. A night at Angeles Abbey typically meant an arrival at sunset and departure at sunrise.

On Friday, February 5, Angus Scrimm wrote:

Kevin's parents, grandparents and little brother all visit to watch our simple scene together: With Kevin strapped upon it, I push a gurney around a mausoleum corner and abandon him in the corridor of crypts. But the spidery old gurney, which must date back to Florence Nightingale, doesn't corner well; we practice many times to get it into precise camera position. I ask Kevin, "Enjoying the rides?" He grins. "Disneyland is better!"

Kerry Prior dangles a silver sphere from a fishing pole.

(Photo courtesy Kristen Deem)

"Look into my eyes..."
(Photo courtesy Kristen Deem)

"I thought Angus was the nicest guy you could ever want to meet," Connors says. "He's the exact opposite of the character he plays. Looking back, I didn't really have that many scenes with him, but he was a very calming, soothing person whenever I did work with him. It seemed like everything he said was a nugget of wisdom. When Angus talked, people listened."

SPHERE ITSELF

With mausoleum filming came the first on set appearance of the silver sphere, now under the direction of Kerry Prior. Where his effects work on *Phantasm II* had been purely optical, Prior's work on *Phantasm III* would be of a more practical nature. There were considerably more spheres this time around, more than in the previous films combined, and much more for them to do. Prior's work began by recreating a staple *Phantasm* scene,

Above: Sphere on a wire.
Bottom: Kerry Prior and Sarah Scott Davis.
(*Photos courtesy Kristen Deem*)

the drilling of Rocky's friend, Tanesha, which was achieved in much the same way as Father Meyers' drilling in *Phantasm II*. "My biggest concern was all of the sphere effects that had to be built, and getting Kerry Prior on board to figure them out," Seth Blair says. "We had to get them all built on a small budget. I think he had one of the toughest jobs on the film. The spheres were as big a part of the film as the actors. In addition, we wanted to do some things with the spheres that hadn't been done in either of the two previous films. So Kerry really had his work cut out for him."

It was here at Angeles Abbey that Prior executed an impressive innovation on the traveling sphere effect, a shot that previous *Phantasm*s achieved during post-production. Prior managed this effect in-camera by swapping out the traditional cable-operated ball for a wireless, remote controlled one and mounting it to a clear sheet of Plexiglas. The result is one of the most impressive sphere effects in the series. Through upgrades such as this, Prior was able to leave behind the archaic method of pitching spheres down corridors and reversing the footage.

Police presence at the Abbey.
(Photo courtesy Todd Mecklem)

A DIFFERENT KIND OF SHOOTING

On a subsequent rainless night, production moved to the Abbey's front lawn, which had been converted into a makeshift cemetery, *Phantasm* style. Across this field a transforming Mike flees at the film's conclusion.

Baldwin displays ghoulishly pale skin and gold spherical eyes for the scene. "Those types of contact lenses weren't all that common back then," Baldwin says. "They weren't soft either. They were hard with a gold mirror surface. An optometrist had to specially fit them to my eyes and then remain on set to put them in and take them out. They could only be worn for about thirty minutes at a time before they started to damage your eyes. It was kind of like wearing sunglasses on your eyeballs. They were uncomfortable and weird, but they do look amazing in that scene."

"I've never been a big fan of going to cemeteries," Gloria Lynne-Henry says. "Even when I was a kid my parents knew that I just didn't go to funerals. So on *Phantasm III* I had to take a moment and realize that while I'm acting, I have to respect my surroundings. If you watch the scene where we're running over tombstones, you can see that I never step on one. I had to rehearse that because no way was I going to step on someone's grave, not even for a movie. It was quite moving to be in that setting and smell death all around you and still have to perform. In between scenes, you get to looking at people's birth dates and death dates and it makes you realize that life is really short."

On Sunday night, February 6, the production was interrupted by a group of unwelcome visitors voicing their displeasure about the filming. "I remember one or two cars pulling up to the exterior gates just as we were in the middle of shooting a scene," Art Director Candi Guterres says. "Then I remember hearing loud popping noises and as I looked around my surroundings, I saw leaves falling to the ground and the crew seemed to have disappeared. The guys yelled something to us from outside the gates, got into their cars and peeled out.

Top: Michael Baldwin at the Abbey.
Bottom: A quiet moment with Bill Thornbury.
(Photos courtesy Kristen Deem)

Playghoul's Reigning Mortician of the Year, 1979 - 2014
(Photo courtesy Kristen Deem)

"People really appreciate that she was a black female in a horror movie who didn't die."

Gloria Lynne-Henry on Rocky

It was then that I realized that we had just been shot at by gang members who were not happy that we were filming and felt that we were disrespecting their dead. I stood there in awe of what had just happened as the rest of the crew, slowly and nervously, came out from behind the trees, the headstones and off the floor."

"They were maybe thirty feet away," Jeff Shiffman says. "Suddenly they yell, *'My sister's buried in there!'* and we're just praying that they'll go away. Well, they don't and things escalate. One of them pulls out an Uzi and starts shooting into the air. But as far as we knew, they were shooting directly at us. The police came shortly after that and we didn't have any more trouble."

Oddly enough, another incident involving firearms took place several days later, albeit under completely different circumstances. The scene involved Kevin Connors, Christopher Chomyn and blanks. "That was right around the time that we had heard about Brandon Lee being shot on *The Crow*," Chomyn says. "This was in the mausoleum when Reggie is handcuffed and Kevin walks in pretty close to the camera and shoots. The wadding from the blank came down and burned the back of my hand. Not badly, but it scared me more than anything. Once I knew I wasn't hurt, I was fine. It wasn't his fault. I was so new to the business that I didn't know what we were doing wasn't the safest. I should've known in hindsight, but I didn't."

"I do remember shooting our director of photography," Connors says. "I wound up catching him in the hand with shrapnel a couple of times. I felt bad about it too. No one ever tells you about that part of movie magic. I remember they had a weapons specialist take me to a firing range to prepare with a real .357 before filming. What thirteen year old

kid wouldn't love that?"

On February 13, the production resumed filming at the North Hollywood warehouse with the booby-trapped interior of Tim's house in a sequence that would feel at home in an R-rated version of *Home Alone*. Stuntman Bob Ivy doubled actor Brooks Gardner for the scene where a knife-adorned clown mannequin falls from the ceiling, barely missing Rufus. "Those were really fun scenes to shoot," Kevin Connors says. "It was like every day on set was Halloween. It was great!"

ROCKY

Where Kevin Connors' Tim was an obvious tribute to an existing character, Gloria Lynne-Henry's Rocky was unique and unlike any character ever seen before in *Phantasm*. Equal parts B-movie exploitation and action heroine, no other role beyond the original film caught on with audiences quite like Rocky. "It's been amazing to have the kind of following that I've had with Rocky," Lynne-Henry says. "People really appreciate that she was a black female in a horror movie who didn't die. On top of that, she was a strong heroine! That wins a lot of enthusiasm from the general public."

As filming continued, Lynne-Henry began to feel a connection to and responsibility for Rocky similar to Angus Scrimm's connection to the Tall Man. "The biggest black action star I knew at the time was Wesley Snipes," Lynne-Henry says. "So I decided that I was going to be a female Wesley Snipes and, by doing that, I probably went over the top a little bit. But my mindset was that I was going to be sexy and kick major butt

Top: Reggie Bannister, Gloria Lynne-Henry, Angus Scrimm, Michael Baldwin and Kevin Connors rehearse.
Bottom: Mark Shostrom checks Angus Scrimm's spear apparatus.

(Photos courtesy Kristen Deem)

with the part. A couple of times wardrobe would say, '*They want you not to be so sexy here,*' and I would just say, '*No, I'm not wearing that. Rocky wouldn't wear that. She's a military girl, but she wouldn't wear that.*'"

Lynne-Henry's input also extended to dialogue. "Don would go, '*Here's what you have to say,*' and I would go, '*Rocky wouldn't say that.*' Being a black female, I know there's certain dialogue that she just wouldn't say. Don was so wonderful in letting me add a couple of slang things here and there, and letting me reword my lines. It made me feel so much more comfortable with the character."

"One of my favorite parts of the film was Rocky's expression in the 'Cuda when we see the pink hearse pull alongside them," Seth Blair says. "Just as we see Rufus, Henry and Edna in the front seat right before the crash, Rocky says, '*Friends of yours?*' That was really funny and it wasn't even in the shooting script."

SPEARING THE TALL MAN

On Friday, February 12, filming moved to the embalming room set for several scenes near film's end. Among these was one in which Mike stumbles from a gurney and over to a mirror. Horrified, he sees what the Tall Man has been trying to extract from his skull – an embedded sphere caked in yellow blood. "That mirror scene was shot by a second unit director, a very nice guy," Michael Baldwin says. "As I recall, the first couple of takes had been much more than what you see in the film. You might call it the Al Pacino School of Overacting if I may just align myself with one of our greatest actors. But that's the way I work. At the beginning, I'm way over the top with too much and then I dial back. I find it's much harder to go the other way and pump up your performance. Later on when I saw the final version, I asked Don why he picked the take he did and not the other ones and he said, '*Dude, those were way too over the top.*'"

"We had to do two setups for that sphere-head scene," Mark Shostrom says. "One was a very tricky appliance on Michael's real head with a hair piece on it so that he could peel it back and be the person looking in the mirror. The other was a gelatin head that we shot much later on. That head allowed us to do a close-up of the sphere sitting in Mike's skull because obviously you can't do that on a real person. It's the same situation we had with Angus in the second movie with the bug coming out of his head. It's the only option you have when an actor can't physically do the gag."

This same evening saw Baldwin and Kevin Connors as Mike and Tim, the past and future, strapped to gurneys in the Tall Man's lair. "Mike was the coolest acting teacher I've ever had," Connors says. "He was definitely the jokester on set. I remember that he had a very outgoing personality. He was a guy's actor, just super cool and always seemed smooth in every scene he was doing. He was kind of like our own George Clooney."

"Kevin was a good little actor, very likable, and we would hang out in-between scenes," Baldwin says. "I think I saw a little bit of myself in him, honestly, but I was much more talented than he was at that age. *Kidding*! I'm kidding! In those scenes where we're both incapacitated in the embalming room, I remember having conversations with him, actor to actor, about trying to create a moment there and working on expanding that moment. Kevin was very professional for someone his age."

It should also be noted that on this night, Scrimm delivered what would become his favorite line in all four films: "*Let me release you from this imperfect flesh that ties you to time and space. All that is unknown will be known to you once more.*"

On Thursday, February 18, filming continued inside the embalming room with a sequence that would put years of speculation to rest. In the original *Phantasm*, a striding Tall Man pauses before the icy mist which billows from Reggie's ice cream truck. The mortician's reaction is strangely ambiguous. The debate vacillates between whether he was experiencing pain or ecstasy. The final answer, now revealed in a deleted ending, is pain. Yet this excised footage would not be available to the fan base on home video until 1999. With *Phantasm III*, Coscarelli planned to freeze the Tall Man and then show exactly the effect this would have on him.

A quiet moment on set.
(Photo courtesy Kristen Deem)

Top Left: The frozen makeup being applied to Angus Scrimm.
Top Right and *Bottom*: Mark Shostrom's Tall Man sculpture before, during and after filming.
(Scrimm photo courtesy Kristen Deem)
(Sculpture photos courtesy Mark Shostrom)

The sequence proceeds with Rocky impaling the Tall Man with a liquid nitrogen-tipped crematory poker. Immobilized by the cold, the Tall Man is pushed back into a freezer wall. Rocky, Reggie and Tim slam shut the freezer door. A gold sphere burrows out from the mortician's frozen cranium and explodes through the freezer door. The Tall Man is no fan of cold.

As the main unit prepared to roll camera, Mark Shostrom was in the back offices fitting Angus Scrimm with an impaled poker. The actor was forced to endure the awkward lance apparatus for hours on end while the set was prepped. To prevent him from accidentally stabbing a crewmember, soda cans were placed on the poker ends that jutted out from his chest and back. When off camera, Kristen Deem and Shostrom took turns supporting the weight of the pole to give Scrimm momentary relief. The actor joked that Deem deserved a *'Spear Carrier for Mr. Scrimm'* credit on the film to which she quickly responded with an alternative, *'Sphere Carrier for Mr. Scrimm'.* Her final credit, however, was as *'Assistant to Mr. Scrimm'.*

Meanwhile on the embalming room set, Gloria Lynne-Henry was readying to film Rocky's encounter with the Tall Man. "I had a spear," Lynne-Henry says. "S-P-E-A-R. Not the other word, not a sphere (laughs). I'm supposed to ram it at Angus and right when they said, *'Action'* I started laughing hysterically, and Don says, *'Cut, cut, cut. Gloria, what's wrong?'* And I told him, *'Don, I'm about to spear the Tall Man! (laughs)'* and I just kept on cracking up. It was crazy and I couldn't help it! So they let me gather myself and we get ready for another take, same scene, and right as they called, *'Action',* I started crying. So Don (frustrated) goes, *'Cut, cut, cut. Gloria. What's wrong now?'* and I go, *'I'm in a movie with the Tall Man!!!'* It was just so overwhelming for me and I could not stop crying. I mean, this is the man that would scare you when you were little and say *'Boy!'* and here I am, all the way from Michigan, standing in this makeshift mausoleum with this beautiful man. Angus' personality is incredible and to be there about to spear him, it was the most moving thing I've felt in my film career."

"I'll never forget Gloria's laugh," Connors says, recalling his co-star. "Her laugh always made me laugh. She's got one of those crazy laughs. Once it starts, it's out of control.

She was just one of those very charismatic kind of people. I remember making jokes with her about the script because there's that over the top, chasin' zombies thing. She had a big heart. I loved hanging out with her."

Later that night, filming moved further inside the set into the morgue freezer. Despite its cold appearance onscreen, the actual environment was blisteringly hot with no air conditioning or ventilation. Studio lights only drove the temperature up more and, worst of all, the icy-looking fog was almost pure carbon dioxide, which made breathing difficult as the shoot raged on. To help the Tall Man appear frozen and not in heatstroke, Shostrom and Dean Gates applied a makeup called zice, which wouldn't run as Scrimm's body temperature and perspiration increased. Gates' ingenious ice crystal makeup consisted of spraying the actor with heated wax from an insect fogger.

"The closer we got to the end of filming, the more we realized just how ambitious the shooting schedule we had was," Jeff Shiffman says. "We ended up with only a couple of weeks left and a whole lot of scenes still to shoot. Our way of getting around that was taking an extra week to film and, on top of that, shooting around some of the more time-consuming special effects because Don could more easily shoot those in post-production with his own miniature unit."

HOSPITAL ATTACK

The company spent Tuesday and Wednesday, February 23 and 24, on the hospital room set capturing the film's introductory scene. A comatose Mike wakes from the dream tunnel scene and is attacked by the demon nurse operative of the Tall Man. Reggie shows up and, after a moment of struggle, a silver sphere bursts from the nurse's head and crashes out through a window.

"My scenes in the hospital were fun but not for the reasons you might think," Michael Baldwin says. "When you're in a hospital bed in a show, you're just lying there. You don't have to stand up so it's rather relaxing and there's plenty of time when you're just waiting around so you can take it easy and

Top: An on set reunion with Reggie Bannister, Kathy Lester and Bill Thornbury.
Bottom: Kerry Prior's bizarre eyeball sphere.
(Cast photo courtesy Guy Thorpe)
(Sphere photo courtesy Mark Shostrom)

even nap. It's better than wasting your time standing around craft services all day."

Even from this early scene, it had become apparent to Baldwin as it would to audiences later that *Phantasm III*'s Mike seemed incongruent with previous films. First an energetic youth and then a romantic heartthrob, this version of the character was mainly a victim; often attacked, kidnapped or chased. The former main character goes missing for the entire second act of the film. "My only complaint with *Phantasm III* was with my own performance," Baldwin says. "I just played Mike too much like a victim and you can't do that when you're supposed to be a hero. If I could go back and do it differently, I definitely would because it's not so much about how the dialogue is written; it's about how you play it. The script is a big part of it, but the actor's take on what is written is what matters at the end of the day. I tried to fix that for *Phantasm IV* and have Mike be the hero again."

"The hospital attack was filmed over a long night that began in early afternoon," Irene Roseen says. "The demon nurse makeup took a few hours and by the time you're on set, you play the *'hurry up and wait'* game because it's a movie set. We were the last ones out of the soundstage that night, the makeup guys and myself. It was around four in the morning when we started taking it off. That process took a long time."

"There was a part of that scene that got cut out," Dean Gates says. "I had rigged a dummy head of the demon nurse with compressed air valves that, when triggered, would spurt out pieces of her skull. That's what you see in the film. The part that got cut was where the sphere inside was shown to have a Sawzall blade as though it was trying to cut its way out of her head. Instead we just cut to Irene with a half-ball appliance on her head flailing around. I've got to hand it to her – she really helped sell that scene with her performance."

"Irene was great and very fun to work with," Baldwin says. "People are always asking me if I was ever scared while making one of these movies or scared of Angus as a kid and I tell them, *'Never'*. But when Irene turned around in that hideous makeup, she scared the shit out of me! It was one of the very few times where I was truly freaked out on a set while

making a *Phantasm* movie. I love seeing actors when they're totally with what they're doing. It just takes your breath away. She was great that entire day."

"He gave me a lot of freedom with that scene," Roseen says of Don Coscarelli. "He blocked it himself and his only other direction was for me to be as sweet and helpful as I could. I was supposed to be spiritually guiding this poor young man over the crossroads and then once he woke up I would just snap. Don said, '*You scared the heck out of me in the audition so I want you to go full-force with it here.*' And then Reggie comes in. Talk about being in the wrong place at the wrong time! He had to get that yellow stuff sprayed in his mouth for that scene. I did not envy him."

"That scene actually went wrong in a good way," Gates continues. "When the demon nurse pulls out the IV, the yellow blood was supposed to hit Reggie in the face. We hid a latex bladder under Irene's neck appliance, the tubing of which ran down to a fire extinguisher filled with that nasty yellow stuff. The pressure going into the bladder was so strong that instead of spurting, it ballooned out like a grotesque boil. It was pretty cool! We hadn't even planned on it happening that way. For the reverse shot of Reggie getting a mouthful of goop, I had fun squirting him with a medical syringe over and over. Then in between shots he uses a magical paper towel to wipe it away and he's clean for the rest of the scene."

The following day character actor Chuck Butto filmed his role as Mike's somewhat shady doctor, a bit part with a subtle twist. "I remember Don had quite a bit of input on my role," Butto says. "We did the scene a few times and any number of different ways. I did want to cast a little bit of doubt in the audience with the role and that was my intention with it. I think that was Don's idea too since it was the opening scene of the picture. We wanted the audience to be not quite sure of this guy."

Cameras returned to the hospital set on Wednesday, March 3 to film several cameos, the first of which brought back the Lady in Lavender character from *Phantasm* as a nurse. Kathy Lester remembers being more than happy to reprise her role. "It was really great to see everyone after so long. I spent all day on set and had so much fun reflecting about the good old days with Bill and Angus. I was kind of hoping when I arrived that Don would say, '*Let's make her the main character and give Elvira a run for her money!*' (laughs) But that didn't happen." Lester's cameo eventually amounted to a single shot at the beginning of the film when the camera dollies into Mike's hospital room. Sharp-eyed viewers can also spot Angus Scrimm as the doctor opposite her in the brief shot. The moment passes so quickly that many fans miss her appearance altogether. "When I went to see the screening," Lester says, "I totally missed the scene. Even I missed it and I'm in it! Not only is it a cameo, it's a blip!"

Another hospital cameo was that of Michael Baldwin's wife, Jennifer Bross, as the receptionist at the nurse's station when Reggie walks past. "You might ask yourself why wouldn't Jennifer hear the monstrous racket going on in the hospital room later on," Baldwin says. "Well, she had headphones on. That was her cameo and she was great in that scene. Don told me how many women were vying for that tiny little part, everyone's wives and girlfriends and it was very sweet of him to choose her." Bross would go on to inspire Coscarelli to create the character of the same name in *Phantasm: Oblivion* several years later.

KIDNAPPING MIKE

Friday night, February 26, saw the production working in different directions. The first order of business was filming the reunion of Mike, Jody and Reggie on the living room set. The reunion, which follows the hospital attack, is cut short when the Tall Man arrives: Reggie is incapacitated, Jody imprisoned within a charred sphere and Mike kidnapped. The black leather Eames chair that spins around to reveal Bill Thornbury is the same prop from the Pearson home in *Phantasm*. Thornbury and Bannister staged a musical reunion on set, much to the crew's delight. A visiting Guy Thorpe commemorated the event by treating the crew to a round of Dos Equis, an inside-joke for those who recalled the brewery's sponsorship on the first film. The day was also sweetened by a surprise visit from Kathy

Lester. It marked the first time in nearly fifteen years that all five performers stood together in one room with their director.

The scene in Reggie's home marked the first major input that Kristen Deem had upon a *Phantasm* film as script consultant. "For *Phantasm II*, I'd made minor continuity corrections," Deem says. "But now I was creatively contributing to the story. To see this coming to life around me on that set was such an incredible, unbelievable experience!" As originally written, the Tall Man was to crash through a window in Reggie's home to kidnap Mike, a move used twice before in *Phantasm* and *Phantasm II*. "I suggested to Don that he re-write the scene so that there's this energy field enveloping the entire house with windows blowing out, fierce winds and electric static. The portal would suddenly appear inside the house and the Tall Man would step through. This indicated that the spacegate wasn't a fixed device confined to the white space/time continuum room. It made the Tall Man scarier because he could now appear instantly wherever he chose. There would be no way to escape him."

Coscarelli liked this idea so much that he reused it in *Phantasm: Oblivion* several years later. The spacegates were now more than just a doorway to the Red Planet. The possibilities were endless. They could lead *anywhere*.

Reggie's den. This room could use a plant.
(Photo courtesy Guy Thorpe)

Elsewhere in the warehouse, a second unit was scheduled to film scenes inside the Tall Man's hearse including the scene where Tim's parents are abducted. Thorpe had arranged for a member of the local hearse club to lend his 1971 Cadillac for the night as he had done on previous exterior shoots. Unfortunately, the hearse owner never showed and Thorpe was unable to find a replacement on such short notice. "What we ended up doing was using the pink hearse," he says. "We were just careful not to show the outside of the car. Surprisingly, it worked, though for the shot of Angus looking in the rear view mirror at Tim, you can almost tell it's a pink hood!"

The following night, filming resumed at the living room set with the Tall Man's dramatic entrance. The scene called for Reggie to be thrown backwards by an unseen force and knocked unconscious. When Reggie Bannister arrived on set to find his role reassigned to stuntman Gunther Simon, he began to protest. After all, he could (and still can) proudly count the number of times he had needed a stunt double in his career on one hand.

Having personally designed the stunt, coordinator John Stewart was firm in his decision to use Simon. "I won't let actors do heavy stunts like the ratchet pull with Reggie. I never do because they'll get hurt. I always let them do fights if they'll work out and rehearse it beforehand, though. I like to let the actors throw a few punches but when it's time to fall down stairs or over a railing, that's when I put a stuntman in there."

Stewart explained to Bannister that the stunt involved Simon being harnessed to a shock cord that ran ten feet over a set wall where several burly grips were waiting to pull it back violently. Recalling his own time on the business end of a shock cord for the spacegate room scene in *Phantasm*, Bannister agreed to using a stuntman.

THE PINK HEARSE STUNT

Saturday, March 6 involved what might be the most unforgettable night of filming on any *Phantasm*. In the film, zombies Henry, Rufus and Edna engage the 'Cuda in a chase,

Reggie Bannister in the makeup trailer.
(Photo courtesy Kristen Deem)

which abruptly ends when their pink hearse slams into a boulder. The brightly colored funeral coach is sent careening through the air and bursts into flames upon crash landing. Designed by John Michael Stewart, the death-defying pipe-ramp stunt was to be performed by stuntman Bob Ivy, a self-professed fan of the franchise.

"Dan Roebuck called me one day saying that he wanted to go pick up a coffin for a Halloween show he was putting on and I had a pickup truck that could transport it," Ivy says. "We went over to this apartment in Hollywood and it was Guy Thorpe's house. He showed me his *Phantasm* collection and I was thoroughly impressed. Then he told me that they were getting ready to make *Phantasm III*. So I went home and called John Stewart who worked on *Phantasm II* and *Survival Quest* and told him that I wanted to work on it and that's how I got the pink hearse stunt."

Staged on Mulholland Highway, the night shoot attracted a sizable crowd of onlookers that included cast and crew, their families, the local hearse club, a camera crew from NBC Channel Four, emergency personnel and the highway patrol. The stunt was to feature a pipe ramp specially designed by Stewart to include a jump-enhancing kicker. The coordinator had the ramp disassembled after filming so that it could not be used again after *Phantasm III*. Stewart was also in charge of death proofing the pink hearse, which included the installation of a roll cage. Channel Four reported the stunt's final price tag at $20,000.

"Just before I did the stunt," Ivy says, "the highway patrol came over to me and said, '*We're going to have a radar gun on you and if you go over the speed limit we're going to shut you down.*' So I was pretty bummed because that was just too slow. As I was getting ready to go to the starting position, Don came over and said, '*I don't care if they shut us down. Just go as fast as you want.*' So that was all I needed to hear."

"That officer was really difficult," Christopher Chomyn adds. "He kept threatening to shut us down and, for the record, his breath smelled a lot like whiskey."

"He kept telling us that we could not go faster than the posted speed limit which was something like 35 miles per hour," Seth Blair recalls. "If the hearse hit the pipe ramp going that slow, it might never have gone off the other end. It might have just have stopped at the top and teetered there. After that representative left the conversation, we had our own discussion regarding how fast we thought the car needed to hit the ramp. Ultimately, I think Bob far exceeded the speed we decided on."

Chomyn had intended to capture the stunt using a multi-camera setup including one operated by himself, one operated by Don Coscarelli and one inside a crash-proof box operated by no one. Chomyn's own camera was positioned several hundred feet in the direct path of the hearse. "I was walking toward my camera and I saw that a stunt guy had parked his van right behind my position," Chomyn says. "He gets out of his van and tells me, '*Look, if that hearse lands on its wheels it's going to come at you like a bullet, and if that happens this van is going to drive in between you and it to stop it.*' I thought that was nuts. I couldn't believe what I was hearing. Then he tells me about this other guy standing there in full harness attached to something on the side of the road. He said, '*If this happens, he's going to pull you out of the way and jump down this slope holding onto you.*' It was the stupidest idea ever, but I was green and also feeling a lot of other pressures at the time, so I just went along with it, not that any of that wound up happening."

"The speedometer on the hearse wasn't working," Ivy says. "But I pretty much floored it all the way to the ramp. I was knocked out immediately. When you see it flipping through the air, I'm already unconscious at that point."

"We had cameras placed a couple hundred feet down from the ramp and it flew over all of them," Stewart says. "When I got to Bob once he landed, it had rung his bell pretty good." As the disoriented stuntman was being pulled from the wreckage, he was reportedly asked if he needed anything and jokingly responded, "*A Coke.*" The distance between the ramp and where the hearse touched down measured one hundred and forty-seven feet. The highway patrolman clocked Ivy at more than eighty miles per hour but for whatever reason, most likely amazement, no citations were issued. Immediately rushed to the hospital, Ivy was shot full of narcotics. "I was in a lot of pain and, unfortunately, these didn't do anything for me,"

"When you see it flipping through the air, I'm already unconscious at that point."

Bob Ivy on the pink hearse stunt

The zombie trio of Brooks Gardner, John Chandler and Cindy Ambuehl (Dean Gates applying makeup)
(Gardner/Chandler photo courtesy Guy Thorpe)
(Ambuehl photo courtesy Kristen Deem)

he says. "For two weeks afterwards, I would have dizzy spells and double vision. Sore muscles and headaches too, but they all went away eventually."

"We were all very relieved that Bob was okay after what we just saw happen," Blair says. "The car prep guys who built the safety cage saved Bob's life. My family was there that night. I wanted them to see what I was doing and what I was a part of. It was a proud moment and I still have a very special souvenir from that crash that can be clearly seen in the movie, but I won't say what it is in case Don wants it back. "

"There was something else special about that night of filming for me besides the stunt," Chomyn says. "Just before the jump, I turned around to see this guy videotaping us. I go to tell him that he should leave because this is a dangerous area. He lowers the camera and it's my father! Somehow, since that morning when I called to tell him about the stunt we were doing, he'd flown from Maine to Los Angeles, figured out where we were filming and showed up on set to support me. I was

blown away. It was unbelievable and overwhelming to me that he would do this. He taped the scene and we pulled it up on his camera afterward to watch it. You see Bob hit the ramp and start to soar and right then the camera hits the ground and you hear my Dad go, "*Holy shit!*" and he wasn't shooting anymore. So he really didn't capture much of it!"

CHANGING MIKES

On Tuesday, March 9, Don Coscarelli began work on a sequence he would ultimately never finish. Following Mike's rescue from the crypt wall, the Tall Man chases our heroes through a bunker on the Red Planet, eventually returning to the campsite where the spacegate severed hands wreak havoc. Rumors circulated that Coscarelli intended to finish the sequence with CGI and re-insert it into the film for its 2007 DVD release, but this did not happen. The Anchor Bay disc did include a brief twelve seconds of chase footage, however. In the final version of *Phantasm III*, Reggie and Mike escape directly from the mausoleum prison to their campsite.

On Wednesday, March 10, filming traveled to Angeles Forest to partially re-shoot and continue the ending of *Phantasm II*, this time using Michael Baldwin instead of James LeGros. The finished film would seamlessly blend old and new material. Paula Irvine had retired from acting by this time, her absence resulting in the abrupt dispatch (and decapitation) of her character. Following the fiery hearse crash, Reggie would engage in a grenade standoff with the Tall Man. Coscarelli's script indicates a seven-dwarf posse lurking behind the mortician; a humorous nod to Snow White.

During the night a long-simmering disagreement finally came to a head. The script originally called for Reggie to threaten his adversary, "*Eight seconds to hell, motherfucker.*" Feeling that such profanity would greatly debase the Tall Man, Angus Scrimm objected to the line quite openly. Scrimm had even faxed Coscarelli a strong letter during pre-production advising against this exchange. Unwilling to omit the line, Coscarelli filmed both the scripted sentence and a revised version, "*Eight seconds to hell, goddamn it.*" No promises were made about which would ultimately be used (the latter).

"It would be really hard to look the Tall Man in the eye and call him something like that without immediately being killed," Kristen Deem says. "Yet Don wanted very much to use it and Reggie took great pleasure in saying the line. Not surprisingly, Angus was furious. He started pacing the set, circling the entire area where we were filming, in this predatory stride. To the crew, he looked *scary*. It had been brewing in the back of his mind for months that this might happen. I just remember it was not a good vibe that night. "

Later in the evening, the Tall Man's 1969 Cadillac hearse from *Phantasm II* made a brief return, having since been purchased by Guy Thorpe. For the shot in which the coach skids to a stop mere inches from the camera, the hearse coordinator himself stepped behind the wheel. "That was pretty terrifying," Thorpe says. "I was trying really hard not to slam into the $50,000 camera they were filming with. It took me a

couple of takes to get it right because I was gun-shy, but we got it on the third take. If you look closely, you can just barely see me peering over the steering wheel trying to see where the camera was."

There was an obstacle, however, in that the opening of *Phantasm III* called for the *Phantasm II* hearse to be overturned and burning as the Tall Man confronts Reggie. "I sure wasn't going to let them destroy my hearse that way! So they came up with a pretty clever solution," Thorpe recalls. "They decided to use the pink hearse that Bob Ivy had just crashed because it was totaled anyway. They had to tow this mangled pink hearse to Angeles Forest, get it down off the tow truck, literally push it across the road because it wouldn't roll and flip it onto its side. Then they painted it black using basic house paint and set it on fire. It was pretty funny to watch all this unfold."

On Friday, March 12, the production completed its filming at Angeles Forest with a shot of Thorpe's *Phantasm II* hearse, containing Mike and Liz, racing away from Reggie. As the vehicle, driven by stunt coordinator John Stewart, went out of camera range the crew detonated a controlled background explosion that simulated a crash and burn. Principal photography officially concluded on this night. Several months more of special effects, insert shots and additional scenes were yet to follow.

OVER SCHEDULE (AND BUDGET)

April through June were spent editing and shooting additional sphere and makeup FX sequences. "My biggest concern was all of the sphere effects that had to be built because we had to get them all done on a small budget," Seth Blair says. "I think Kerry Prior had one of the toughest jobs on the film because the spheres were as big a part of *Phantasm III* as the actors. Especially when you consider that we wanted to do some things with the spheres that hadn't been done in either of the two previous films. Kerry really had his work cut out for him."

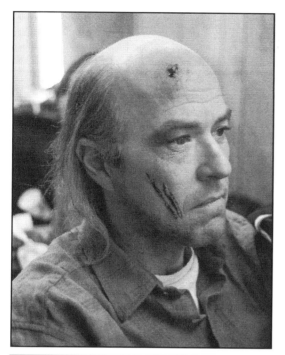

Top Left and *Right*: Reggie Bannister and Angus Scrimm at work on *Phantasm II* continuation.
Bottom: The dwarves unmasked!
(Bannister/Scrimm photos courtesy Kristen Deem)
(Dwarves photo courtesy Guy Thorpe)

Do you sphere what I sphere?
(Photo courtesy Kristen Deem)

"The schedules changed pretty dramatically on *Phantasm III*," returning special effects maker Wayne Beauchamp says. "I came to be on call while I was working on another feature and couldn't give them the new time they'd requested. It was getting to the point where we were there all night and the scenes I was to work on never got shot. I had to pass it off to Kevin McCarthy two days before wrap because I just couldn't do it anymore. They were literally running out of money."

"Obviously, the demise of the Tall Man was the capper of *Phantasm II* and *III* and Don wanted to get rid of him in a different way for each film," Mark Shostrom says. "In this case, he was to be frozen. When it came to actually making the sculpture of the Tall Man's head, I handled that part myself but it had to have some slick, perfect hair work. Because it was a rigid, plastic head, we couldn't punch hair into it." The only other option was to have a custom wig handmade for the scene. Shostrom immediately thought of Karin Hanson who had made wigs for films ranging from *Planet of the Apes* to *The Godfather: Part II*. "She was the best," he continues, "but she was also expensive."

Not wanting to drop the bomb on Coscarelli in terms of cost, Shostrom arranged for him to meet Hanson at his studio. "Eventually, the question from Don's mouth came out, '*How much is this going to cost?*' and Karin answered in her commanding voice, '*Three Thousand Dollars*,'" Shostrom recalls. "Don kind of did a little jig and spun around in his chair. I thought he was going to fall over, honestly. But they did come to an agreement and Karin did the wigs and they looked beautiful in the film. Towards the end, though, Seth had to be the bad guy when the production money ran out. My department also ran out of money and they had cut my partner, Dean Gates. So I was at my shop for the last few weeks doing five different things at once, working until midnight and trying to get this stuff ready. I called the office and told them that I had to have more money to continue and they said they couldn't do anything. I told them that they had better figure something out because I wasn't going to work out of my own pocket for the next two weeks and they still weren't responding. Then I told them to be more forthcoming with the cash we needed to finish this or else I was going to take the Michael Baldwin heads I had made, put them in the alley and run over them with my truck. That got their attention and things improved shortly thereafter."

"You've got to laugh when you're on a show like *Phantasm III*," Jeff Shiffman says. "Every crew member from

181

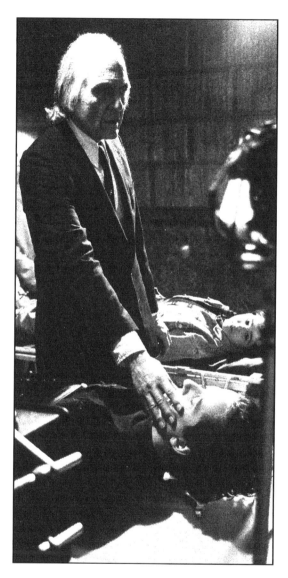

The Tall Man and his boys.
(Photo courtesy Kristen Deem)

A NEW ENDING

By early April, the poor state of the budget was also spelling trouble for the film's original ending wherein the Tall Man's gold cranial sphere was to be forever buried in ice, forever defeated (until one factors in global warming as Reggie Bannister jokes). A previously slated field trip to Alaska to shoot on-location was now financially impossible. Not wanting to give up his Arctic ending, Don Coscarelli attempted to shoot close-ups of Bannister and Connors burying the gold sphere, hoping to later integrate these with stock footage of a snowy wilderness. The close-ups were staged in the parking lot of the North Hollywood warehouse on a hot, sunny day with the cast decked out in parkas and icy-looking makeup.

"I do remember shooting that ending and filming in those parkas," Connors says. "That's actually the only thing I remember doing in post-production. I really liked that ending because it had that sense of finality to it that I thought was really cool. But obviously, when you're making a series of movies, I knew they'd need more of an exciting cliffhanger. And I knew that one day they'd make a fourth one. It was Reggie, myself, Don and the director of photography. There may have also been a makeup person, but it was a very small crew that shot that."

In late April, Coscarelli informed his cast that he was opting out of the original ending in favor of a new one that would allow the Tall Man to live. As Rocky, Reggie and Tim reentered the Boulton mausoleum, they would find that a new Tall Man had already arrived through the spacegate. After a swarm of spheres fatally pins Rocky to the wall, she warns Tim and Reggie that it's all over. As the freezer doors swing open to reveal the Tall Man, he tells them, *'It's never over.'* Tim is then pulled backward through a window by an unseen figure before the scene cuts to black. The only problem with this new ending was that Coscarelli wouldn't be ready to film until sometime in mid-June, long after Scrimm's contract with the production had ended. The Tall Man performer would graciously return for the new ending without pay or contract. For this he wore the original Tall Man suit.

craft services on up is putting in incredible hours and the fatigue level is so high that you're actually shortening your life. So there's no reason to have a miserable set. The very least you can ask for is to have a funny set and to keep the humor going. That's what is going to keep crew morale up."

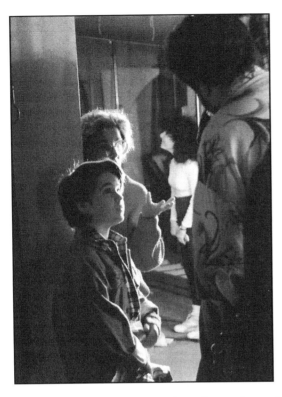 

Filming the new ending with Kevin Connors/Don Coscarelli (*left*) and Angus Scrimm (*right*).
(Photos courtesy Kristen Deem)

"I remember that they had a test screening and they asked the audience what they thought of the Rocky character," Lynne-Henry says. "They said that they liked her very much and at this point, I was going to die. They were going to kill me off. Because of the audience's response, they decided to change it so that I could drive off at the end of the film and live to see another day."

"I like the new ending better," Baldwin says. "I would always prefer we do a cliffhanger ending on these films because then there's a possibility of coming back someday."

Work on the new ending commenced the following month. Thursday, June 17, marked Angus Scrimm's last day of filming which, coincidentally, made his final scene the last of the picture, an anomaly in filmmaking as most productions shoot out of order. Scrimm's only shot for the entire day entailed the freezer doors swinging open and the camera dollying in for a close-up as he warned, '*It's never over.*' The line was suggested by Coscarelli's mother. By 2 PM, Scrimm had wrapped all of his scenes for *Phantasm III*. Elsewhere in the warehouse, Bannister was being adorned with more than a dozen silver spheres for his character's multi-sphere attack.

The last material to film for the day also happened to be the final shot in the film. Still sporting bruises from his pink hearse stunt several months earlier, stuntman Bob Ivy stood in for the graver that breaks through a window to grab an unsuspecting Tim. "I was a little bit anxious about the scene where the guy grabs me through the fake glass because I'd never done anything like that before," Connors says. "I was mostly worried about where the glass was going to go. I just didn't know what to expect but it was fine. Scary, but fine."

Reggie was less victorious in the new ending.
(Photo courtesy Kristen Deem)

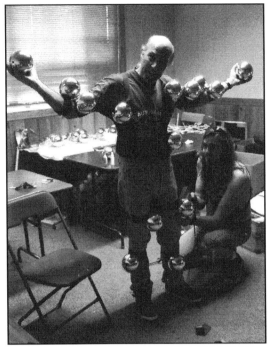

Top Left and *Right*: Reggie Bannister and the new ending.
Bottom: Michael Baldwin on set.
(Getting Ready/Baldwin photos courtesy Kristen Deem)
(Pinned Bannister photo courtesy Guy Thorpe)

WEEKEND OF HORRORS

On May 1, 1993, <u>Fangoria</u> held its annual Weekend of Horrors convention in Los Angeles where *Phantasm III* was to have a strong presence. Angus Scrimm appeared as a presenter at the Chainsaw Awards alongside *Mindwarp* co-star Bruce Campbell, who joked onstage that he was taller than the Tall Man (but only when he stood on his toes). Elsewhere at the event, Michael Baldwin and Reggie Bannister narrated a behind-the-scenes slideshow to a crowded ballroom of fans, giving them a rare glimpse of the discarded Arctic ending.

"I was miserable at that show," Baldwin says. "My agreement to do it had been only if Angus and Don were going to show up and we all do it together. We all had to be there for me to show. But they bailed and no one told me because I would've bailed too. At the time, I just didn't understand the whole fan-convention thing and maybe it freaked me out a little. I totally get it now, though. That weekend wound up being just Reg and me onstage trying to charm our way through a slideshow, which was not the most exciting way to promote our new film."

Top: Michael Baldwin and Reggie Bannister on stage.
Middle: Bruce Campbell tries to be taller than the Tall Man.
Bottom: Conversing after the show.
(Photos courtesy Kristen Deem)

HEARSE FLEET

On Thursday, June 24, Don Coscarelli and a skeleton crew traveled to Agoura to shoot insert shots of the Tall Man's fleet of hearses. Coordinator Guy Thorpe made his biggest impact on the film this night when he wrangled nearly two-dozen funeral coaches. Personally phoning members of the Los Angeles Hearse Society, Thorpe was able to round up volunteers who wanted to have their vehicles featured in the film. "We followed each other up to Agoura and then we put ourselves in a holding pattern," he says. "Once we caught up with each other, we slowly drove up into the complex in formation. I'll never forget the look on Don's face when he saw twenty hearses drive onto his set. He was so happy to see everyone arrive." The location was only a few hundred yards from the hanging tree from *Phantasm*.

Once the hearses were in position, Coscarelli captured the scene where Reggie, Tim and Rocky drive up on several gravers amid the hearse fleet. Bob Ivy stepped in as the graver sent flying after being hit by the 'Cuda. As the night drew to a close and the sun began to rise, post-production photography was now complete.

CUT TO PREVIEW

The following week was spent busily editing several last minute scenes into the film in advance of its first test screening on Thursday, July 1. The film would be screened at 7 PM on the Warner Brothers lot in Burbank for an audience that was largely random, although a handful of fans and hearse society members were present. Don Coscarelli attended with his parents. Kristen Deem, Guy Thorpe and Bob Ivy attended, arriving in style on the backlot in the *Phantasm II* hearse. Cast members were not allowed to attend for fear of falsely influencing the audience, but Angus Scrimm did slip in once the lights had dimmed and then out again before they came back on. The print used for this screening was rough and missing finished effects and score.

Bottom: Guy Thorpe with Baldwin and Scrimm.
(Photo courtesy Kristen Deem)

Even so, the audience cheered at the first appearance of the Tall Man striding through Perigord's fiery embalming room.

On Thursday, July 1, Kristen Deem wrote:

It is wonderful to see P3 from start to finish on screen. It looks better than I expected! It's fast-paced and filled with action and great SPFX. Michael Baldwin and Bill Thornbury look wonderful acting together again. Reggie steals the show as comic relief. Angus is great as the Tall Man. [...] Some fans complain that Reggie is too much like Rambo and that P3 turned out to be his story when it should have been Mike and the Tall Man's story. One audience member is quite blunt that Coscarelli leaves the ending too open and is hinting too much at a Phantasm IV. The young man complains that he wants answers NOW and doesn't want to wait for yet another sequel. Overall, though, the audience likes the film and is quite kind.

Although positively received, several problems with the film were now apparent to Coscarelli, some of which were fixed with the addition of exposition regarding the Tall Man. Unable to remove or change the zombie stooge/pink hearse scenes that divided audience opinion, Coscarelli instead focused on choosing more effective dialogue takes.

"That was a great screening," Thorpe says. "We had to contain our excitement whenever the hearse scenes came on. We thought it was just hilarious that we had driven there in the very hearse we were seeing up on the big screen. This was a good year before it got released and the mood was a little more optimistic. We weren't sure it was headed to theaters, but it wasn't entirely ruled out at that point."

The following week saw the North Hollywood world of *Phantasm III* start to crumble as sets were demolished and the warehouse cleared. This was concurrent with Scrimm trimming away the Tall Man's long locks. The cast and crew moved on to other projects. The production was officially complete.

"The most rewarding aspect of working on the film for me was the day I left the project," Seth Blair says. "I had just given someone I didn't know ten months of my life. I gave Don and the production everything I had to give. Everything else in my life at that time was secondary. And, in turn, Don put my name on the movie poster. That made it all worth it. I have the poster beautifully framed and still hanging in my office to this day."

On July 24, *Phantasm III* was screened for the MPAA, who naturally objected to the film's gore content. Their issue was not with shotgun blasts, impalements or decapitations but with the same sphere drilling scene they had objected to twice before in *Phantasm* and *Phantasm II*. Coscarelli once again attempted to make a case that his scene was identical to *Phantasm*'s drilling scene, which they had permitted with an R-rating, and even presented a frame-by-frame comparison of the two scenes. The MPAA rejected his argument, however, and refused to assign his film the desired R-rating. Coscarelli dialed back the drilling scene and was finally granted an R-rating on November 16.

The revised R-rating certificate.
(Certificate courtesy Guy Thorpe)

DISTRIBUTION

Upon completion, *Phantasm III* sat idle in the hands of MCA/ Universal for the remainder of 1993, the studio seemingly unsure what to do with it. Despite positive test audience responses, the movie was ultimately given a limited theatrical run the following year before a direct-to-video rollout in the days leading up to Halloween. Perhaps the recent commercial failure of *Army of Darkness* had some bearing on MCA's reluctance, especially in light of *Phantasm II*'s meager earnings. Neither 1993 nor 1994 were particularly strong horror years for the studio; *Phantasm III* marked MCA's only horror genre output for 1994.

Despite being spun as "chillingly successful" to home video retailers, *Phantasm III*'s limited theatrical run failed to inspire a wider release. The studio did emphasize, however, that it out-grossed *Serial Mom, Cops and Robertsons* and *Bad Girls* in "some regions." MCA was also quick to tout the return of *Phantasm*'s original cast as well as Angus Scrimm's recent induction into the Fangoria Hall of Fame. The film's eventual arrival onto home video occurred with minimal fanfare, though it now bore a peculiar subtitle: *Lord of the Dead*. The new *Phantasm* received none of the lush marketing that had been afforded *Phantasm II*. Instead, it featured as part of a bizarre promotion wherein video retailers who ordered three or more units of the film would receive a Tall Man clock with plastic sphere blades as clock hands. The home video release was unable to even approach the runaway sales of *Jurassic Park*, released a week earlier.

MCA/Universal paraded Scrimm through several media appearances to promote the film. The star was flown cross-country to their Orlando, Florida theme park as a presenter alongside Beetlejuice for the 1994 Halloween Horror Nights telecast. Just prior to Halloween, Scrimm hosted a segment of Extra! wherein he counted down his top five Halloween movies, number one of course being *Phantasm III*. The humorous segment began with Scrimm sandwiched between two monster rivals: "Forget about that wimp, Freddy

Top: An introspective Michael Baldwin.
Bottom: The Tall Man senses a disturbance...
(Photos courtesy Kristen Deem)

189

Krueger, and that hoax in the hockey mask, Jason… *I* am the high lord of horror this Halloween!"

With the reduced visibility of a direct-to-video release came far fewer reviews. Daniel Schweiger notably wrote in <u>Fangoria</u> that *Phantasm III* was "the wildest *Phantasm* of all." He went on to praise its "brain-blowing effects" and called the reunion of original cast members "a horror fan's wet dream."

In a rare bright spot following the direct-to-video release, *Phantasm III* was nominated for and won the Fangoria Chainsaw Award for Best Limited Release Film of 1994. The award was presented onstage to Don Coscarelli at the annual Weekend of Horrors convention in Los Angeles.

Right: Embalmer for hire.
Below: Michael and Reggie at Fangoria with Ted Raimi.
(Reggie photo courtesy Todd Mecklem)
(Convention photo courtesy Kristen Deem)

THE END?

In a major blow to series morale, *Phantasm III*'s challenging production had been followed by a halfhearted release from an indifferent distributor. This turn of events was all the more unfortunate because the sequel was a worthy series entry with a unique sensibility all its own. Had the new film dropped the ball, so to speak, a home video release would have been appropriate. Even with its abundance of black humor, *Phantasm III* stood tall as an action-packed thrill ride every bit as slick and polished as its predecessor, an impressive visual feat given the further reduced budget. The story is aggressively advanced with interesting characters both old and new. The strange mythology of the Tall Man and the silver sphere is also satisfyingly expanded.

With so much to like in the film, a direct-to-video fate was hardly warranted. *Phantasm III: Lord of the Dead* would be just one of dozens of home video sequels that year, alongside forgettable such fare as *Children of the Corn III*, *Ghoulies 4* and *Witchcraft 7: Judgement Hour*. Worse, the direct-to-video downgrade cast doubt upon the distribution of potential sequels, if not their very existence.

"I never felt that *Phantasm III* was going to be the final film, mainly because it didn't tie up loose ends," Kristen Deem says. "It felt like the middle of a story where you haven't yet reached the climax. The sequel was building towards something. Only at the end of the film did I feel we were beginning to get somewhere—with Mike's metamorphosis. Of course, there was concern about whether *Phantasm III* even merited another sequel."

While hosting the film on TNT's *MonsterVision*, horror host Joe Bob Briggs praised Kevin Connor's "grade school Rambo" and Gloria Lynne-Henry's "crewcutted black Amazon Kung Fu queen." In his recommendation of the film, he noted, "It's no *Phantasm II* but it's still pretty dang decent."

"What little recognition the film brought me after we made it amazed me," Gloria Lynne-Henry says. "It didn't happen that often, but it definitely happened. People would notice me, sometimes just from my voice, on the subway or at the mall, and tell me how much they liked the movie. Men in bars would buy me drinks. It was insane!"

"I don't think the timing of it was right for a big screen release," Kevin Connors says. "Had it been released some other time, it might've done better. Being my first movie, I was just excited to see it made at all."

"It was great," Seth Blair says. "It was collaborative, it was adversarial, it was full of fun and it was full of tension. There were days that never ended and days that ended too soon. All things that go into making a movie! I worked on this project for ten months and I learned a lot about filmmaking and I learned a lot from Don. I got to direct and shoot some inserts and 2nd unit shots, and I even got to act in a scene and use my body parts for some of the close-up shots. Don knew that I was a muscle car enthusiast so he often let me take the 'Cuda home. It was little things like that which made me work as hard as I could for him."

Gloria Lynne-Henry at a 2010 *Phantasm III* screening.
(Photo courtesy Kristen Deem)

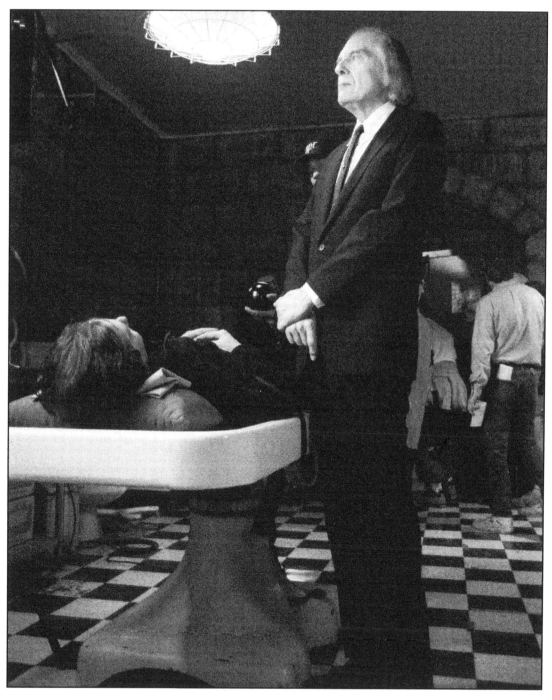

Whither *Phantasm IV*?
(Photo courtesy Kristen Deem)

Chapter 4:
Oblivion

PHANTASM 1999

Following his 1994 Academy Award win for Best Screenplay on *Pulp Fiction,* Roger Avary set his sights on an unusual follow-up project – penning the ultimate sequel to *Phantasm.* The Canadian-born writer, a self-professed "phan," contacted Don Coscarelli with plans to create a big-budget action/horror sequel that would reveal the Tall Man's vast devastation of the United States of America, and depict Reggie's last-ditch effort to stop him. This would mark the first time in the series that Coscarelli's name would be absent from a *Phantasm* script byline, though he still intended to direct. The series creator would give the project his full support, championing it for years to come. Early drafts were titled *Phantasm 1999,* but as the millennium ended it would be renamed *Phantasm 2013* and finally *Phantasm's End.*

Avary's story envisioned the United States in post-apocalyptic ruin from a devastating "bag plague" that caused its victims' heads to swell enormously and burst, raining sharp bone fragments and contaminated blood. Reggie sets out to find and rescue his friend, Mike Pearson, now trapped in the quarantine zone of the central United States. With weaponry and an armored 'Cuda, Reggie embarks on a one-way mission deep into the Tall Man's lair of desolation and disease…

Phan response to the project was immensely enthusiastic, particularly on the Internet where Coscarelli regularly allowed story details and concept art to be posted. The genre community was especially pleased to hear that Avary had written a commando role specifically for Bruce Campbell, who first confirmed but later denied his involvement in the film. Had fans actually been able to read what was being suggested, their reaction might have skewed closer to that of studio executives who found much to criticize about the proposed sequel. Potential backers hesitated not only at the eight million dollar price tag but also at the script itself, voicing their concerns to Coscarelli. Problems within the script ranged from the nitpicky (the Tall Man speaks "backwards-Vietnamese" to his dwarves) to the nearly insurmountable (a screaming monkey named Titi

Avary's script began with the Tall Man chasing a victim through the "Plague Zone" toward quarantined civilization.
(Photo courtesy Guy Thorpe)

saves Reggie by clawing out the Tall Man's eyes).

The script would divide *Phantasm*'s cast, several of whom genuinely favored Avary's bold new direction. Others disliked where the franchise was headed but kept silent so as not to hinder *Phantasm 1999,* which was poised to help the series bounce back from the direct-to-video slump incurred on *Phantasm III.* One anonymous cast member put it bluntly: "I couldn't understand why this writer, who apparently was such a big *Phantasm* fan, would create something so very non-*Phantasm.* That didn't make any sense to me. All of a sudden, it was all about these commandos, but he's Roger Avary, so what are you going to do?"

Although rife with questionable plot choices, the script was not entirely without merit. Fans longing for concrete answers regarding the Tall Man's origin would surely have received it – the Tall Man was to be the product of a "corpuscular projector" controlled by the "Tall Mankind," a grotesque oversized Tall Man head not unlike Oz in *The Wizard of Oz* (the script's own comparison). The *1999* draft also saw Mike Pearson split into "Good Mike" and "Bad Mike," which made for a chilling confrontation. An interesting concept used in later drafts entailed the Tall Man's enormous mausoleum comprising a hyperdimensional tesseract. This meant that corridors existed outside of normal time and space. Depending on what corner he turned, Reggie could conceivably run into himself from an earlier/later time or even enter an alternate dimension!

High among the project's faults was the lack of attention given to main characters other than Reggie. In the *Phantasm 1999* draft, the Tall Man has a five-page introduction before disappearing for a whopping ninety-four pages, then resurfacing only a scant twenty-six before the end. Mike Pearson was shuffled even further into the background, not appearing until page eighty-four and spending the script's remaining thirty-eight pages in Reggie's shadow. In a later *Phantasm 2013* draft, Avary committed the cardinal sin by dropping Mike from the storyline altogether and reassigning what little dialogue he had to other roles. The main character of *Phantasm* had now been reduced to a non-speaking cameo as a mummified corpse. Jody, last seen following his brother into the darkness in *Phantasm III*, was inexplicably absent from the story's action. A later draft would see Jody cameo as another mummified corpse.

Price tag and script issues aside, the changing winds of the horror genre spelled further trouble for the project. Despite valiant efforts, the sequel languished without a backer in the dawning age of *Scream*. A plan was even devised to deliver the film for about half the originally proposed budget but this failed as well. Potential suitors such as New Line Cinema and October Films ultimately passed on the script. Avary would eventually depart the project to direct his own *Rules of Attraction*, leaving Coscarelli to mount a new, scaled down sequel of his own design.

"*Phantasm 1999* was a well written, apocalyptic *Mad Max* affair; a search-and-destroy story mixed liberally with comedy," Kristen Deem says. "Most definitely it was a showcase for Reggie. It would have been a blast for him! He certainly deserved the opportunity after all these years. Yet I couldn't help thinking how this was not a *Phantasm* movie. It had little of the foreboding aura; virtually none of the brooding, nightmarish moments that caused the first movie to get under my skin. The Tall Man and Mike Pearson were hardly in it. It isn't a *Phantasm* movie if the story doesn't revolve around those two characters. *P1999* could have stood on its own, something entirely apart from *Phantasm*. With a different title, it might have been extremely successful."

While Avary's script may indeed have pleased the action movie crowd, it ultimately lacked that Coscarelli magic that had made previous *Phantasm*s so special. The series creator was not only noticeably absent from the script's byline but in the pages that followed as well.

THE NEW SEQUEL

By 1997, Roger Avary's sequel seemed to have lost all momentum going forward. Sensing the need for a new direction, Don Coscarelli opted to write a new script. One strong influence on the new direction was a January 10, 1995 treatment by Kristen Deem (her sixth script consultation on a Coscarelli project) that suggested the series refocus on the Mike/Tall Man relationship. Her pitch found Jody and the Tall Man showing an evolving Mike "visions from his past in a battle of good vs. evil for Mike's soul/mind." From this rudimentary premise, Coscarelli penned a sequel screenplay that juxtaposed new story developments with outtakes from the original *Phantasm*. The first draft was dated March 4, 1997 and titled *Phantasm Fourever*, though subsequent drafts went by the code name *Infinity*. It would eventually see release as *Phantasm: Oblivion* per horror author Richard Elkin's suggestion.

Picking up the story from *III*, the new *Phantasm IV* finds Mike fleeing to Death Valley, frightened and confused by the transformation now upon him. Although warned by the Tall Man to stay away, Reggie follows after his friend at

Jody's insistence. Amid sporadic appearances by his spectral brother and the Tall Man, Mike begins to master his newfound abilities and traverses time and spacegate to better understand his nemesis. He discovers that the Tall Man took the guise of 19th century undertaker/inventor Jebediah Morningside and that perhaps they've been playing this game longer than Mike even remembers. The film climaxes when Mike faces off against Jody and the Tall Man, who succeed in painfully extracting the sphere from his skull, killing off his human form. In the film's final enigmatic moments, Mike and Reggie circa 1978 ride away in the ice cream truck while the dying whispers of present-day Mike permeate the night breeze.

In a journal dated 9/25/97, Angus Scrimm wrote:

> *This is the best Coscarelli script I've read. It gets back to the eerie qualities of the first film in scene after haunting scene. Plus, there's a deepening and enrichment of the four main characters that will be fascinating to play.*

It was clear from the outset that Coscarelli was changing course from the direction in which Avary had hoped to send the franchise. Where *Phantasm 1999* had been big, loud and overly explanatory, *Oblivion* would be introspective, cerebral and offer fewer answers. Mike and Jody were rightfully reinstated as main characters. Both the bag plague and the commando unit were jettisoned. The moment of the Tall Man's creation would feature prominently, but the forces behind him would remain a mystery. The script derived influences not only from Deem's treatment, but also from her earlier *Phantasm III* script critique. These contributions included ideas for Jebediah Morningside, the fortune teller's return and the Civil War flashback. The latter, as first envisioned, would have introduced an even bolder twist to the *Phantasm* mythos than seen in the final film.

"I originally envisioned the Tall Man as a kindly doctor, not an alien, attempting to save the life of one soldier - who turns out to be Michael Pearson," Deem says. "Instead, Mike is the alien, bleeding yellow, who inadvertently infects

Back in control of the franchise.
(Photo courtesy Paul Miser)

the human field surgeon! When Don handed me the *Phantasm III* script in 1992 to critique, and the Tall Man tells Mike, *"You've found your way back to where you started,"* I suggested a battlefield flashback in my notes to him. This would have added an entirely different dimension to their relationship, Mike and the Tall Man coming full circle with Mike being the creator of his nemesis! Versions of my Civil War flashback and the kindly doctor, albeit a bit revised as inventor Jebediah Morningside, ended up five years later in Don's *Phantasm IV* script. I was honored."

A great deal of *Oblivion*'s charm owes to the inclusion of the aforementioned *Phantasm* outtakes, which few had ever seen before. The footage was in relatively good condition, though new sound mixing was in order. The outtakes were also stripped of Fred Myrow's original score and fitted with new music by Christopher Stone. The hanging scene audio track necessitated Angus Scrimm re-recording the Tall Man's entire dialogue with Mike. This and another scene also required new pickup shots for completion. Of the nine *Phantasm* outtakes scripted for inclusion, only five made it into the finished film.

"I was ecstatic when I found out we would be using footage from the first film," Production Assistant Chris Malinowski says. "I was passing through the office one day and walked right past Don and Michael screening outtakes on a monitor and couldn't believe what I was seeing. Who else even knew this material existed after all these years? I appreciated their inclusion because they helped develop the characters more this time around. For me, the deleted scenes from *Phantasm* were the best part of *Oblivion*."

"I thought it was brilliant of Don to weave a story around those deleted scenes," returning hearse coordinator Guy Thorpe says. "I can't think of any other time in film history where that's been done so effectively. I mean, where else do you have an actor that's thirteen in one scene and thirty-three in the next? Never! I was really happy that fans would finally get to see that footage. I knew we were onto something great here and yet I kind of had the feeling that we were making the last *Phantasm* movie all along. Even then, I was perfectly okay with that. If *Oblivion* is how we go out, I'm satisfied."

Whether or not this was going to be *Phantasm*'s swan song became a point of confusion surrounding the production. Despite Coscarelli and the cast lamenting *Oblivion* as hindmost in a Fangoria cover story titled "The Tall Man's Final Ball," it was not truly planned this way as additional sequels were scripted and one even rehearsed on tape in the years that followed. In fact, Coscarelli's sequel was carefully written to be compatible with *Phantasm 2013* should Avary's screenplay have eventually found financial backing. Simply put, *Oblivion* was never truly planned as the final *Phantasm*. It was only marketed that way.

TEAMBUILDING

Solid though the new script may have been, its fortunes were directly tied to the return of the four main cast members. Luckily, they were all agreeable to one more outing, though the film's scheduling did force Angus Scrimm to decline a role in *The X-Files* movie. The only two new characters were Jennifer, a hitchhiking femme fatale, and a demonic state trooper in the employ of the Tall Man. Don Coscarelli cast actress Heidi Marnhout as Jennifer in only her second feature film role. Returning stuntman Bob Ivy was picked for the demon trooper since the role required a stunt-savvy performer for its fiery demise. Ivy would also serve as stunt coordinator.

"Honestly, I didn't have any great motivation to come back for *Phantasm IV*," Michael Baldwin says. "There's not a heck of a lot of money in these movies and the hours are grueling. So in order to make it more interesting for me, I made a deal where I said that I would produce the show *and* star in it, which was challenging as hell. Looking back on it, I was more like a line producer than your average producer who is just sitting in a chair. My job was much more practical than that. It was a very rewarding experience and I'm proud of the film we made for how much we made it on."

"I can remember Coscarelli first telling me that he was ready to do another one," Bill Thornbury says. "I read the script he sent me and I immediately called to tell him that I'd be happy to do it. I wouldn't say there was pressure to come

Top: The Ice Cream Man and the Hearse Man.
Bottom: Michael Baldwin - star and co-producer on *Phantasm: Oblivion*
(Photos courtesy Kristen Deem)

back, but I could tell that he really wanted to get his original cast back together one more time. I think that's what was missing from *Phantasm II* and he might have sensed that. I still had no intention of getting back into acting by the time that *IV* rolled around but I was more than happy to play Jody one more time. I consider it an honor to have been asked back, honestly."

Behind the camera, nearly a dozen crewmembers returned for *Phantasm*'s fourth. Christopher Chomyn was back as director of photography, Jeff Shiffman as first assistant director and Scott Gill as editor. Sphere master Kerry Prior returned for his third stint as ball handler on a *Phantasm* film. Guy Thorpe once again wrangled hearses and twice found his way before camera in cameo appearances. Kristen Deem was hired on as script supervisor and bestowed with the additional duties of managing props and wardrobe.

"I first heard about *Oblivion* getting the go-ahead from Don himself," Thorpe says. "He called wanting me to meet him with my hearse at this tiny warehouse up in Northridge to

see if it would fit inside, which it just barely did. Then Don gets into the driver's seat and asks me to sit cross-legged in the rear of the hearse and he starts looking at me in the rear-view mirror and from different angles. I knew nothing about the story at this point and didn't have a clue what we were doing. I later realized upon reading the script that we were staging the hearse ride between Mike and the Tall Man."

"I had worked with Michael Baldwin on a film called *With Friends Like These*," Production Designer Naython Vane says. "I wasn't aware of who he was at first. *Phantasm* had scared me as a kid but I didn't immediately connect him to the film. Just as they were gearing up for *Phantasm IV*, he invited me to have lunch with him and Don Coscarelli. I was so hungry for the opportunity to production design my own film that I jumped at their first offer. I knew going in that I was up against a struggle with the budget, but that's why Don chose me for the job. He knew I was willing to accept the challenge. A more experienced production designer would've said, '*No, thank you.*

Don Coscarelli scopes out the Northridge warehouse with Guy Thorpe.
(Photo courtesy Guy Thorpe)

I don't need to work quite that hard.' But as a kid from Kansas City who drove out to Los Angeles and lived in a van for six months, I couldn't have been more excited to do it."

One sequel vet not tapped to return was effects artist Mark Shostrom, who had since committed to *The X-Files* movie and *Men in Black*. As a favor to Coscarelli, three of Shostrom's former assistants volunteered to handle the film's limited effects order on the cheap. They were Bob Kurtzman, Greg Nicotero and Howard Berger, all of whom had since formed the award-winning KNB Effects Group.

Bill Thornbury in Melanie Kay's makeup chair.
(Photo courtesy Kristen Deem)

CALM BEFORE THE SHOOT

Having satisfied his agreement with Universal Studios on *Phantasm III*, Don Coscarelli was free to direct the fourth *Phantasm* however he wanted for whomever he wanted. But in the wake of the previous film's humble earnings, another multi-million-dollar sequel would be a hard sell. In an effort to attract new investors at the 1997 American Film Market, Coscarelli debuted a clever teaser trailer for his new film assembled from deleted scenes from the first three *Phantasm*s. Set to an epic version of Fred Myrow's theme, it could (and did) easily fool the uninitiated into thinking they were seeing footage from an entirely new film. For those not enticed by the trailer, Coscarelli had Redondo Beach model Heidi Lamar lure visitors into the *Phantasm IV* suite by wearing a bra of silver spheres, drill-bits protruding. His pitch worked and the film was financed for less than a million dollars, the lowest budget since the original.

With so little money, *Oblivion* would have to be cost-savvy at every turn. It would rely heavily upon isolated filming locations and a shorter production schedule. Vehicles, props and wardrobe pieces from previous *Phantasm*s could be employed at no cost. The Northridge warehouse, which was akin to a garage, was so small that it could only house one set at a time, not that *Oblivion* could afford to build many. There were only two full sets (Jebediah's laboratory and the hotel room) and two partial sets (Boulton and Morningside mausoleums).

The crew would be smaller but their director's expectations of them would remain high.

"*Phantasm III* was a huge film given the budget," Christopher Chomyn says. "Even more so when you consider the inexperienced crew. It was certainly bigger than anything we were accustomed to and maybe even should have been involved with. By *Phantasm IV*, we all had more experience and therefore more trust in one another. So it didn't feel like Jeff Shiffman was yelling at us quite as much on *IV*. It felt like he was pushing us because he knew what we were capable of."

"Don involved me in *Oblivion* from the very beginning," Bob Ivy says. "He told me how he was looking for a weird, desert landscape and I told him that he needed to look into Lone Pine because it's just one great hill after another. So he rented a car and we went on a road trip for two or three days. We checked out Lone Pine, Death Valley and the sand dunes in Baker, mostly places that wound up being used in the film. They're great locations to film at. Anyone who sees them in

Phantasm: Oblivion's modest lodgings.
(Photo courtesy Guy Thorpe)

person is immediately going to go, '*Wow*'."

Desert filming would bring the production four hours north of Los Angeles to scenic Lone Pine. Here the company would be headquartered at the rustic Dow Villa Motel, known for housing film crews all the way back to the 1920s. Lone Pine's production history includes films such as *Gunga Din, 3 Godfathers, High Sierra* and *Bad Day at Black Rock* along with more recent films *Gladiator, Django Unchained* and *Man of Steel*. Among *Oblivion*'s locations were the Alabama Hills, Death Valley and the Owens Lake Bed, which had previously contained water until it was drained in 1924. Just as on the original *Phantasm*, location filming would occur first to allow ample time for set construction back home.

"I arrived in Lone Pine with Bob Ivy a few days before the crew got there," Guy Thorpe says. "We had to drive each of the hearses up, both the hero hearse and the exploding hearse, in order to have them ready for filming. Bob towed the

trooper car on a trailer behind his hearse. Getting our coaches to location was a real challenge. The dirt roads we took were quite narrow. In certain spots, there was only a foot of space on either side of the car as I drove past the canyon walls. Luckily, we made it. I suppose it was even luckier that we were able to make it back!"

INTO OBLIVION

On Thursday, October 23, 1997, filming began on *Phantasm: Oblivion* with a sunrise-for-sunset shot of Reggie suiting up in his ice cream threads (an outfit not seen since the original *Phantasm*) and striding into Death Valley, four-barrel in hand. The day's second location was Horseshoe Meadows Road where Reggie first drives past Jennifer. By all accounts, this first day of production was miserable. Neither craft services

Kristen Deem standing in a dangerous spot.
(Photo courtesy Guy Thorpe)

nor mobile bathroom facilities reached location and the actors' contractually promised RV wound up being commandeered for storage by the crew. What was intended as a private dressing room now contained lights, C-stands, cords, boxes and makeup kits. Though bathrooms would arrive the following day and craft services the day after, the desert shoot would offer few comforts for cast and crew.

"Our location played a part in my bad attitude," Jeff Shiffman says. "I didn't enjoy it up there. The accommodations weren't fantastic and, of course, those were the days when I was being spoiled on big productions with four-star hotels and being taken care of. *Oblivion* was like taking a camping trip with your buds up to Lone Pine. It's not the most fun place in the world. It was cold and we were high up in the stratosphere. It was an experience, for sure. I can't say I've been back. My better memories are from *Phantasm III*, to tell you the truth."

"For me, the problem with going on location had

nothing to do with the harsh conditions," Michael Baldwin says. "Harsh conditions I can do just fine. Bring on the desert, I say. My problem with going on location was in how ridiculously far away our locations were. If you get up to Lone Pine and realize that you left something back in Los Angeles, you've got to find a way to get along without it because it's a several hour drive back. That's a trip you want to make as few times as possible."

"Making a film sometimes is like being in a war," Kristen Deem says. "You're down in the trenches. It's dirty and hot with grueling hours. The work can be pretty thankless until you see the final result — the magic — playing up on the silver screen. So it's the cast and crew, the people around you all night long, that get you through a shoot, that make things fun. There were a lot of good people on the *Phantasm IV* crew that made the experience endearing and got me through each day."

While this marked Heidi Marnhout's first day on a *Phantasm* set, she was not entirely unfamiliar with her cohorts.

She had recently appeared in *Vice Girls*, an action/drama written, produced and co-starring Baldwin with effects by Kerry Prior (it was executive produced by B-movie king Jim Wynorski who frequently cast Angus Scrimm). Marnhout would reunite with Don Coscarelli on his 2002 film *Bubba Ho-Tep*.

In a journal dated 10/23/97, Angus Scrimm wrote:

> Warning comments on the call sheet: "Be prepared for climactic extremes! It'll be darn cold and darn hot. Don't play with the reptiles!" I'm to go up Saturday for the Tall Man's first day's shoot Sunday. Late tonight, Kristen Deem phones from Lone Pine. Variously a storyboard artist, script analyst, publicity/casting assistant and troubleshooter on previous Phantasms, Kristen is script supervisor on Phantasm IV and overseeing wardrobe. She's seen no reptiles, but warns me to bring thermal underwear and a heavy topcoat: "The nights will freeze your eyebrows off!" Lord help us – the Tall Man with no eyebrows?!

Although much of the film is set in Death Valley, the production spent only a scant three hours filming there on Thursday, October 23. To reach location, the cast and crew braved the three hour journey from Lone Pine through miles of uninhabited desert, neither a gas station nor cell phone signal to be found. The only scene captured here was of Reggie spotting Jennifer at the Emigrant Pass rest stop area.

Desert filming with Bannister and Marnhout continued on Saturday, October 25 with the rollover crash/explosion of Jennifer's car as she swerves to avoid a tortoise (an armadillo in Coscarelli's script). The car stunt was entrusted to Bob Ivy and the subsequent fireball to pyrotechnics expert Gary Beal. It would be the first of three vehicles blown up for *Oblivion* and the only one for which Ivy didn't have to be set on fire. The explosion was delayed by strong desert winds which can be seen beating down the flames in the film.

"It was just a basic wooden ramp that I drove Jennifer's car onto," Ivy says. "I took that scene a lot slower than most of my other car stunts. I didn't even have a roll-cage installed because at that speed you don't really need one. You just need a seatbelt on to keep you inside the car. You can't tell this from watching the movie but I actually landed the vehicle back on its wheels. Don wound up cutting around it so that it looks like I landed it upside down."

In a journal dated 10/25/97, Angus Scrimm wrote:

> My volunteer driver on the trip up is friend Guy Thorpe, longtime Phantasm fan and Motion Picture Academy staffer who functions as hearse coordinator on this film (as on PIII), rounding up the required long black coaches through his Hearse Society connections. I fully expect to ride up in a hearse but we make the trip in a rented Chevy Malibu and arrive at sundown at the Dow Villa Motel. Almost immediately the Phantasm IV cast and crew spill into the lobby, red-faced but exhilarated from a long day's work in the desert sun. Don, Mike, Reggie and I greet each other with the bemused "Well, here we are again..." grins of a foursome who've been doing that Phantasm thing together for two decades.

A HANGING IN DEATH VALLEY

Although he'd been on location as co-producer from the start, Michael Baldwin's first day back before camera came on Saturday, October 25 for the scene in which his character tries out his newfound powers of telekinesis. Mike first tries crushing a scorpion (originally a tarantula) using a rock, and then a dwarf using a boulder. In the same sequence he wanders through the desert rock formations, unaware of a graver (played by Bob Ivy) watching him nearby. Baldwin was joined by Angus Scrimm the following day to film Mike's suicide by hanging, which reverberated the infamous cut scene from *Phantasm*. The location's uniquely gnarled centerpiece was an actual tree hailing from the lyptus species. Both it and the dwarf-crushing boulder were acquired from Green Set's Plant and Prop Rentals.

"That scene was a logistical nightmare," Baldwin says. "Because there aren't any perfectly picturesque trees just standing out in the desert waiting to be filmed. We had to rent that tree, drive it up from Los Angeles on a giant tow truck and convincingly plant it in the ground. None of that process was particularly cheap, mind you, and we were a low-budget film."

"As star and co-producer on *IV*, I thought Michael was very down-to-earth," Christopher Chomyn says. "I remember him and Jeff Shiffman literally dragging the tree Mike was to be hung by across the dry lakebed to get it in place. There was no sense of boundary to what his job as co-producer entailed. On a larger show where your star is also producing that would never have happened. Someone else would've done it. I respected Michael a lot for working shoulder to shoulder with the crew."

"Michael brings such depth to the character of Mike Pearson," Kristen Deem says. "On *Phantasm: Oblivion* he became producer. I could tell it meant a lot to him to branch out and do something different. He took on so much responsibility and worked hard at it. He was always answering phones and trying to solve all sorts of problems. I admired him for that. He had much more on his shoulders than most of us!"

Above: Don Coscarelli directing in the desert.
Below: "Hanging" out between takes.
(Photos courtesy Guy Thorpe)

Tightening the noose.
(Photo courtesy Kristen Deem)

As the noose tightens, Mike begins to pass out and envisions the *Phantasm* outtake wherein he and Jody lynch the Tall Man. Coscarelli trimmed the sequence to exclude any mention of the mortician's hold on the sun, which is how he lured Mike back to him (Mike originally woke late morning to total darkness, "Where is the goddamn sun?"). His return to the Tall Man in 1978 was purely to bargain for the sun's release. In *Oblivion*, young Mike wakes during the night to hear the Tall Man's whispers in the night air, "Cut me down, boy." Waking from this vision in the present day, Mike spies the Tall Man watching him from afar. The noose breaks and Mike falls to the ground.

In a journal dated 10/26/97, Angus Scrimm wrote:

> *Guy Thorpe drives me within yards of the distant rise and warns me to be careful crossing the treacherous lake bed. As I climb to position, he drives off. I stand, conjuring the Tall Man, and ponder that I'm doubtless the only person in the world at the moment standing on a rock in a dry lake bed in the blazing sun with a camera trained on him from a quarter-mile away. Ah, movies! [...] Tonight Bill Thornbury drives in from Fresno, accompanied by his 10-year-old son Ben. They join Don, Kristen, Guy, Bob Ivy and me for dinner at Smoke Signal. Ben has inherited Bill and Sharon's good looks and social ease. He chats affably with us at the table, and he and I take a snapshot together. Back at the hotel, Bill tells me that Ben said after dinner, "Dad, you're scarier than Angus!"*

"I had a great time taking my son Ben down to filming with me," Thornbury says. "Don rented us a Toyota Corolla. We threw some bags in the back, stopped at 7-11 for snacks, and hit the open road, just father and son. I wanted him to see what moviemaking was like firsthand. He loved the whole deal. He ate too many snacks from the craft services table and wound up getting sick but we had a good time otherwise. He really took a liking to Angus who was such a gentleman to Ben, always very attentive and made him feel very special."

"Come, boy. We have things to do."
(Photo courtesy Kristen Deem)

Desert photography.
(Photo courtesy Kristen Deem)

YOU I CAN'T TRUST

On Monday, October 27, the company traveled farther into the Alabama Hills for several establishing shots and to capture the final daytime exterior: an ominous exchange between Jody and an increasingly suspicious Mike. Flashing back to another *Phantasm* outtake, Jody explains that he didn't leave town years before – he was taken. Mike is unconvinced and begins to notice the desert floor below filling with spacegates. The film omits the brothers' final scripted exchange here wherein Jody warns, "Soon there will be thousands. The invasion is about to begin and it will be a blight upon this land." Gazing down into the portals, Mike was to have coldly responded, "So be it."

"Bill did an extraordinary acting job in *Oblivion*," Kristen Deem says. "He maintained a sense of ambivalence with the role so that the audience would always wonder, '*Which side of the fence is Jody on?*' Is he a mere puppet of the Tall Man? Is that truly even Jody? Or is this the Tall Man in one of his shape-shifting guises, luring Mike over to the dark side? At times, Bill was quite chilling in the role. There were also moments when his brotherly love, the old Jody Pearson, shone through."

These scenes between the Pearson brothers, however brief, mark a momentous turning point for Baldwin's character. No longer a standby player in his own story, *Oblivion*'s Mike begins to distrust his brother's specter and rebels against the Tall Man. While journaling his plight, he notes that while he can't kill his nemesis, he might be able to prevent him from ever existing. His request later on that Jody take him back to "where it all started" is not a fact-finding mission but an assassination attempt. Failing that, Mike constructs his own lethal sphere

Top and *Bottom:* A bad place to have car trouble.
(Photos courtesy Guy Thorpe)

"My goal with *Oblivion* was to do right by that character."

Michael Baldwin on Mike Pearson

using parts from the hearse's engine in a feat of ingenuity not seen since the hammer-shotgun cartridge explosion of the original *Phantasm*.

"My goal with *Oblivion* was to do right by that character," Michael Baldwin says. "Don and I would play tennis together over on the west side of town near Century City. Whoever was driving, we would go back and sit in the other one's driveway and chat about *Phantasm IV* and where it might go, all of the possible directions. I think this was after we knew Roger Avary's script wasn't panning out. In those initial talks with Don before he had started writing the film, I asked him to please not have Mike be so much of a victim this time around. I didn't like where we took that character in *Phantasm III* and wanted to correct it for *Phantasm IV*. So from the beginning, it was my intention to restore Mike to where I liked him best."

The desert scenes with Mike and the hearse feature several recycled props from past films. The black Jody sphere is an obvious carryover from *Phantasm III*. The dagger Mike finds in the glove compartment belonged to the Tall Man/Lady in Lavender in *Phantasm*. The casket at the rear of the hearse was repainted black from its previous turn as the sheriff's casket in *Phantasm III*. Even the coach itself was reused from another sequel: it was originally the zombies' pink hearse in *Phantasm III* (the one that wasn't wrecked). The hearse would reappear years later in Don Coscarelli's *Bubba Ho-Tep*.

Shortly after location filming commenced, special effects makeup coordinator (and future Mrs. Reggie Bannister) Gigi Fast Elk Porter felt that negative vibes of the landscape and weather were hindering morale and production and that, eventually, this would result in someone being hurt. There had already been several close calls including a near vehicle-crewmember collision, a falling set light that had not been properly weighted down, and the ever-present choking dust winds. Porter, a Native American Comanche/Osage, performed an onset medicine ceremony one desert evening and gifted sage-filled medicine bags to the crew. The shoot would conclude with cast and crew relatively unharmed.

SOME COPS CAN BE REAL ASSHOLES

As desert exterior shooting switched from day to night, the company began work on Reggie's deadly encounter with the Demon Trooper. After a fierce battle, Reggie shoves his adversary into a patrol car and blasts the vehicle to smithereens by introducing a lit flare to the gas tank. Much of the battle was filmed Thursday, October 30 with the explosion staged the following night, Halloween. Close-ups and vehicle interiors were captured later in the Northridge warehouse against a black backdrop. In the film, the scene cuts seamlessly between location and warehouse footage multiple times.

As originally written, the Demon Trooper confrontation contained several details that were either omitted or changed. After being engulfed in flames, the Trooper was to have a flaming sphere burst from his skull and soar off into the night, not unlike the Demon Nurse from the opening of *Phantasm III*. As the trooper burned, Reggie was originally to quip, "That was for Rodney [King]." This was also cut. Reggie Bannister improvised a coda to his scripted line, "If you think I'm gonna help you find your brother Mike, you're wrong. Dead wrong, *which as I recall is not a big deal for you.*" Reggie getting gooped in the mouth with yellow Demon Trooper blood was filmed five times, with Gigi on pouring duty. The first take was the one that made it into the final film. The yellow blood this time around was an unappetizing cocktail of Karo syrup, sorbitol and food dye.

"The demon trooper makeup took an hour," Bob Ivy says. "That was just a basic mask I put on and then makeup would be filled in around my mouth and eyes. Most of that hour was spent blending the mask with the makeup so that it would appear seamless."

"*Phantasm IV* had such a limited budget that we had to make do with whatever we were offered," Kristen Deem recalls. "This included special effects. One night, out in Lone Pine, we opened a box and inside was the Demon Trooper mask. I'm not even sure it was made specifically for P4; possibly it was a hand-me-down from the SPFX studio. It looked a lot like Freddy Krueger. One of the A.D.'s groaned, "*That is the Demon Trooper? THAT'S what they're giving us?!*" We had to work with it. The makeup folks shined it up. Bob Ivy donned the mask and really made that character come to life because of how he moved and that crazed gleam in his eyes!"

"I hadn't done anything like the police car explosion before," Ivy says. "I was burned pretty good because the flammable chemical that we painted on the car rubbed off on my boots once I got inside. I usually don't need flame retardant socks and I wasn't wearing any. When the car blew up, my boots immediately caught fire. I never plan on taking bruises for the *Phantasm* series going into these jobs, I just know that my work involves a certain level of risk and I accept it."

"Bob Ivy is such a cool guy to work with," Michael Baldwin says. "He's a big *Phantasm* fan from way back and as a professional stuntman, he always goes the extra mile. *Always.* The night of the trooper explosion was a rough one because he was supposed to be in the car when it exploded, get out, stagger and then fall down. Now that's nerve-racking tension for everyone, setting up for and pulling that one off."

Beginning Halloween, Baldwin's report-to-set time as star and co-producer is listed on the daily call sheets as being "ALL DAY, ALL THE TIME."

The original Demon Trooper mask now resides in the vast genre collection of Daniel Roebuck.
(Author photo)

ALL IN HIS HEAD

The first week of November was spent capturing desert night exteriors set near film's end, including Reggie's dwarf battle and the final confrontation between Mike and the Tall Man. Don Coscarelli's daughter, ten-year-old Chloe, stood in as the dwarf that attacks Reggie. This scuffle, which played out on the red dirt floor of the Alabama Hills, spelled trouble for the character's white ice cream suit. Reggie Bannister's wardrobe would require multiple applications of baby powder to preserve continuity. The week of night shoots culminated in the Tall Man's enigmatic final scene and the hearse explosion prior to it that engulfs him, prompting a regenerated Tall Man to appear through the spacegate.

Don Coscarelli, Christopher Chomyn, Joe Waistell and Angus Scrimm on set.
(Photo courtesy Kristen Deem)

In a journal dated 11/4/97, Angus Scrimm wrote:

> More Mike/Reggie/Tall Man action in the brooding
> Alabamas. A significant moment for me – shot well out of
> sequence, as is the way with movies – is the Tall Man's final
> close-up in the film and what may be his last ever moment on
> screen. These few frames will provide the audience with their
> final clue to the Tall Man's real identity; demented mortician,
> space alien, nightmare chimera or the Grim Reaper himself?
> I'm sure each viewer will reach a highly personal conclusion
> based on the way life has conditioned him to regard mortality.
> How can I most subtly assist? I remember director Rouben
> Mamoulian's suggestion to Garbo on portraying the ineffable
> in Queen Christina: "Think of absolutely nothing." Good
> advice is good advice. Roll 'em!

The theatrical realization of the Tall Man's final scene skips a
few details found in Don Coscarelli's original screenplay. Reggie
was to originally hand Mike a grenade necklace in case the *"fit
hits the shan"* so that the Tall Man wouldn't be able to collect
their corpses. The ice cream man's parting lines to a dying Mike

were also different in the script. Rather than *"I'm coming back
for you,"* Coscarelli had Reggie say, *"Goodbye, buddy. I'll see you
in hell."*

The scene called for the Tall Man to be standing
next to the rigged hearse as Mike detonates his self-engineered
explosive device. Since Scrimm would obviously be unable to
tackle this stunt himself, Bob Ivy was an ideal pick to double
him for the explosion. The only problem was that Ivy's visage
looked nothing like Scrimm and the production was unable
to afford an expensive custom-made mask. Fortunately, Guy
Thorpe was in possession of the next best thing.

"I loaned Don a rubber life-mask of Angus that
was taken for Jim Wynorski's *The Lost Empire,*" Thorpe says. "It
was perfect because it even had the Tall Man scowl on it. So
when they were discussing how to make Bob Ivy look like the
Tall Man, I told Don about this mask I had. I took it over to
KNB Effects Studio and they added some hair to it and got it to
location. When I got it back, it was a bit charred. I didn't mind
because it was a souvenir for *Oblivion* in addition to being in
Lost Empire."

In a journal written on 11/6/97, Scrimm wrote:

When I reached location tonight, I find the Tall Man has preceded me, and is chatting purposefully with Coscarelli and Chomyn. But out of his mouth comes the Texas drawl of Bob Ivy, in Tall Man mask and wardrobe. With Gary Beal handling pyro FX, and Lone Pine's fire department looking on, Bob stunt doubles the Tall Man in a huge hearse explosion that blasts away the darkness for miles around. When the enormous fireball subsides, there's Bob, being hosed down by Gary and the crew. His wardrobe is ash, but the fire-retardant garments beneath have left him sweaty but unharmed. I then suit up and valiantly, courageously, bravely step before the dying flames for my part of the sequence.

"I'd never done a stunt like the hearse explosion before," Ivy says. "I decided to talk to a special effects friend of mine to see what he thought about it. I told him what I wanted to do – stand beside a car as it exploded – and he told me, '*No, you can't do that. The gasoline will splash onto you and get into your clothes.*' I didn't really think that was the case so I went ahead and did it anyway. It turns out that I was right because the gasoline didn't seep through my clothes. When the explosion goes off, the gasoline comes out and immediately ignites. If you freeze-frame that scene you can see it spray out of the hearse and then ignite into a fireball. It all happens very quick."

In the film, the explosion and rising fireball violently knock Mike and Reggie off their feet. Moments later, a new Tall Man emerges from the spacegate to retrieve the gold sphere from Mike's skull. With prize in hand, the new Tall Man walks back to the spacegate and turns to give the fiery scene and our world one last glance before vanishing through the portal. The only mystery greater than what the mortician might have been thinking was where he might have gone…

"I know exactly where the Tall Man went," Scrimm says. "Straight to my dressing trailer to get the location's nighttime chill out of my bones and to pour the stiff whiskey Reggie expected me to hand him when he soon followed."

Reggie comforts a dying Mike before the flames, raises his four-barrel and chases after the Tall Man through the

Don Coscarelli on set.
(Photo courtesy Kristen Deem)

gates. The film then cuts away to Reggie giving teenage Mike a ride in his ice cream truck. As the two drive along, the faint dying whispers of an older Mike can be heard in the night air. Reggie asks if his young friend heard something to which Mike smiles and cryptically replies, "It's only the wind."

"It's not for me to say what my take on the ending is," Michael Baldwin says. "The people that have watched all of the *Phantasm* films can have their own take on it. I think certainly you can view it as the series coming into a sort of loop, a horizontal figure eight of shadow and dream."

"I thought it was the perfect ending," Writer and Bannister collaborator Todd Mecklem says. "Ending each movie with the Tall Man in control was fine, but after four films it was time for something more enigmatic. Those old scenes that were integrated into *Oblivion* were remarkable, and I loved that shot of them riding off—not into the sunset, but the darkness.

Does it mean…full circle, back to where we began? It's open to interpretation, like so much in the *Phantasm* films."

And so November 5, 1997 concluded night exteriors in the cold desert for *Oblivion*. "Guy Thorpe drove me up to the Death Valley location for my week-or-so shoot," Scrimm says. "But when my final scenes were completed, Guy wasn't available to take me back to Los Angeles so production coordinator Jason Savage offered me a lift on one of his runs back south. On the exceedingly early morning drive – it was still dark most of the way – Jason and I had lots of time to chat and at one point best boy electric Danny Vecchione's name came up. *'Danny thinks you're a great actor,'* Jason volunteered with a chuckle. To which I replied, *'Danny has such perception.'* Jason almost drove off the road."

AND SO IT BEGINS

The company returned to the Northridge warehouse a week later on November 12, 1997 to begin filming on Jebediah Morningside's laboratory set, which boasted an antique version of the spacegate. The role of the kindly inventor was a unique opportunity for Angus Scrimm to challenge the audience's preconceived notions about his iconic role. This gentler alter ego would be used sparingly in *Oblivion*; enough to intrigue but not demistify. In a nod to the Tall Man's trademark accessory, Kristen Deem created Jebediah's cuff links from the same red Czech glass used in the mortician's tiepin.

"I don't think Jebediah Morningside made the Tall Man less scary at all," Bill Thornbury says. "I think, if anything, it made him more interesting. It clues us in to the history of the character and shows that he's been around for years, a lot longer than a normal human being. It shows the Tall Man is possibly even immortal. It does refer back to the first film where we see Angus on the horse drawn carriage, which was a scene I always loved."

"I liked that Jebediah shook things up and gave Angus a chance to do something different," Todd Mecklem says. "I don't think it detracts from the Tall Man at all. Jebediah

used technology to explore realms better left unexamined, a deft nod both to Lovecraft and to steampunk fiction, and unleashed the Tall Man and his minions on an unsuspecting world. Was Jebediah transformed into the Tall Man? Did an other-dimensional being first devour his soul and then mimic his form? Or is the Tall Man simply playing with Mike's head, as he does repeatedly, sometimes literally, throughout the series? Like the characters in the films, we're left to try to decide what it all means…or die trying."

In a journal dated 11/12/97, Angus Scrimm wrote:

After a week's hiatus, we're now at the Northridge soundstage, where production designer Naython Vane (from Wichita) and art director Michael Roth (Atlanta, GA) have created the study and laboratory of one Jebediah Morningside, 19th century embalmer and dabbler in science. These sequences input key clues into the ongoing Phantasm mysteries, and Nate and Michael's intriguingly detailed sets ingeniously capture the ambience of their bygone time and place.

Kristen Deem and Jebediah Morningside
(Photo courtesy Kristen Deem)

A clue to the Tall Man's origins...
(Photo courtesy Kristen Deem)

"The incredible thing about *Oblivion* was that our art department only had two guys in it," Michael Baldwin says. "That's crazy small. It's so cool now to look at that tiny warehouse and see what they were able to create. Those sets looked like they were from a $2 million movie when *Oblivion* was made for well under one million. Sheer talent."

"We filled Jebediah's lab with the most interesting props we could find," Vane says. "Some of it came from this old prop house on Main Street in Santa Monica and the rest came from History for Hire, which specializes in antique and historic props. If you go into that store today and browse around, you'll see much of what we used in Jeb's lab sitting around."

"I thought the art department did a beautiful job with Jebediah's lab," Christopher Chomyn says. "The floors really looked like they were made of wood. It wasn't until I actually set foot on them that I realized they had just painted the concrete floor to look that way."

"One of the finest sets ever was Jebediah's lab," Deem says. "Naython did such an incredible job creating this! The wood floors, the antique furniture and lab equipment, the fake sunlight filtering through the curtained window… I remember wandering alone through that set, touching everything, completely spellbound! There was a violin and xylophone on top of one shelf. Cool Victorian period chemistry equipment. Dusty old tomes and various correspondences in several foreign languages. A bizarre black "coffin chair" which I've since seen used in other TV horror shows. The set had an uncanny feel as though I'd truly stepped back into the 19th century, to Morningside Mortuary the way it used to be. Imagine how surreal it was for me to sit at Jeb's old rolltop desk, to witness Angus walking around in Victorian garb! Years later my mom and I were walking down Main Street in Santa Monica, and in the windows of Jadis Props, we spotted Jeb's prototype spacegate! I was so amazed to see it again!"

The Jadis Prop house that stocked Jebediah's laboratory has twice supplied props for Dr. Frankenstein's laboratory in both *Gods and Monsters* and *Van Helsing*. Additionally, Jadis has supplied props to films such as *The Artist*, *The Prestige* and *X-Men: First Class*.

Getting into character.
(Photo courtesy Kristen Deem)

VISIONS OF FUTURE PAST

The following day, Thursday, November 13, saw the production back on location; this time at Leo Carrillo State Beach for two scenes, one of which revealed what might have been had the Tall Man never existed. In it, Mike and Reggie drink Dos Equis by the 'Cuda as Jody plays guitar, the sun setting on the beach horizon. This tender break from the nightmare world of *Phantasm* is so endearing that it is sometimes mistaken as outtake footage from the original. It is through dress and demeanor that the cast look many years younger than they actually are. The golden hour shoot almost didn't happen; Reggie Bannister was late arriving to location and did so with only minutes to spare before sunlight ran out. Don Coscarelli ordered three takes using the remaining daylight with Bill Thornbury strumming '*Sittin' Here at Midnight*' on the first two and the *Phantasm* theme on the third take.

"I think it's a really nice scene," Michael Baldwin says. "It's such an awesome part of the film. It's also sentimental and there's not much sentimental energy in these films, which makes it poignant. It only works for people who are fans of the franchise because other people aren't going to get what's going on. That day at the beach, which was north of Malibu, we woke up in the morning and it was raining everywhere. We had to shoot it at a state park and it takes a special permit and lots of money to shoot there so we couldn't afford to go back and get it some other day. We drove out in the pouring rain, which was depressing, but it cleared up just in time to film."

"I really enjoyed shooting the scene where it's just the three of us at the beach," Thornbury says. "That day was such a laid back affair once we got going with it. It's probably because we really were drinking Dos Equis throughout it. The weather, at that point, was beautiful as well. I don't know that there was that much acting going on in that scene because we really were just hanging out, playing some music and drinking beer. It's one of my fonder memories from that film."

Don Coscarelli, Michael Baldwin and Angus Scrimm.
(*Photo courtesy Guy Thorpe*)

1860 CONTINUED

On November 16, the company traveled fifty miles west to the Camarillo Ranch House for the exteriors of Jebediah Morningside's home. The porch scene where Jebediah offers Mike a glass of lemonade would be his first appearance in the film. The Camarillo property wasn't the first location pick, however. Don Coscarelli had originally hoped that Dunsmuir house, last seen as Morningside Mortuary in the original film, would serve as Jebediah's home. Guy Thorpe contacted the Oakland estate in early autumn and found them quite receptive to the idea of *Phantasm* returning so many years later. In her response letter, Dunsmuir's Executive Director even offered to negotiate a lower location fee than their published figures to secure *Phantasm*'s return. The production quickly realized, however, that such a distant shoot would be terribly costly and require 400 miles of travel plus overnight accommodations for both cast and crew, all to capture one brief scene.

In a journal dated 11/16/97, Angus Scrimm wrote:

We're shooting sunup to sundown at a sprawling Victorian-style farm home in Camarillo, CA with a gracious veranda on two sides and a big red barn with horses, chickens and peacocks. Kristen Deem invites me to come along in her new red Honda Civic and we start up the Ventura Freeway in the 5 a.m. darkness. Dawn Stewart directs us to park near the dressing trailer and when Kristen unloads her costumes, she asks, "Did you remember to bring the Tall Man's pants?" I panic, having totally forgotten that I'd worn them home after Thursday's shoot. Fortunately, she finds spares left over from Phantasm III and, the dressing room trailer being locked, I sidle behind a refrigerator on our host's back porch and try on several pairs till I find one that fits.

"Jebediah is another winner in terms of ideas," Michael Baldwin says. "It's another reason to bring *Phantasm* into the daytime and I always enjoy that because it seems to me that most horror films are set at night. It was also just great to come around a corner and see Angus acting as that character. It's so unexpected and really throws you for a loop. The thing about that scene and what most people don't know is that Jebediah was the invention of Kristen Deem. Also, I don't know where we got that old woman from, but she was fantastic. She might as well have been the original fortuneteller actress because she looked exactly the same. Of course, she's not. My wife at the time, Jennifer Bross, provided the cackling voice of the old lady in *Oblivion*. So that puts her in two *Phantasm* movies, forever immortalized."

"I think I was floating the whole day we were doing the porch scenes," Deem says. "There was a sense of amazement and gratitude that Don had incorporated various ideas I'd offered. It was a childhood vision very close to my heart. Imagine my joy, watching over Baldwin's left shoulder,

Makes the best lemonade.
(Photo courtesy Guy Thorpe)

DUNSMUIR HOUSE & GARDENS HISTORIC ESTATE
2960 Peralta Oaks Court
Oakland, CA 94605
510-562-0328 * FAX 510-562-8294

DATE: **September 16, 1997**

TO: **Guy Thorpe**

FR: **Lynda Guthrie, Executive Director**

RE: **PHANTASM'S MORNINGSIDE MORTUARY**

Thanks for your call this morning. It is my understanding that you might be interested in doing one day of filming at Dunsmuir sometime in mid November. As we discussed, we would need to have a commitment as quickly as possible in order to adapt our exterior Christmas decorating to your schedule.

I am enclosing the Filming at Dunsmuir information packet for the Director's review. As I noted this morning, our base fee is $1,000 for a full day of filming outside. The published minimum is $750 for less than a full day.

The Director should feel free to make a proposal. We would enjoy working with you and will give consideration to whatever you might be able to offer.

Thanks!

Top and *Bottom: Phantasm* very nearly returned to the Dunsmuir House.
(Photo courtesy Kristen Deem)
(Letter courtesy Guy Thorpe)

as Angus poured a glass of lemonade and handed it towards us! Don was the one who mainly created Jebediah, named him and made him an inventor. It was his preliminary vision, that eerily moving sepia photo in *Phantasm,* that had dramatically influenced my adolescent dreams, which in turn were now influencing *Oblivion*."

BATTLEFIELD

The Civil War battlefield sequence was filmed later in the day at the same Camarillo property. As first conceived for *Phantasm III* by Kristen Deem, it was to feature Mike's alien ancestor infecting the human Jebediah, causing his transformation into the Tall Man. In incorporating this idea, Don Coscarelli swapped out Jebediah for the Tall Man and changed Mike's ancestor from an alien to a human soldier undergoing a painful live embalming. The scene would continue to evolve across multiple script drafts. Theatrically, this vision appears to Mike as he sleeps in the hearse, whereas an earlier draft saw Jody guide his brother back through time to witness it firsthand. Jody's exposition about the Tall Man's early exploits was omitted when Coscarelli re-contextualized the scene as a dream. Jody would have revealed that by following Sherman's Army, the Tall Man was able to lay to rest "thousands in a single day."

"That was a really fun day," Michael Baldwin says. "Certainly it was one of the biggest days on our production, that's for sure. It was also the kind of day where if you're going to invite someone to a *Phantasm* set, you do it then because there are dead bodies everywhere and your friends get cameos. It seemed like everyone got in on that scene."

"Naython and Mike, the art guys, pulled up with two coffins on their truck," Kristen Deem says. "One of the coffins was rather short. They were bemoaning the rental, wondering who would even fit into the smaller coffin, and I immediately chimed, "I know *just* the person!" That coffin was made for Guy Thorpe! I knew he'd be tickled to play a dead soldier; to be in a *Phantasm* film. Sure enough, he fit perfectly. Guy had a wonderful close up at the start of that scene!"

The other coffin opposite Thorpe's was filled with another recognizable face, one that belonged to Roger Avary.

"Some of the "soldiers" were laid out on the ground as corpses," Todd Mecklem says. "I was lucky enough to get a live role charging across the field of battle. I was issued a rifle. My fears of being cut out of the film—which had always happened on previous extra gigs I'd done — faded as I realized that the young soldier who'd be running just behind me was Andy Coscarelli, Don's son! It was a complicated shot with Bob Ivy riding by on horseback, Andy and I crossing in front of the camera, other soldiers charging as the camera took in the corpses of the fallen and moved towards the tent where, strangely enough, a field surgeon who looked just like the Tall Man was preparing to operate on Mike. I mainly concentrated on not screwing up the shot, simple as my part was."

"I love that scene," Christopher Chomyn says. "Even though we were limited both in budget and schedule, we were somehow able to make that battlefield feel bigger than it actually was. In reality, it wasn't that big at all. We had a couple tents, a couple horses, a couple soldiers and some dead bodies. Then we smoked the perimeter so anything beyond the foreground action was obscured. It worked out fantastic. It was also great shooting that reel on black and white film stock as opposed to just shooting in color and then bleeding the color out for the transfer. From a negative cutting point of view, shooting in black and white film stock made things complicated because we were working with different base materials, but it was worth it in the end. If you look closely in that scene, you can see our colorist from Fotokem, Robert Tomashefski, as one of the dead bodies. He was so thrilled to be asked to do that. He worked with us well into post-production with the final color grading of the film."

The Civil War reenactment looked terrific on film," Naython Vane says. "I wish I could take more credit for it but I really did very little. Don knew a group of top-notch Civil War re-enactors who really knew their stuff. They came out with costumes and gear and pitched their own setup. I only supplemented a few antique-looking pieces for it. The spread they brought with them was definitely impressive."

Top: Reggie Bannister, Morningside recruiter.
Bottom: Last known photo of the 13th Morningside Infantry.
(Photos courtesy Todd Mecklem)

Top: Naython Vane and a dead Roger Avary.
Bottom: Todd Mecklem with Jebediah Morningside.
(Photos courtesy Todd Mecklem)

RETURN TO BOULTON

Continuing a series tradition, *Oblivion* began where its predecessor ended, which now meant deep inside the Boulton Mausoleum with the Tall Man letting Reggie live to fight another day. "The final game now begins," announces the mortician, warning Reggie that his end draws near. The character's end was seemingly already at hand with *Phantasm III*'s ending. *Oblivion* rectifies this by having the spheres, in an unprecedented move, simply hold Reggie up with blades retracted. Early script drafts had the Tall Man deliver a different warning as he departs. The mortician first thanks the "little man" for delivering Mike to him but adds that Reggie's "services are no longer required." The Tall Man then warns that if he tries to see his friend again, Reg will suffer "horribly."

"The mausoleum we recreated from *Phantasm III* was only a tiny sliver of a set," Naython Vane says. "Don only needed a few insert shots to match the *Phantasm III* footage and we built as little of the set as we needed to pull it off. It was helpful that Don had kept pieces of that *Phantasm III* mausoleum setup so that we could better match the colors and textures. I think the switch between *Phantasm III* and our film is pretty seamless."

A frequent complaint leveled at *Oblivion* criticizes how the film disregards young Tim from *Phantasm III* who was last seen being pulled backwards through a freezer door. As *Oblivion* opens the scene continues between Reggie and the Tall Man, but with absolutely no mention of Tim or his fate. An early draft would have featured a pack of ravenous dwarves feasting upon the boy's gruesome remains. Reggie was to raise his four-barrel toward the dwarves to avenge Tim's death but reluctantly stand down knowing the Tall Man is still nearby and would likely object. After a pause, he fires at the feeding pack anyway, cuing the film's title card (the series' only computer-generated swarm of spheres cue the title card in the actual film). The decision to forego showing the mutilation of another beloved character, as happened to Liz in *Phantasm II,* was deemed more prudent.

Reggie faces down a sphere.
(Photo courtesy Kristen Deem)

"I don't think Don needed to explain what happened to Tim," Todd Mecklem says. "Ever since we watched Reggie die in the first movie, and in the next scene we found that Reg was alive and it was really Jody who died, we knew we shouldn't expect logical explanations in *Phantasm* films!"

"I definitely would've come back to *Phantasm* if Don asked me," Kevin Connors says. "It would've been a lot of fun to reunite with everyone on a fourth movie. But I realize that too much time had passed for me to play that same character again at that same age. You could bring the other actors back for a fourth movie and everybody's going to look enough the same that it wouldn't matter. There were no hard feelings about my not being asked back. I understood."

Peace, man.
(Photo courtesy Kristen Deem)

NOT THE
HONEYMOON SUITE

On November 19, the production switched to the hotel room set for scenes with Reggie Bannister and Heidi Marnhout's characters. The motel room was constructed on top of the Boulton Mausoleum set that appeared in the film's opening, which explains the mausoleum tile flooring behind Jennifer as she undresses. The motel exterior was captured guerrilla-style under the cover of darkness at an abandoned property. The motel sign the production team outfitted the building with was subsequently left behind after filming.

"If you pay close attention and really study our sets, you can see little details that reveal how we were making these sets in the same space every time," Naythan Vane says. "The motel room set was the result of pillaging and scraping whatever we could find. We'd find pieces of wood in dumpsters and find a way to make it part of the set. It's just what you do when you haven't got the money."

The motel room set was home to one of *Oblivion*'s most infamous scenes. Reggie unbuttons a sleeping Jennifer's shirt to find half-emerged silver spheres where her breasts once had been. Jennifer screams as the spheres burst out and attack Reggie. Arguably the most misogynistic moment in the series,

Showdown in Boulton.
(Photo courtesy Kristen Deem)

the sphere-tits gag originated in Roger Avary's *Phantasm 1999* script. In that version of the scene, a prostitute named Kathy attacks Reggie in a nightmare scene.

When Don Coscarelli first conceived of the sequence, he did so with Jennifer Bross in mind. In the first version of the motel scene, a sleeping Reggie was to flashback to Bross' cameo in *Phantasm III* as the nursing receptionist. Upon realizing that he had met this hitchhiking femme fatale before, he would wake to find Jennifer in sphere-breast attack mode. The dream epiphany for Reggie that Jennifer was an operative of the Tall Man became untenable when Bross passed on the role. Instead, Reggie dreams of Mike as a Tall Man and wakes to find Jennifer in attack mode.

"It's true that Don had my wife in mind for the role of Jennifer," Baldwin says. "That's why the character was named Jennifer. Truthfully, though, I did not want her to do the scene. I was in love with and married to a woman who was utterly adorable and I just did not want to see her breasts explode with silver spheres. I had a talk with Don about that and by the end of it I think he understood where I was coming from. Jennifer was flattered that he would write a role just for her but she politely declined and we all moved on."

The final scene called for one of the boob-spheres to impale Reggie's hand. As originally scripted, the Tall Man was to appear in the ball's reflection as it began to drill, reminding Reg that he was warned to stay away. Now, the mortician continued, there would be "hell to pay."

Shortly after the motel material, the production captured a brief pickup needed to complete a cut scene from the original *Phantasm*. The fire-extinguisher attack on the Tall Man needed one final shot of the mortician exploding in a burst of yellow goo. Although the pickup was filmed and the scene completed, it was omitted from *Oblivion*'s final cut. The original 1978 scene and the 1997 pickup shot can be seen as a bonus feature on the *Phantasm* DVD release.

"I helped out towards the end by rigging the fake Tall Man head with explosives," Ivy says. "It was just a little piece of primer cord that I set off. Don actually had the original wallpaper from the first movie's mausoleum to use as

background. He keeps everything from these movies. He's got something like six storage units filled with props and wardrobe. He took me to one of them once and it was filled with *Phantasm* and *Beastmaster* props."

"That was one of the very last things we shot," Vane says. "I remember when Don explained to me that we were going to be recreating part of the mausoleum from *Phantasm*, I was taken aback because the contact paper and drapes all had to match perfectly. I wasn't prepared for that. I went, *'Okay, I can do this but I'm going to need some time to line up what I find with the first film's look.'* Don kept coming back to me every few days with newly found pieces of set dressing he had from twenty years ago. I'd be looking for something and he'd go, *'Oh, yeah. I have that in storage. I'll bring it to you tomorrow.'* I was blown away that he still had that stuff, like *'Wow, thanks! That makes my job a lot easier!'*

ABBEY AGAIN

On Saturday, November 22, 1997, *Phantasm* again returned to Angeles Abbey. There, scenes set near the end of the film were scheduled for shooting. In them, the Tall Man would surgically operate on a prone Mike Pearson to remove the gold cranial sphere revealed at the end of *Phantasm III*. Both Jody and the Tall Man are swiftly paralyzed, however, by a tuning fork given to Mike by Reggie moments before. Mike uses this advantage to plunge the Tall Man's buzz-saw sphere into Jody's carotid. A badly wounded Jody confesses that he actually perished in a car accident years earlier. The Tall Man revives and telekinetically seizes the tuning fork. Mike flees through the spacegate back to the desert and his only remaining ally, Reggie.

This night was significant because it was originally intended to close the story arc on Bill Thornbury's character (until *Ravager* came along). Momentarily freed from the Tall Man's control, Jody achieves redemption by confessing the truth about his demise. Earlier drafts of the screenplay had the character live to retract this revelation and continue the pursuit. After Jody's admission, a "sinister force" would reclaim Jody so that he would crush the tongs of the obstructive tuning fork (rather than the Tall Man taking it). Jody would chase Mike back to the desert to find Reggie waiting, four-barrel in hand. Mike demands that Reggie shoot Jody. When the ice cream man hesitates, Mike warns, "It's him or me. Choose now." Reluctantly, Reggie blasts his old friend back through the spacegate.

"Honestly, I would've preferred that the Pearson brothers always be true to one another," Thornbury says. "I never wanted to see Jody lie to Mike or deceive him because they really did care for one another in the original film and I wanted it to stay that way. I thought that was the strength of *Phantasm*; the relationship between the brothers. But the story has to eventually change and go different places so I understood the direction Don was taking us in. I did appreciate my final scene because it felt like an attempt to set things right. I think we owed it to the Pearson brothers by the fourth film, especially after all that had happened. We also needed to do it for the fans, you know? It was a redemption that restored the character to where I always liked him best, which was on Mike's side."

"I vividly remember the yellow blood bubbling from his throat as Jody attempted to speak," Deem recalls. "In the hour before dawn, I had tears in my eyes listening to his parting words. Bill played it with such sincere love. I wondered if I was witnessing the final time he would ever play Jody. A chapter of the *Phantasm* saga was closing there before us."

"I seem to remember mausoleum filming being near the end of our shoot," Naythan Vane says. "Angeles Abbey really didn't need much in terms of set dressing. It looked pretty creepy all by itself. Strange that such a gothic-looking place was situated in the middle of Compton, which as you can imagine, was not the nicest neighborhood to be in."

Chatting over a scene at the Abbey.
(Photo courtesy Kristen Deem)

"I think we were very fortunate to get back into Angeles Abbey," Bill Thornbury says. "Even though it was still kind of run down. The neighborhood was rowdy as all get out, sirens going off every ten seconds. I remember that we had to do a lot of audio looping with those scenes because there was a big party going on at a house adjacent to the mausoleum and nobody wanted to go over and tell them to knock it off. We probably could've sent Angus over as the Tall Man to quiet them down. He would've cleared the place out! I always preferred the fake mausoleum

"Honestly, I would've preferred that the Pearson brothers always be true to one another."

Bill Thornbury on the story

on the first film to the real one in the sequels. The fake ones were much cleaner and controllable. The one in Compton was beautiful but it wasn't very well maintained."

Abbey filming called for yellow blood to spray from Jody's neck as Mike plunged the Tall Man's sphere into Jody's throat. Not wanting to be downwind of the gushing yellow blood, Michael Baldwin was doubled by Guy Thorpe in his second *Oblivion* cameo. For the close-up wherein Mike's hand jabs the sphere into his brother's neck, the appendage is that of Thorpe not Baldwin. For Guy the scene entailed literally baking on the embalming table under hot set lights while being occasionally doused in yellow blood.

"I still have the scars from that scene to prove it," Thorpe jokes of the hot lights. "I was able to stand in as Mike for that scene because they didn't want Michael's costume to get stained with Jody's yellow blood. I just happened to be wearing all black that evening so I was in the right place at the right time. When I got to move Angus' hand holding the buzzing-sphere up to Jody's neck it was a blast, literally! That's when the spray of yellow blood came out. Fortunately, it was more of a fine mist than a wet spray so it wasn't *that* messy, but it would've

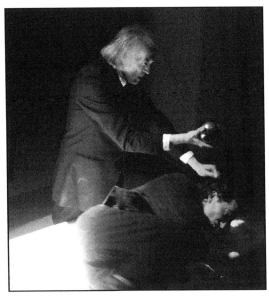

Michael Baldwin barely escapes attack.
(Photo courtesy Kristen Deem)

definitely been a problem for Baldwin's costume."

On this night a disagreement erupted between Angus Scrimm and his director over whether the Tall Man should joke during such a serious scene. The line as written, "This won't hurt a bit. Well, maybe just a little bit…" struck the actor as too humorous a quip for the Tall Man as he prepares to slice into the skull of the franchise's main character.

"Don had written the line comically but Angus wanted to revise it," Deem recalls. "Don is generally amenable to such suggestions but on this night they stonewalled. Don insisted on filming the line exactly as it was in the script. The two of them stormed off to different areas of the mausoleum, fuming. It was three or four in the morning and filming stopped cold. We were all exhausted. It was tense, the waiting… The scene itself was really tense too. During practice takes Baldwin's screams had been piercing; absolutely gut wrenching in volume and pathos. We were all holding our ears as the echoes rang through the marble halls. There was nothing funny about the scene."

In a journal dated 11/22/97, Angus Scrimm wrote:

> There follows an animated discussion between two highly opinionated old friends, with much chortling, guffawing and backslapping, about the virtues of both lines, with the actor insisting that brevity is the soul of wit and moreover, the Tall Man is a man of few words, and the director steadfastly maintaining that the script version is funnier and at last suggesting, "Let's film it both ways, and we'll see which works better in the editing room." Well, I've won hands down, obviously.

"Don is always in control of his sets," Todd Mecklem says. "But if he's a dictator, and a director has to be, he's a benevolent dictator. The movies are a creation of his mind—in other words, it's his universe, and on the set we're all living in it. For the cast and crew, of course, it's also a job, and a tough one at times. But the core cast, and some of the crew, go back so far that each movie is almost like a family reunion. I never saw Don lose his cool, or rant and rave like some directors do. There could be

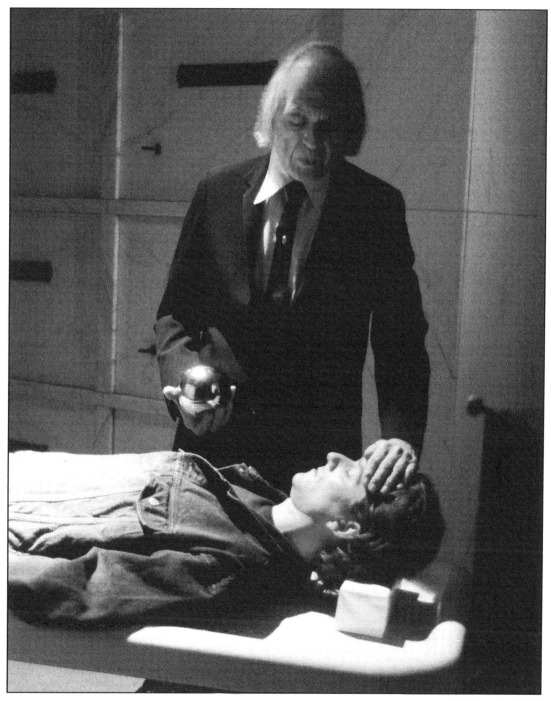

It's all in his head.
(Photo courtesy Kristen Deem)

tense moments, of course, during seemingly endless all-night shoots, but that's unavoidable. I was very impressed by the care that Don—and the cast and crew—put into their work, regardless of the budget restrictions and the hassles of tough location shoots."

As it would turn out, Coscarelli won. The scripted version of the line made it into the final film.

CEMETERY FACEOFF

On Sunday, November 23, 1997, the cast and crew assembled in Chatsworth Park for *Oblivion*'s final night of production. The evening's first scene found Mike, having escaped Jebediah's parlor, spacegating to a nondescript cemetery with his brother in tow. Jody grabs Mike's throat and a struggle ensues. Producing a dagger, Mike slices his brother's hand to reveal yellow blood and confirm his suspicions. With this Jody's true nature revealed, Mike overpowers him but is ambushed a moment later by a second Jody who drags him through the gate to a waiting Tall Man. In true *Phantasm* style, the burial ground brawl contains a skillful deception as a second Jody appears in the foreground whilst the dead Jody lies in the background.

"I was able to double Bill Thornbury for one reason and one reason only," Christopher Chomyn says. "We both have the same male pattern baldness! It was not something we had planned far out in production. My recollection is that someone either the day before or the day of filming said, '*Chris, you're bald like Bill,*' and suggested I double him for the scene. It worked out great because we didn't have to cut from a shot of Jody lying there to another shot of him grabbing Mike. By having me as Jody already in the frame, the last thing you expect is for the character to re-appear in the foreground to grab Mike. It also harkened back to that classic *Phantasm* theme of temporal space."

The evening's second scene was written in tribute to the original *Phantasm* and even filmed in the same Chatsworth Park area used two decades earlier. Waking to find his bed in the middle of a cemetery à la young Mike, Reggie follows the

sound of children's laughter in the darkness. Moments later, he spins around to see Mike looking very Tall Man-esque looming over him before waking up in his hotel room. That Reggie heard children's laughter in his nightmare could well symbolize the ruin of Mike's childhood, guilt over Tim's death or the loss of his own family in *Phantasm II*.

"I really liked that scene a lot," Michael Baldwin says. "Even though I'm only in one shot of it. It was fun. As soon as that idea came up it was obviously a winner and something we had to do. As I think on it now, there was a possibility that I could actually play, not the Tall Man, but my character could morph into something else in the future because of that scene, something like the Tall Man. I don't know how I would ever sustain that intense look for a whole film, though."

"One of the sweetest memories I have of the Bannisters is during that final night of principal photography," Kristen Deem recalls. "We were up at Chatsworth Park South, and the night was getting steadily colder. The dewy grass became so wet that it soaked through my boots and socks. I was numb to the bone – still hours before dawn – and I could tell others on the crew were equally miserable. Around midnight Gigi and Reggie started setting up a Thanksgiving feast at the craft services table. It was so amazing, far superior to the craft services fare we'd been getting. A huge, delicious hot meal on such a chilly night! The best medicine possible! The Bannisters had that special gift for making everything alright; making us all feel like a cozy family!"

The night's final task was to capture a hearse cruising through a foggy graveyard for the film's opening. Neither the script nor the film reveal who is actually behind the wheel or how they got there. The driver is presumably Mike, having escaped following the events of *Phantasm III*. Earlier script drafts included a scene in which Mike hotwires a hearse outside the Boulton Mausoleum, thus explaining the acquisition.

The final shot of principal photography, which was to become the film's first, wrapped at 5:50 AM on Monday, November 24, 1997. The evening's call sheet references the upcoming Thanksgiving holiday with: "We give thanks that this is over!"

Bill Thornbury in the makeup trailer.
(Photo courtesy Kristen Deem)

THANKSGIVING ON WILSHIRE

Although principal photography had wrapped, one of the script's most ambitious sequences remained. As Mike traverses the spacegate, he lands in a major city completely ravaged by the Tall Man. The air is eerily still and the streets empty, save for the approaching mortician in the distance. To properly secure such a massive location would have meant shutting down streets, sidewalks and businesses in a payout equal to or larger than *Oblivion*'s entire budget. The ingenious workaround to this was to film the Miracle Mile district of Wilshire Boulevard at a time when it would be naturally void of people – dawn on Thanksgiving Day. Don Coscarelli would capture the shot guerrilla-style utilizing a skeleton crew and without filing for a permit with the city. The result is as clever as it is breathtaking.

"When people talk about guerilla filmmaking," Michael Baldwin says, "they're very boastful about it like, '*We did this*' and '*We stole this shot from here.*' I happen to think we did guerilla filmmaking here in a way that was classy, unobtrusive and nondisruptive. It was no small accomplishment that we shot that on one of the busiest thoroughfares in one of the largest cities in the world without any cops or permits. I just think it's cool! Back then, I lived on the west side not too far from Wilshire Boulevard so we decided everyone would come to my place so we could caravan to location together. Angus showed up at my house at something like four in the morning and greeted me at the door in a gravelly voice, '*Hello, Michael.*' It was kind of startling but also funny because the Tall Man is the last person you want on your doorstep that early! (laughing) I was like, '*Come on in, Angus. We're already ready to go. Want some coffee?*'"

Wilshire filming was not without risk. The undercover filmmakers were nearly caught in the act when a police cruiser suddenly rolled into the shot. Thinking quickly, Angus Scrimm turned from his mark and began picking flowers in the median as naturally as anyone could in full Tall Man costume and makeup. The officers, apparently not *Phantasm* fans, found nothing objectionable about this and continued on their way.

"They were cruising along very slowly," Christopher Chomyn recalls. "As they passed by, they actually waved to us. We just waved right back and they never stopped to question what we were doing there. I guess we looked like we belonged. I definitely think it was to our benefit that Angus, who was made up as the Tall Man, was a good ways down the street from the camera setup we were using. Had he been any closer, he might've raised suspicion."

"There's one thing about that scene that pisses me off," Chomyn continues. "The bag lady on the side of the frame. She slipped past us when we were editing the film. It would have been an easy fix too because the camera was locked down. Had it been caught, we could have frozen that part of the frame either before or after she showed up. It's one of the easiest digital cleanups out there. Fortunately, I think most people are focused on the Tall Man during that shot so she quite often goes unnoticed. I notice her every time."

POST-PRODUCTION

Post-production efforts on *Phantasm: Oblivion* continued into early 1998 with Scott Gill returning from *Phantasm III* as editor. Although several originally scripted flashback sequences were omitted, only one new scene was cut involving Mike and Jody escaping the deserted Wilshire Boulevard. Future Coscarelli-cohort Daniel Schweiger outfitted an early cut of the film with a temporary score utilizing music from films such as *Lost Highway* and *Full Metal Jacket*. Composer Christopher Stone returned to

Have you seen it? Reggie Bannister has.
(Photo courtesy Paul Miser)

voice the dwarves and provide music. Despite being mentioned in early sales art for the film, *Phantasm* theme creator Fred Myrow did not return to join his former collaborator.

One surprise musical addition to the film came from Reggie Bannister, who had included a *Phantasm* tribute song on his latest album, *Fool's Paradise*, which also contained humorous liner notes by Angus Scrimm. His song '*Have You Seen It?*' played over *Oblivion*'s end credit scroll and was teased on the official *Phantasm* website as "having answers to some of the *Phantasm* mysteries." While short on answers, Bannister's song was a fun rock ballad written from his character's point-of-view. Best of all, it featured a rockin' rendition of Myrow's familiar eight-note theme.

In *Oblivion*'s end credit scroll, Coscarelli would credit each of the fourteen Civil War battle scene extras as a 13th Morningside Volunteer Infantryman. Roger Avary was credited for his Civil War coffin-cameo as Yrava Regor, his name spelled backwards. Additionally, Richard Elkin would receive thanks for naming the film, and Jennifer Bross for voicing the fortuneteller. *Phantasm* stalwarts Paul Pepperman, Roberto Quezada and David Gavin Brown were also thanked, likely for their contributions to the original *Phantasm* footage used in this film.

ORION DIMS BUT THE LION ROARS

Distribution rights to *Oblivion* initially went to Orion Pictures, the acclaimed but financially troubled studio behind *Silence of the Lambs*, *The Terminator* and the *Robocop* series. Having only recently emerged from bankruptcy, Orion toyed with the idea of releasing *Oblivion* theatrically and even tested it in four markets. Unfortunately, they would soon relegate the film to direct-to-video. Also hampering the sequel's situation was that Orion was in the process of being purchased by Metro-Goldwyn-Mayer. This acquisition accounts for the discrepancy of early advertising materials containing the Orion logo while home video releases displayed the MGM logo.

Phantasm: Oblivion - the sequel with balls.
(Photo courtesy Kristen Deem)

Although MGM made no attempt to reverse *Oblivion*'s non-theatrical fate, the studio did express an interest in pursuing future sequels should the film perform well on home video. In 1999, MGM Home Video would release the original *Phantasm* onto DVD, porting over most of the 1993 special edition laserdisc's bonus features.

"Naturally, you always hope for a theatrical release when you do a film," Bill Thornbury says. "Even though *Phantasm III* didn't get that we still had hoped that *IV* might go that route because it was worthy. The excitement around a new *Phantasm* film was and has always been huge. Needless to say, it was disappointing when *IV* went straight to video."

In January 1998 Don Coscarelli and the main cast flew to Fangoria's Weekend of Horrors in New York to promote the film. "It was better than my Fangoria appearance for *Phantasm III* because we were all there together this time," Michael Baldwin says. "I insisted upon that if I were going to attend."

"That trip was a blast," Bill Thornbury says. "We had an evening off and I was getting ready to go see the Bulls play the Nicks because Madison Square Garden was right across from the hotel. I was just heading out and I ran into Angus and

The man with the answers.
(Photo courtesy Paul Miser)

The premiere was introduced by Don Coscarelli and Angus Scrimm, who also fielded audience questions afterward. During the Q&A, the writer-director explained that fan criticism of previous sequels greatly influenced the film's direction, the chief complaints being too many characters and too much humor.

AintItCool.com reported that the audience enjoyed the film and ran two reviews from the premiere, one positive and one negative. The latter sharply condemned the film's script and meager budget. It did note, however, that Scrimm was still "one mean-looking son of a bitch onscreen." The negative review ended by calling the sequel "a rather sad, disappointing and confusing conclusion." The positive review, which surprisingly hailed from an admitted non-fan, called it "great" and "visually exciting." The reviewer acknowledged that while some may find *Oblivion* confusing, he found that it "cleared up a lot of questions… from the earlier movies."

As *Phantasm*'s second direct-to-video release, *Oblivion* was largely ignored by critics in the mainstream media. The sequel did, however, receive its customary <u>Fangoria</u> cover story in issue 176, a magazine that could have easily led with *Halloween H20*. The few reviews *Oblivion* did garner were encouraging. John Powell of Jam! Showbiz called the film "a highly atmospheric thriller," before concluding that "pictures really do speak a thousand words, especially when Coscarelli is the one pointing the camera." Powell closed his review by saying that if this was the final *Phantasm*, "it was one hell of a ride."

Several weeks after its North American premiere, *Oblivion* debuted across the pond at the Fantasy Film Festival in Berlin, Germany where the *Phantasm* films enjoy a cult following. The event began in the afternoon with a marathon of the entire series that culminated in the film's European premiere. *Oblivion* was domestically released to videocassette and laserdisc on October 13, 1998. A cast and crew premiere screening was held that same night at Fotokem in Burbank.

One troubling component of MGM's marketing included the mailing of thousands of promotional screeners of the film to video stores and media outlets for use in contests and giveaways. This led to *Oblivion* being readily available – not as a workprint but in its finished form – well in advance of its

he says, '*Bill, how about some New York Pizza? I'm buying.*' How could I turn that down? So as much as I wanted to go to the game I said, '*I'd love to, Angus,*' and we just went jamming down the boulevard. It was a very relaxing, very cool evening, just the two of us hanging out. I felt very secure at night walking down the streets of New York with Angus by my side."

Oblivion had its world premiere on August 6, 1998 before a packed house at the Bloor Cinema in Toronto, Ontario, Canada as headlining film of the FanTasia Film Festival.

"As far as I'm concerned, *Phantasm: Oblivion* is my favorite beyond the original."

Michael Baldwin on the series

release date. The sequel was soon pirated throughout the globe.

In March 1999 the film proved to be a popular entry at the Brussels International Festival of Science Fiction, Fantasy and Horror. Accompanied by Scrimm, the film premiered late on a Friday night to a packed theater. The Tall Man performer was greeted onstage with an immediate standing ovation. When he began to address the audience in their native French tongue, he received a second ovation. Translated, he told them: "The films of Don Coscarelli are impregnated with mystery, the mystery of life and death. Some of you will not understand it, others will. Some of you will be afraid, but don't worry. I'll be watching the film with you and holding your hand."

REFLECTING ON OBLIVION

It's a rare moment in filmmaking history when a writer/director and his cast of four are able to return to their posts more than twenty years later. It's downright unprecedented for that film to contain scenes wherein the cast ages and regresses twenty years. Having explored the vast world of *Phantasm* across the past two decades, Don Coscarelli reins in *Oblivion* to become his most personal entry yet, and this film belongs to Mike, Reggie, Jody and the Tall Man. Although the film's continuity requires *Phantasm II* and *III* to exist, it is largely a direct sequel that bookends the original *Phantasm* and, as such, remains incredibly endearing.

As a motion picture, *Oblivion*'s miniscule budget worked against it almost as much as the stigma of being a direct-to-video sequel. Yet Don Coscarelli and company have much to be proud of where production values are concerned.

Christopher Chomyn in particular shoots *Oblivion* like an apocalyptic John Ford film. DVD Active reviewer Gabe Powers notes the director "gracefully makes *Phantasm: Oblivion* look like at least two million bucks." Continuing, he comments that the film "does many things right, including a deeper look at the series' mythology."

"We had less time, less money for locations and sets, a smaller stage, a smaller crew, less film to shoot, and lots of fun," Christopher Chomyn says. "Of course there are creative compromises on every film. I don't know which ideas were killed for financial reasons and which for creative reasons. I know I often come up with ideas – sometimes unusual – and sometimes Don likes them, and sometimes he looks at me like I've lost my mind. In the end, he is the final word on what goes into his films, and I am sure that there were times when he wished we had more money, but I know that he put every penny of his budget onto the screen. If Don likes an idea, and there is a way to do it with the budget, he will make it work."

"As far as I'm concerned," Michael Baldwin says, "*Phantasm IV* is my favorite beyond the original. I worked so hard starring in it and co-producing. I also just think it's a really well made film and I say that as objectively as I possibly can. Although I do see people ragging on it sometimes, I do appreciate the fans that both get it and like it."

Interestingly, *Oblivion* wasn't the only twentieth-anniversary horror sequel released in 1998. There was also *Halloween H20* which saw Jamie Lee Curtis return to the role that made her famous. Tracing the histories of these franchises reveal two very different paths leading up to their 1998 sequels. Although both began as low-budget independents, *Halloween* went with the prevailing genre winds, a byproduct of its

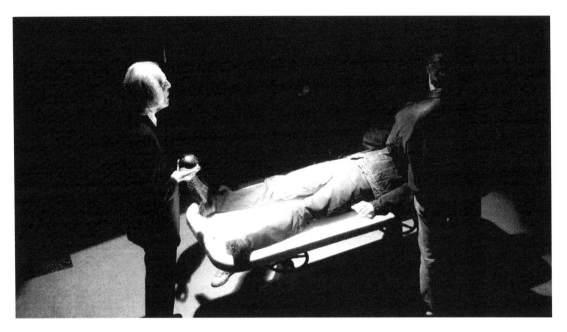

This won't hurt a bit.
(Photo courtesy Kristen Deem)

constantly changing creative team. Tonally, *H20* has more in common with *Scream* than its own forefather and requires viewers to forget the three films that preceded it. *Phantasm*, on the other hand, managed to both retain its original creative team and remain true to itself. Although each new sequel boasted a unique personality, threads exist in each calling back to the first film. *Oblivion* is so spiritually connected to *Phantasm* that it literally ends where the franchise began back in 1979.

Then again, *Oblivion* suffered a quiet direct-to-video issue and *H20* went on to gross more than $55 million at the domestic box office alone (if only Coscarelli had recast Reggie with LL Cool J). Perhaps that is the cost one pays at the crossroads of integrity and continuity, having to exist on the outer fringes of cult cinema and, occasionally, on the direct-to-video shelf. *Oblivion* need not be ashamed; it is a fine sequel.

Another spot in their journeys where *Halloween* and *Phantasm* diverged was in how much was revealed (or convoluted) with each new sequel. In *Halloween*, Michael Myers becomes variously comatose, psychic, superhuman, the instrument of a druid cult, a product of child abuse and – in the case of *H20* – a detective rivaling Columbo in order to track down his sister. *Phantasm*, conversely, offers up more questions than answers as it moves forward, eschewing a linear narrative in the process. Being both the most philosophic and cerebral entry yet, much of the film is open to interpretation, having inspired much fan discussion through the years. These qualities have, at times, been frustrating to some viewers. *Oblivion* stands out from its predecessors as the only *Phantasm* not to conclude with a jump scare, but rather a poignant moment between old friends. For many, this begs the question; where does that ending leave the franchise? Was it all just a dream?

Perhaps Brutalashell.com's Sam Hawken says it best: "*Phantasm IV* brings us back to what the series has ultimately always been about: dying. Everything and everyone dies regardless of how much they are loved or love in return. Death is the eternal constant: inescapable and implacable. It may seem threatening, but in fact it just is. And in the end, *Phantasm IV* wants you to come to terms with that."

Phantasm V?
(Photo courtesy Kristen Deem)

Chapter 5:
Spacegate to Ravager

Despite *Phantasm*'s apparent conclusion, phans had no desire to let the series slip into oblivion. The films rose steadily in popularity following the franchise's fourth outing, with new generations discovering *Phantasm*'s surreal and spellbinding universe. Hungry for more adventures with Mike, Reggie and the Tall Man, the "phandom" community has been persistent in its fervent demand for a new *Phantasm* film, which has struggled to get off the ground despite continued efforts.

PHANTASM-ANIA

In 2000, writer and film aficionado Stephen Romano put together an event celebrating *Phantasm* at Austin's Alamo Drafthouse cinema. Dubbed *Phantasm-ania*, it promised screenings of all four *Phantasm* films throughout April Fool's weekend. The event, boasting the tagline "The film festival with balls!" was attended by Don Coscarelli, Angus Scrimm, Reggie Bannister and scores of enthused phans. *Phantasm-ania* culminated in the United States theatrical premiere of *Phantasm: Oblivion* in 35mm, which has seldom graced theater screens.

　　"Seeing the sequels up on screen was gorgeous," Kristen Deem recalls. "DVD's just don't do those films justice, especially Chomyn's sweeping desert panoramas in *Oblivion*. The best night for me was the first *Phantasm*. I looked over and there in the darkness at my side was the Tall Man. He was sitting where my father had been in June 1979. I felt such a mix of awe and contentment in that moment. It was the perfect closure for me, coming full circle to where it all began."

　　The attending phamily members introduced the films, fielded audience questions and autographed all manner of collectible. Bannister took to the stage to play his music (including the *Phantasm*-inspired 'Have you seen it?') and to personally serve ice cream to phans. Coscarelli gave attendees a special glimpse into his own personal *Phantasm* archives with rare footage including trailers, outtakes and even a tape of Brad Pitt's *Phantasm II* audition! The event also gave phans an opportunity to purchase hard to come by *Phantasm*

Friends to the end.
(Author photo)

memorabilia such as publicity stills, buttons and posters, not the least of which was artist Robert Long's striking limited edition 20th Anniversary art print.

　　"Best of all, there was this wonderful, zany, hilarious writer named Stephen Romano who picked us up at the airport and showered us with such praise and creative ideas for *Phantasm*," Deem says. "He was so talented and made such an impression on us! He later became a very important member of the phamily."

　　Phantasm-ania's legacy extends far beyond being the only event solely dedicated to the franchise. The festival was directly responsible for leading to the writing partnership of Coscarelli and Romano which would fuel *Phantasm* for the next several years. The event organizer is said to have pitched a *Phantasm* cable series to its creator with three episodic screenplays. Although the show never materialized, Coscarelli was so impressed with the pitch that he let Romano develop another *Phantasm* project while he tended to *Bubba Ho-Tep*.

THE PHANTASM COMIC

Summer 2002 brought whispers of a *Phantasm* comic series, which would debut early the following year from publisher XMACHINA. The premiere issue, the first in a four part miniseries, was titled *Phantasm: Overminds*. The book featured a script by Stephen Romano and artwork by Mike Broom, Noah David Henson and Ricardo Bernardini. *Overminds'* print run was limited to 2,000 copies, all of which were autographed by Don Coscarelli. *Phantasm*'s creator would also pen an afterword for the issue titled "When's the Next One? A Note from Don Coscarelli."

Picking up from *Phantasm: Oblivion*, *Overminds* found Mike waking in the company of dream research specialist Dr. Quezada in the year 2040. Nearly naked and hooked up to a massive sprawling computer, Mike learns that he has been in a strange coma since 1979 and that Jody has been dead for twenty years. The doctor reveals that his experiments have allowed him to watch Mike's dreams (the events of the four *Phantasm* films) just as the audience has been able to. The comic soon re-introduces Rocky to the series, now proficient with a katana, as well as an army of upgraded spheres with nasty new accouterments. The issue closes with a revelatory conversation between Mike and Dr. Quezada after which the latter reveals his true identity in a cliffhanger ending.

E.C. McMullen Jr. of FeoAmante.com was initially skeptical of the series. "My own fears that this comic would butcher the movie series were unfounded," McMullen wrote. "Stephen did an excellent job and my only complaint is that there is too much story here for just one comic. There is enough in the first issue to have continued into two and maybe even three issues. [...] That said, *Phantasm: Overminds* is a good start with a beautiful rendering of story, art, and production values."

To promote the comic, Coscarelli and Romano appeared alongside Angus Scrimm and Reggie Bannister at the 2003 Fangoria Weekend of Horrors convention in Burbank.

You know, Don is a pretty *tall* fellow himself.

(Photo courtesy Paul Miser)

The Tall Man has been waiting a long time for this.
(Photo courtesy Scott Pensa)

PHANTASM (2005)

The March 10, 2005 edition of <u>The Hollywood Reporter</u> carried a surprising front page story: New Line Cinema would soon be producing a *Phantasm* remake! The studio press release stated that negotiations had been underway for more than a year and were in the final stages. Championed by Jeff Katz, the bold executive later known for developing *Freddy vs Jason vs Ash*, this *Phantasm* was planned as the first installment of a new trilogy that would span Mike's coming of age. It was hailed behind the scenes as "the *Star Wars* of the horror genre." Having chased the rights to *Phantasm* since 1978 when AVCO Embassy first acquired them, "the house that Freddy built" was closer than ever to owning a piece of the franchise. In addition to Katz, *Phantasm (2005)* was to be overseen by George Waud and Stokely Chaffin. Don Coscarelli would return to produce but not direct.

"I'm thrilled to have this opportunity to introduce a new generation to the saga," Coscarelli said in a press release. "I'm happy that Jeff Katz, who was very aggressive, and New Line are intent on staying true to the original spirit."

Scripted by Coscarelli and Stephen Romano, *Phantasm (2005)* was anything but your typical remake. Featuring return appearances by Mike and Reggie, the project was set long after the events of *Phantasm: Oblivion* and centered on a new generation of characters and their fight against the Tall Man. Mike Pearson, having beaten his own personal phantasm years before, was something of a Jedi-esque mentor for the new characters. No longer on the run, he was now Professor Pearson and the author of a book about his experiences. Never having reunited with Mike, Reggie remained on the road, now the leader of a mercenary group pursuing the Tall Man. Series elders aside, the incoming generation of characters were to be the focus of the remake and also of the Tall Man's wrath. This re-telling of *Phantasm* within its original continuity suggested both that history repeated itself *and* got better with time.

The long brokered negotiations between New Line and Coscarelli would fall apart shortly after the project's

XMACHINA teased the second issue here with posters of Reggie, who was largely absent from the first issue, decked out in military gear. Above *Phantasm's* faithful sidekick were the words *Play the Game*, the second issue's original title. This moniker was quickly changed to *The Game of Fear* when disappointed phans began mistaking *Play the Game* posters for an upcoming *Phantasm* video game that did not exist.

Unfortunately, *The Game of Fear* never saw release and XMACHINA eventually disbanded altogether, leaving the remaining issues in limbo. No official explanation has been given as to why the *Phantasm* comic series was halted. Although all four books were scripted, only the first three were illustrated. The *Phantasm* camp has since remained silent as to why the series was abruptly halted. The comic's death knell was likely the legal dispute that arose from Universal Studios, which still held rights to half the franchise.

The Lady in Lavender... putting the fatal in femme fatale.
(Photo courtesy Paul Miser)

announcement. The press release announcing the remake has since disappeared from New Line's Media Relations website.

In a 2013 interview with sModcast.com, Katz revealed that one frontrunner to direct the project was longtime series admirer J.J. Abrams, which is not surprising given the filmmaker's phan status. He had cast Scrimm in a recurring role on *Alias* years before. An episode of Abram's sci-fi hit series *Fringe* also guest-starred Kenneth Tigar and included a surprise reference to "Agents Scrimm and Coscarelli."

PHANTASM FOREVER

The next project that followed *Phantasm (2005)* was another attempt at a *Phantasm V* called *Phantasm Forever* from a script by Stephen Romano. Less about action set pieces (though it certainly contained them) and more about exploring the mythology of the series, *Forever* was poised to become the

ultimate *Phantasm* sequel. The film's bold conclusion unfolded in such a way that, if realized, would have been entirely compatible with *Phantasm (2005)*'s script.

The sequel's cast roster was a veritable *Phantasm* phan's dream come true; Michael Baldwin, Reggie Bannister and Bill Thornbury were all slated to return as their original characters. Angus Scrimm would again juggle dual-roles as the Tall Man and Jebediah Morningside – not the kindly inventor last seen in *Phantasm: Oblivion* but Mike's physician in the present. Dr. Morningside's true nature would remain a mystery... for a time. *Phantasm*'s own Lady in Lavender, Kathy Lester, would return as a seductive hospital administrator working with Dr. Morningside. Fan favorite Gloria Lynne-Henry would also return as Rocky. Even *Oblivion*'s Heidi Marnhout was back, this time as Celeste, a character first referenced in *Phantasm II* but never seen in the flesh.

The screenplay was separated into four very distinct acts, each with its own title card. The opening segment found

Mike Pearson waking from a very long coma at Morningside Psychiatric Hospital with Jody by his side, Reggie having died many years ago. Much to Mike's dismay, everything appears to have been a dream... until a visit with Dr. Morningside. The second act would have switched realities to a happier universe where Mike lives with Reggie and Jody really did die in that car accident years ago, although the peace is short-lived. The third act would have plunged Mike into a post-apocalyptic future ravaged by the Tall Man and in the fourth act... all would have come full circle back to Morningside Psychiatric Hospital. Cast members assure that the script included numerous winks to the previous four films, both subtle and overt. Thornbury was set to again perform '*Sittin' Here At Midnight.*'

One of the more interesting twists of *Phantasm Forever* would have featured a tense scene between Baldwin's Mike and James LeGros' *Phantasm II* Mike (referred to here as "Id Mike") in the film's third act. In a scene that would have explained that film's recasting as though it were somehow intentional, Baldwin's character is puzzled at the strange appearance of his so-called doppelgänger. Mike remarks that Id Mike doesn't look anything like him to which Id Mike replies, "You're damn right I don't!" Mike's evil twin would go on to suggest that his *Phantasm II* counterpart was the clear superior version, culminating in a showdown between the two Mikes.

Whether LeGros would have agreed to appear in the film remains unclear. He declined participation in the UK's *Phantasmagoria* documentary, the *Phantasm II* BluRay release and multiple convention reunions. (For what it's worth, he also first declined, then accepted, then again declined participation in the book you're now holding. No hard feelings, James.)

Romano's script was universally praised by the cast who read it. Baldwin dubbed it "the thinking man's *Phantasm*" while Scrimm hailed it as being "full of rich dialogue." By imaginatively expanding the series' mythology in a way that honored the four preceding films, the script was reported to be tonally like a Coscarelli creation and, more importantly, like a *Phantasm* film.

Don Coscarelli's enthusiasm for *Phantasm Forever* was so great that he financed an elaborate table read version

of the film. The entire main cast was in attendance with the exception of Marnhout, who was unavailable due to prior commitments. She was replaced at the last minute by *Hellraiser* heroine Ashley Lawrence. Armed with props, the cast performed the entire *Phantasm Forever* script across a sixteen hour day. Shot against a green screen using a three camera setup, the footage was later polished with digital backgrounds, computer-generated effects and musical score. What resulted was a feature-length rough draft of the movie.

"Mum's the word," Scrimm says. "It was supposed to be a secret. I will say the script was almost pure Stephen Romano and it's always fascinating to read the words that emanate from that corruscatingly brilliant mind, especially with Don Coscarelli's own shrewdly masterful input. Always great too to be reunited with so many *Phantasm* series cohorts. And Don's wife Shelley catered a lavish spread of tantalizing munchies of all kinds we nibbled at throughout the day. Now, not another word."

"Michael and I hadn't seen each other in years," Lynne-Henry says. "We had a pretty intimate scene together

Michael Baldwin keeping the *Phantasm V* faith.
(Author photo)

where Rocky has to die and I'm in Mike's arms. The scene is really close-up on my face and I wasn't feeling it the first time we did it. It just wasn't clicking. I wasn't even that comfortable. So we go to do the take again and Michael whispered something in my ear. It was the most perfect thing to say to me and from that I was able to just let go and do the scene. It was wonderful. No, I'm not going to tell you what he said! (laughs) But for that moment, I really thought we connected brilliantly. He helped me through a difficult scene."

The world would receive a sneak peek at the cast read footage in 2007 by accident. Coscarelli used fifteen seconds from the project in a farewell tribute to the doomed Alamo Drafthouse Cinema. The video, which was intended to be shown only once at the Alamo, surfaced the following day on YouTube. Although the video was taken down almost immediately, it was too late; the Alamo tribute had been saved by quick phans and reposted multiple times over. Coscarelli eventually embraced the leak by featuring the video on the main page of *Phantasm*.com.

As is so often the case, the funding for *Phantasm Forever* never came through. In several interviews Coscarelli suggested that Anchor Bay Entertainment was beginning to fund feature films and might back the project, but this too never materialized.

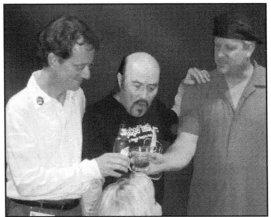

FLASHBACK WEEKEND

In August 2008, Chicago was home to the largest *Phantasm* reunion ever. As part of Mike Kerz's Flashback Weekend convention, Don Coscarelli joined Angus Scrimm, Michael Baldwin, Bill Thornbury, Reggie Bannister and Kathy Lester. It would mark Baldwin's first public appearance at such an event since the 1998 Fangoria Weekend of Horrors convention for *Phantasm: Oblivion*. Also in attendance was Robert Kurtzman, who had worked with Mark Shostrom on *Phantasm II*.

Saturday night in Chicago.
(Photos courtesy Scott Pensa)

Top: Onstage together at the Q&A session
Bottom: Phamily photo at the Saturday night cocktail party.

(Photos courtesy Scott Pensa)

For one weekend, the Crown Plaza Hotel was overrun with *Phantasm* phans. The parking lot featured numerous hearses and even a pair of 'Cudas. Crown Plaza's information channel looped *Phantasm* trailers for three days. Graphic designer Chad Savage designed buttons declaring "I Love Mike/Reggie/Jody/Tall Man," allowing phans to declare their allegiance(s). Flashback arranged screenings of *Phantasm* and *Phantasm III*, preceded by cast intros and a Q&A session. The weekend's beverage of choice, Dos Equis, was in plentiful supply.

The *Phantasm* autograph tables lined an entire wall of a Crown Plaza ballroom that featured an elaborate backdrop of wall crypts and a spacegate. Located at the far end of this line was Anchor Bay Entertainment's booth where phans could score free *Phantasm* and *Phantasm: Oblivion* posters. All six autograph lines came to an abrupt halt Saturday morning when an impromptu musical performance broke out. A convention attendee had given Thornbury an acoustic guitar which the actor then used to play '*Sittin Here At Midnight*' with Bannister backing on vocals. It was a *Phantasm* phan's dream come true.

While introducing *Phantasm* Saturday night, Coscarelli and cast joked and reflected on their work three decades later. "I don't know what *I'm* doing here… *I've* seen this movie!" Scrimm quipped to great laughter. "But as long as I am here, thanks to Don for creating something that's brought us all together this weekend, something brilliant that came almost unbiddenly out of his head and has been so remarkable."

"I was shocked and amazed," Lester says. "I thought maybe there would be a few people who remembered me but I was really overwhelmed by how many there were! It was very emotional for me. After the first night, I got back to my hotel room and actually teared up. They were tears of joy because I really felt the love from these people. It was exhilarating and draining at the same time. So many people coming up and sharing memories and then telling you how much they loved the movie and love you in it, how old they were and who they were with when they saw it the first time. It was so awesome."

RAVAGER

As this book goes to print, the next chapter of *Phantasm* rapidly nears completion. Principal photography has ended and postproduction is underway. The most covert and micro budgeted series effort to date, *Phantasm: Ravager* arrives to audiences an astonishing sixteen years after the release of *Phantasm: Oblivion*, far besting the nine years that separated *Phantasm* and *Phantasm II*. Although Internet whispers of a secret *Phantasm* project date back to 2009, *Ravager* wasn't officially acknowledged until March 25, 2014 as Aintitcool. com previewed an online poster. Two days later on the eve

(Logo courtesy George Todoroff - http://georgetodoroff.com)
(Convention button courtesy Chad Savage - http://sinistervisions.com)

Reggie Bannister jamming on what would later be the set of *Phantasm: Ravager*.
(Photo courtesy Kristen Deem)

of *Phantasm*'s 35th anniversary a teaser trailer debuted on <u>Entertainment Weekly</u>'s website. Phan response was immediate and overwhelmingly joyous.

Ravager includes a major changing of the guard as a new director, David Hartman, helms the production. *Ravager* marks the feature film debut of the Emmy-nominated animation director. Don Coscarelli remains highly involved with the film, serving as co-writer and producer.

Hartman, a notable *Phantasm* phan, is no stranger to Coscarelli's repertoire. He created striking visual effects for both *Bubba Ho-Tep* and *John Dies at the End*. In a nod towards *Phantasm*, Hartman snuck a blink and you'll miss it Tall Man cameo into his visual work on *Bubba Ho-Tep*: When Bruce Campbell's Sebastian Haff reads from the Book of the Dead, an on-screen illustration contains a giant soul-eater lording over a house. At the bottom of the page, donning a top hat and speeding away in horse drawn carriage, is the Tall Man. Hartman also was responsible for compositing backgrounds

and effects into the *Phantasm Forever* read-through footage.

Coscarelli explains in a preliminary press release, "I felt it was time to let someone else play with my train set. David and I go back to my film *Bubba Ho-Tep*. He did terrific visual effects on that, and more recently created a wild animated sequence and some amazing visual effects in my most recent film, *John Dies at the End*. Our aesthetics are in sync and he's quite an experienced director in his own right."

Hartman acknowledges, "Having worked with Don before, and being a huge fan of the entire *Phantasm* franchise, it was a great honor to do *Ravager* with him. This film is a real turning point in the series. There's real closure for the core characters that I hope fans will respond to. We were fortunate to shoot amazing new sequences with horror icon Angus Scrimm — he has terrific scenes with Reggie and Mike that are truly powerful."

Ravager's origins are somewhat complicated. Although the film's press announcement noted that filming had

Top: Jebediah's nemesis? No, it's Baldwin as The Conjurer in *It Came From the Dead (2013)*.
Bottom: Baldwin in Benjamin Ploughman's makeup chair for *Phantasm: Ravager*
(Photos courtesy Justin Warren - See ICFTD at http://tinyurl.com/itcamefromthedead)

occurred across 2012 and 2013, the production actually dates all the way back to 2008 when it began as *Reggie's Tales*. Originally envisioned as a spinoff webseries about the misadventures of everyone's favorite ice cream vendor, *Reggie's Tales* would serve as the basis for *Ravager*. Across the next several years, new scenes were added to help it reach feature-length. The newly shot footage incorporated cast members Angus Scrimm, Michael Baldwin, Bill Thornbury and Kathy Lester. Coscarelli familiars Daniel Roebuck and Daniel Schweiger also put in appearances. Although previously referred to as "test" or "experimental footage" by the cast, material from the 2008 webisodes featured in *Ravager's* first teaser trailer.

If any of that seems an unorthodox way to make a movie, consider the unorthodox conditions under which the original *Phantasm* was made and the incredible film that resulted. In that sense, *Ravager* mirrors the unusual production of its forebear. What differs now is the utilization of digital video in place of 35mm celluloid, and computer effects instead of Paul Pepperman's ingenious homebrewed creations. As to be

expected, the new *Phantasm* remains both a family affair *and* a phamily affair.

Location filming included Reggie Bannister's beautiful, rustic home in the mountain community of Crestline, California. The crew also returned to the memorable Angeles Abbey in Compton, California. *Ravager* features classic *Phantasm* elements such as the spacegate, the silver sphere, dwarves, the Regman's four-barrel and the classic 'Cuda. Those phans disappointed with *Phantasm: Oblivion's* lack of a traditional drill-kill will be pleasantly surprised. Early word is that *Ravager* will reveal what happened moments after Reggie vanished through the spacegate as Mike Pearson lay dying on the desert floor.

Though too soon to be certain, the new sequel appears to draw no direct inspiration from the *Phantasm (2005)* remake or *Phantasm Forever*. It does bear some passing similarities to Roger Avary's *Phantasm 1999* script, however. The reversal of Mike and Reggie as leading man and supporting player is very reminiscent of the project (although no longer

Action on the set of *Phantasm: Ravager*
(Photo courtesy Justin Warren)

a strict spinoff per *Reggie's Tales*, *Ravager* is still largely a vehicle for Bannister's acting talents). Other similarities with *1999* include the heavily armored 'Cuda, the post-apocalyptic landscape and an extended sequence on the Red Planet (called the "Negative Zone" in Avary's script). This marks the first time since *Phantasm II* that the otherworldly locale has been featured — and the first time ever that phans will witness the Tall Man walk its hellish landscape.

For six years Hartman and Coscarelli have ardently kept the project a secret. Sharp-eyed phans did notice, however, that Hartman planted a humorous "easter egg" hint within the set dressing of *John Dies at the End* with a prop DVD jacket entitled *Phantasm: Ravager* (a *Phantasm II* publicity shot of Reggie features on the spine). *Ravager's* title appears to pay homage to Kat Lester's 2009 haunting song "Lady in Lavender" the chorus of which teases, "I may be a ravager..."

The implications of this new sequel (promised to be the finale of the story arc) are yet to be seen. Undoubtedly, *Phantasm: Ravager* will inspire the inevitable question: "When is *Phantasm VI* happening?" In the thirty-five years since *Phantasm's* historically indelible release, never has it been more apparent that the franchise will prove as immortal as the Tall Man himself. As our beloved mortician is prone to intone, truly,

"It's never over!"

Ravager's Daniel Roebuck next to his horror host alter ego, Dr. Shocker
(Author photo)

Cameron Norris (1st AC), Michael Baldwin, Justin Warren (2nd Unit DP/DIT),
Andrew Baird (2nd Unit Cam Op/Gaffer), Benjamin Ploughman (2nd Unit Special Effects Make-Up Artist)
(Photo courtesy Justin Warren)

THE PHAMILY

(Photo courtesy Paul Miser)

(Author photo)

DON COSCARELLI

In the time since *Oblivion*, Don Coscarelli has remained a master of the horror genre. In 2002, he directed an award-winning adaptation of Joe R. Lansdale's *Bubba Ho-Tep* which pitted an elderly Elvis Presley (Bruce Campbell) and an African-American J.F.K. (Ossie Davis) against a mummy (Bob Ivy). In 2005, he directed another Lansdale adaptation, *Incident On and Off a Mountain Road*. *Incident* served as the premiere episode for Showtime's *Masters of Horror* anthology series. In 2012, Coscarelli directed another cult-hit, *John Dies at the End*, adapted from the novel by David Wong. Newcomers Chase Williamson and Rob Mayes paired with veteran actors Paul Giamatti, Clancy Brown, Doug Jones and Daniel Roebuck for the film.

ANGUS SCRIMM

Angus Scrimm has been very busy since *Oblivion* having appeared on stage, on screen and in several radio plays. He continues to appear in Don Coscarelli films including his turn as Buddy in *Incident On and Off a Mountain Road* and a surprise cameo as a priest in *John Dies at the End*. His work with Glass Eye Pix has also been of particular note with 2006's *Automatons* and 2010's *Satan Hates You* (both by James Felix McKenney) as well as 2008's *I Sell the Dead* (Glenn McQuaid directing). On the small screen, Scrimm appeared in six episodes of *Alias* as interrogator Calvin McCullough including Jennifer Garner's directorial debut episode. In 2003 and 2004, he was celebrated for his Los Angeles stage performances as the old family butler Firs in Anton Chekov's *The Cherry Orchard* and in dual roles in Ray Bradbury's *Let's All Kill Constance*. In 2010, Scrimm narrated the chilling Glass Eye Pix radio drama, *The Grandfather*, part of their *Tales from Beyond the Pale* audio drama series.

(Author photo)

(Photo courtesy Scott Pensa)

MICHAEL BALDWIN

Following *Oblivion*, Michael Baldwin moved to Austin, Texas where he taught acting and developed several projects from behind camera. In 2012, he returned to acting and the horror genre as the lead protagonist in Michael Patrick Steven's *Brutal.* In 2014, he made another genre appearance in Jeremy Sumrall's *The Pick-Axe Murders Part III: The Final Chapter*, a love letter to eighties slasher films. Baldwin has warmly embraced his *Phantasm* reputation in the years since *Oblivion*, appearing at numerous conventions and alongside Don Coscarelli in a 2013 episode of *Graveyard Carz* that sought to recreate *Phantasm's* classic 'Cuda.

BILL THORNBURY

After his brief return to acting for *Phantasm's* fourth, Bill Thornbury returned to central California where he teaches music to children at a private Catholic school. He has since been honored by having a classroom dedicated to him ("The Bill Thornbury Music Room"). Thornbury has also performed with western music band, The Sons of San Joaquin. The group was inducted into the Western Music Hall of Fame in 2006. In 2007, he released a contemporary Christian CD *Torn Little Page*. In 2010, Thornbury contributed twenty-two songs to a new musical production, *Rancho Tesoro*, which played in Visalia, California. Although his acting days are now rare, he still enthusiastically reunites with his *Phantasm* cohorts for screening events and conventions.

(Photo courtesy Scott Pensa)

(Photo courtesy Paul Miser)

REGGIE BANNISTER

Reggie Bannister has arguably been the busiest phamily member following *Oblivion*. He has since appeared in more than three dozen productions. Most notable are his appearances as the Rest Home Administrator in Don Coscarelli's 2002 *Bubba Ho-Tep*, Ben in Robert Kurtzman's 2007 *The Rage,* and King Clayton in Paul Bunnell's 2012 *The Ghastly Love of Johnny X.* He also reunited with Angus Scrimm in 2010 for James Felix McKenny's *Satan Hates You.* Musically, Bannister released his second folk rock CD, *Naked Truth,* in 2007. As with his fellow *Phantasm* castmates, he is no stranger to the convention circuit.

KATHY LESTER

Following her cameo appearance in *Phantasm III,* phans have been clamoring for more of the Lady in Lavender… who has only grown lovelier with the passage of time. In 1995, Lester released her first CD, *Purrsistance,* now a collector's item. In 2010, Lester debuted her second CD, the cabaret jazz inspired *Boudior Rouge* by Le Kat, to great critical acclaim. The release contained a sultry musical tribute to her *Phantasm* character with extremely clever lyrics: "My sole amigo is my alter ego/ And as far as we know/He's rather *tall.*") Although Lester has toured the world with her music, all the way to Paris and back, she still makes time for the occasional *Phantasm* reunion.

AFTERWORD

You're probably here because you're a *Phantasm* phan. I'm here for the same reason. The four classic *Phantasm* films captured my adolescent imagination and have yet to let go. If ever a franchise deserved a making-of book, it surely was this one. In the absence of such a tome, I impetuously took it upon myself to create one. Writing my first book was incredibly challenging, mostly for reasons unrelated to writing. I intially wondered if pulling back the curtain on *Phantasm* would diminish my enjoyment of it. As it turns out, delving into it has only bolstered my appreciation. I hope this book will have the same effect on you.

The genius of Don Coscarelli, I've found, extends beyond his writing and directing to the like-minded people with whom he surrounds himself. This is in large part what makes the *Phantasm* films so special. That I was able to include so many of these luminaries in *Exhumed* pleases me to no end. I'm also excited to include a chapter on *Jim the World's Greatest* and *Kenny & Company*. If you haven't seen these, you must search them out. You will not be disappointed.

Phantasm phans have a proud tradition of creating engaging works. Early on, there was Nazir Ali's coveted *Phantasm* magazine. Then there was Richard Elkin's *The Sentinel* fanzine and *Phantasm: Further Excursions Into Oblivion* anthology book. There was also John Klyza's *Netherworld* fanzine and his long running *Phantasm Secrets* website. In the spirit of these memorable tributes, I humbly submit to you *Phantasm Exhumed*. If it thrills you half as much as these previous creations thrilled me, it will have all been worth it.

I am forever indebted to the phamily for their participation in this project, especially to the incomparably gracious Angus Scrimm, the extraordinarily talented Kristen Deem and the dependably loyal Guy Thorpe. The support of wonderful folks like Michael Baldwin, Bill Thornbury, Kathy Lester and Mark Shostrom has also been an incredible boon. With friends like these, I felt as though no setback could truly set the book back.

It occurs to me in retrospect that the title of this book is rather tongue-in-cheek. *Phantasm Exhumed*. You can't really exhume something that isn't dead and buried. In this 35th anniversary year, it has never been more apparent to me that *Phantasm* is no more dead and buried than the Tall Man at each film's conclusion. The pulse of this franchise beats strongly and that of the phan-base even moreso. I guess that's why some call it *The Never Dead*. Thanks for reading, boyyyy!!!

Cordially,

Dustin McNeill

Above: Angus Scrimm lends me a hand.
Opposite Left: Chilling on the Red Planet.

ACKNOWLEDGEMENTS

Highest Thanks to

Don Coscarelli for creating so many engaging and intriguing films.

Eternal Thanks to

Angus Scrimm, Kristen Deem, Guy Thorpe & Mark Shostrom

Special Phamilial Thanks to

Michael Baldwin, Bill Thornbury, the Bannisters & Kathy Lester

Special Thanks to

James Balsam, Mike Baronas, Wayne Beauchamp, Jeffrey Berk, Seth Blair, Chuck Bhutto, Christopher Chomyn, Bruce Chudacoff, Sean Clark, Bill Cone, Kevin Connors, Steve Cotroneo, Doug Cragoe, Alan Deem, Carol Deem, Robert Del Valle, Philip Duffin, Lynn Eastman-Rossi, Steve Elders, Betsy Fels, Larry Fessenden, Troy Fromin, Ed Gale, Dean Gates, Señor Corky Gil, Candi Guterres, Nathan Hanneman, Gloria Lynne-Henry, Guy Himber, Del Howison, Bob Ivy, Jim Jacks, Kristy Jett, Kenneth Jones, Jennifer Jones, Brian Keene, Darrell Kitchell, Dennis Kitchell, Beau Lotterman, Mark Anthony Major, Chris Malinowski, Stuart Manning, Rodd Matsui, Steve McKenzie, J. Patrick McNamara, Todd Mecklem, Brian Scott Mednick, Paul Miser, Ben Ohmart, Daryn Okada, Dennis Pavlenko, Scott Pensa, Samantha Phillips, Kerry Prior, Roberto Quezada, Andrew Reeder, Robert Rehme, Ralph Richmond, Daniel Roebuck, Irene Roseen, Chad Savage, Daniel Schweiger, Jeff Shiffman, George Singer Jr., David Jackson Smith, John Michael Stewart, Kenneth Tigar, Tony Timpone, Tony Todoroff, James Vale, Nathan Vayne, James Warren, Justin Warren, John Zumpano

And to the users of PhantasmCommunity.com for their support.

Book Naming Thanks to

Jay Poole

Personal Thanks to

My parents David and Karen, sister Andrea, maltese Chance
and girlfriend Lindsay Carol Squires for their support and encouragement.

Opposite Top: Co-conspirators McNeill, Scrimm and Deem. (*Author Photo*)

Opposite Bottom: Guy Thorpe and a Tall friend. (*Photo courtesy Kristen Deem*)

IN MEMORIAM

In thirty-five years, the *Phantasm* phamily have lost some very special people.
May we never forget those who gave us so much to remember.

Forrest J Ackerman (The First Phan)

Horace Bannister ("Priest" - *Phantasm*)

Rob Blattner (Universal/MCA President - *Phantasm III*)

Ray Bradbury (Author - *Something Wicked This Way Comes*)

John Davis Chandler ("Henry" - *Phantasm III*)

Shirley Coscarelli (Production Designer, Makeup Artist, Wardrobe, Novelist - *Phantasm*)

Ruth Engel ("Grandma" - *Phantasm II*)

Willard Green (Sphere Effects Creator - *Phantasm*)

Scott Magill (Assistant Editor - *Survival Quest*)

Fred Myrow (Composer - *Phantasm, Phantasm II & Phantasm III*)

Steve Patino (Sphere Effects Creator - *Phantasm II*)

Malcolm Seagrave (Composer - *Phantasm*)

John Stolfi (Production Coordinator - *Phantasm II*)

A NOTE ABOUT SOURCES

Numerous sources were consulted during the research for *Phantasm Exhumed*. These included an array of production materials such as treatments, script drafts, call sheets, shooting schedules, memorandums, storyboards and correspondence, in addition to more than one hundred interview hours with cast and crew along with personal journals and scrapbooks. Vintage interviews with Angus Scrimm and Reggie Bannister by Todd Mecklem were also featured.

•

Every attempt has been made to cite magazine and newspaper sources within the text when used. Back issues of Fangoria were an enormous help in initial book research, particularly issues 2, 75, 76, 125, 130, 134, 174 and 177. Other helpful magazines included: Fear Magazine #9, Femme Fatales V7 #8 and G.A.S.P. Magazine V2 #5.

Printed in Great Britain
by Amazon.co.uk, Ltd.,
Marston Gate.